r before the last date
equested by other
n, in writing or by
e number on the

D1332640

THE END
OF
IRISH-AMERICA?

Globalisation and the Irish Diaspora

FEARGAL COCHRANE
Lancaster University

IRISH ACADEMIC PRESS
DUBLIN • PORTLAND, OR

First published in 2010 by Irish Academic Press

2 Brookside,	920 NE 58th Avenue, Suite 300
Dundrum Road,	Portland, Oregon,
Dublin 14,	97213-3786
Ireland	USA

www.iap.ie

British Library Cataloguing in Publication Data
An entry can be found on request

ISBN 978 0 7165 3018 3 (cloth)
ISBN 978 0 7165 3019 0 (paper)

Library of Congress Cataloging-in-Publication Data
An entry can be found on request

Printed by The Good News Press Ltd, Ongar, Essex

To the Irish people –
whoever and wherever they are

Contents

Abbreviations

AIHS	American Irish Historical Society
ANC	African National Congress
ANIA	Americans for a New Irish Agenda
AOH	Ancient Order of Hibernians
CBP	Customs and Border Protection
DMV	Department of Motor Vehicles
DUP	Democratic Unionist Party
EIIC	Emerald Isle Immigration Center
ESRI	Economic and Social Research Institute
FDI	Foreign Direct Investment
FDNY	Fire Department of New York
FEC	Fair Employment Commission
GAA	Gaelic Athletic Association
GDP	Gross Domestic Product
GFA	Good Friday Agreement
GLBT	Gay, Lesbian, Bisexual and Transgender
GNP	Gross National Product
IAUC	Irish American Unity Conference
IFI	International Fund for Ireland
ILGO	Irish Lesbian and Gay Organisation
ILIR	Irish Lobby for Immigration Reform
INA	Irish Northern Aid
INC	Irish National Caucus
INLA	Irish National Liberation Army
INS	Immigration and Naturalization Service
IPC	Irish Pub Company
IRPWA	Irish Republican Prisoners Welfare Association
ISA	International Studies Association

NGO	Non-Governmental Organisation
NIFC	National Irish Freedom Committee
NYPD	New York Police Department
NYU	New York University
ONH	Óglaigh na hÉireann
PIRA	Provisional Irish Republican Army
PLO	Palestine Liberation Organisation
PSNI	Police Service of Northern Ireland
SPL	Scottish Premier League
TBI	Tourism Brand Ireland
UCD	University College Dublin
UUP	Ulster Unionist Party
WASP	White Anglo-Saxon Protestant

Foreword

There is always a touch of displacement in the sense of being Irish. We never feel quite as good about it at home as we do abroad. That is because Irish identity is so much in contention. It is only when the Irish are in Europe or America they feel comfortable about who they are, among people who do not challenge their own assessment of who they are. Our songs are all about wild rovers coming home, drinkers and tinkers; when we look for a stereotype of our collective experience in song and mythology, it is always of the traveller, the one who was never relaxed and at ease at home, never at home in foreign lands. You have to get out of Ireland for these questions to lose some of their complexity and bite.

The integrity in Feargal Cochrane's book is that it starts with reflections grounded in his own experience of being a migrant in England. I could chip in one or two of my own. On my first day in England, an Irish born barman told me that I could be happy there. He said: 'The English don't care who you are, so long as you keep your head down.' One of the valuable insights in this book is the way in which the Irish migrant in Britain has to choose still between being British or Irish, whereas in America, being Irish can entail the fullest sense of being at home, not having to be on your best behaviour. Migration, says Cochrane, is one of the leitmotifs of being Irish but he observes that the character of the Irish diaspora in America is changing.

The older Irish-Americans, with their memories of having to construct a replica of Irish culture in their new home, are a bit disgruntled to find that the new Irish migrants, framed by different experience are not sentimental about the chauvinistic artefacts and strands of culture. They don't need to construct a way of being Irish in America because they never need to wholly lose touch with Ireland. Indeed, there is an anomoly for the Irish who stayed at home in the 'old country' that when their cousins return from the far richer and more populous America, it is those cousins who seem old-fashioned, more reverential of Irish culture and the Catholic church. We may take our cultural leads from American music and film, but, to us, the American sense of being Irish, among those older immigrants, seems uncomfortably dated.

This is a beautiful and insightful book. But is it good news or bad news that the displaced and anarchic Irishness that grew out of unhappy history is now a marketable brand? Better pastiche than the real thing. *The End of Irish America?* reminds us that many of the descendants of migrants have fully assimilated and give the island home little thought. Indeed, we didn't concern ourselves much about them until the peace process when Irish-America played a spectacular hand and stepped right into west Belfast and gave us an importance we never thought we had.

Political possibilities seemed limitless in those innocent days when we all seemed naturally part of the indomitable and global Irishry. If Irish-America evolves further as Cochrane foresees, that is a moment that will not be repeated. And we may feel smaller and more alone here, having only just noticed how many cousins we had.

Malachi O'Doherty
January 2010

Preface

This book has been gestating for a long time. It emerged in one sense from my own experience of growing up in Belfast, Northern Ireland, where I was surrounded by issues of political and cultural identity. This raised (or imposed) a number of key questions for myself and those around me. Was I Irish? Was I British? Was I Irish-British? What qualified me to call myself Irish as a Catholic growing up in a Protestant area of Belfast, where flags, emblems and anthems suggested the opposite? Definitions of identity in this environment were certainly more than just an esoteric exercise, woven as they were (and still are) into the fabric of life. Questions such as: 'Who are you?' 'Where are you from?' 'Where do you live?' can take on a more threatening context when asked at gunpoint, either by a member of the British army or by a paramilitary gang. Such questions still jar today because even when innocently asked, they are about locating and placing us politically, culturally and socially. 'Which part of Northern Ireland are you from? ... Oh Belfast! ... Which part of Belfast *exactly*?'

Growing up in Northern Ireland during the 1970s and 1980s there was certainly no shortage of cues defining what Irishness encompassed (and what it did not) at both political and cultural levels. Both the school that I attended and the church that I went to as a child were bombed by those who claimed to be British. Ironically the latter had to be protected by barbed wire fencing and by a unit of the British army on Sunday mornings during the 1970s, until the congregation had dispersed. While it was made quite obvious to me from an early age that I was not British, I was also clearly different to the Southern Irish ... the 'real' Irish. The people I met on summer holidays who smiled at me, but did so nervously, who treated me like family, but more the awkward distant cousin than cherished sibling.

The book has also been generated by my experience of growing up in a changing Ireland, both North and South. I left Northern Ireland in 1998, shortly after the Good Friday Agreement was reached and Mary Robinson had just stepped down as president of Ireland. For better or worse, both parts of Ireland had changed hugely during these years and it had become a region that people wanted to go to rather than get out of. During the 1990s Ireland became less violent, more prosperous, more liberal and arguably more desirable. Miraculously, it became *chic* to be Irish and for all of its faults the Celtic Tiger roared out optimistically across the world, not least in the United States of America, which had played a small but important role in helping to devise a political agreement in Northern Ireland between unionists and nationalists in the 1990s.

During this period, I moved from Ireland to work in Britain, never thinking for one moment that I was 'emigrating'. It was a temporary stay until I got a job back 'home'. A year at most, eighteen months at a push. I let out my beautiful house in Portstewart, County Antrim, moved into rented accommodation in Lancaster, kept my bank account in Belfast and told everyone to expect me home within the year. That year turned into twelve years. I sold the house in Portstewart, bought one in Britain, got married, and it suddenly hit me … I had left. I was an emigrant. I was a member of the much talked about Irish diaspora. This brought on an existential crisis when people asked me where I was from, which required long and tiring circumlocutions where I explained that yes, while I had a Lancaster post code and had lived there for years, I was not actually *from* there and was not even from Britain; I was Irish, and yes, I meant Northern Ireland and yes that was part of the UK and yes … it was complicated.

But hold on, hope remained! My wife Rosaleen is first-generation Irish with parents who originate from Wicklow and Donegal and thus is just as Irish as myself, even if currently suffering under a false consciousness that she's British! My main bank account is still in Belfast, facilitated by online technology. I have an Irish passport (a birthday gift from my wife who hoped that it might stop me complaining about living in Britain) and I can travel back to Ireland regularly due to cheap air fares. I can watch 'Good Evening Ulster' and listen to 'Talkback' on BBC Radio Ulster when I choose to, thanks to digital satellite television and the internet, and I can even buy my potato bread in Sainsbury's now

– though not the really good stuff that they used to make in the Ormeau bakery in Belfast. In this sense therefore, despite the territorial separation, I haven't really left Ireland at all. Modernity has allowed me to live both at home and away from home, tapping into various aspects of my identity beyond the geographic borders of Northern Ireland.

Of course this last point raises a sensitive issue when it comes to definitions of diaspora and migration, as territorial borders are often contested. Indeed, such disputes can often be the cause of migratory flows in the first place. So – am I a member of the Irish diaspora or not? Well that depends perhaps on your political outlook. I have, after all, simply moved from one region of the United Kingdom (Belfast, via Downpatrick and Portstewart) to another, Lancaster. I have not moved jurisdictions, polities or states, as Ulster unionists would be quite right to remind me. However, I have moved from Ireland to Britain and through another political lens, from a temporarily occupied part of Ireland to another nation. Leaving the politics aside, many would accept that even if I have not emigrated in the political sense, I certainly have in cultural and social terms. I have done so, however, gradually, imperceptibly and pragmatically. Crucially, I have not felt that my move to Britain has compromised my political or cultural identity and, due to the enabling aspects of digital technology, in some ways my sense of being Irish has actually been enhanced, despite being physically removed from the territory itself.

This set of experiences, assumptions and beliefs led me to the subject matter of this book. I wanted to examine contemporary patterns of Irish migration to see if modernity has changed what it means to be a member of the Irish diaspora. The country that brought all of this together for me was America. Irish-Americans are synonymous with the history and politics of Irish migration and continue to build the close relationship between Ireland and the United States. From the accepted starting point of mass Irish migration (the Great Famine of 1845–50) through to recent times, America has been a favoured destination for Irish people seeking better fortunes overseas. Irish-America interested me because it was a developed diaspora, one which had evolved over time and has had a chance to move from beleaguered immigrant community into the American mainstream. In other words, Irish-America has had time to settle in and move forwards in a way that other diaspora groups have not. This passage of time has allowed

Irish-America to blend and twist its notion of Irishness, to hang onto some elements of identity while letting go of or radically altering others. Some of this has led to a disjuncture between political and cultural attitudes in Ireland, and those of Irish-Americans in the United States. In general there is a warm relationship between the two countries but tensions are there too. The Irish are irritated by hyper-real Americans who seem more Irish than the Irish themselves, and by the fact that they need them as tourists in large numbers to bolster their own economy. In political terms, post-9/11 developments in US foreign policy, especially the 'war on terror', led to a chilly atmosphere between Ireland and America, as Irish public opinion was overwhelmingly against the war in Iraq and the human rights abuses that were engaged in by the Bush administration. More broadly, Irish-Americans are sometimes annoyed by the fact that Ireland has changed and become 'spoilt' by its own modernity. There is also a sense among some that Ireland has become ungrateful for the role that America played in taking in Irish emigrants when they were desperate for shelter. While there have been, and will continue to be, tensions between the Irish and Irish-American communities, the cross-fertilisation between the two countries is undeniable. Countless American presidents, including the present incumbent, Barack Obama, have found an Irish heritage, while many of those born in the US have played crucial roles in Irish politics and culture over several generations, not least Éamon de Valera. Irish-America therefore encapsulates the historical, political, cultural and economic journey of the Irish diaspora and connects their story to the enabling aspects of globalisation.

Acknowledgements

This book could not have been written without the help of those who were interviewed for it. I am indebted to everyone who gave me an interview and to numerous others who provided opinions or asked questions which helped me to define the boundaries of the project and develop many of the ideas within the book. I would particularly like to thank Jake MacNicholas of the NYPD, who met me in New York in 2004 despite difficult personal circumstances at the time. Among the other people who helped enormously in providing ideas and information for the book were: Niall Burgess, William Cobert, Siobhán Dennehy, Tom Deignan, Vincent Doherty, Éamonn Dornan, Barry Doyle, Cassie Farrelly, Brendan Fay, Kelly Fincham, Patricia Grogan, Michael Hand, Pat Hughes, Jack Irwin, Martin Kelly, Liz Kenny, Joe Lee, Emma Madigan, Larry McCarthy, Seán McCarthy, John MacDonagh, Christina McElwaine, Mary McGlynn, Kathleen McGreal, John Francis Mulligan, Seán Murphy, Niall O'Dowd, Ray O'Hanlon, Niall O'Leary, Eileen Reilly, John T. Ridge, Niall Stanage, Ciarán Staunton and Pauline Turley.

I would also like to thank my friends at Lancaster University, including my colleagues within the Richardson Institute and the Department of Politics and International Relations. In particular, I would like to thank Patrick Bishop, Nina Caspersen, David Denver, Vicky Mason, Kynan Gentry and Graham Smith for their friendship and perspectives on some of the ideas and arguments in the text. I would like to acknowledge and thank the Lancaster University Research Committee for providing much needed financial assistance for fieldwork conducted in New York.

Beyond Lancaster, I would like to thank other friends and colleagues, including Kenneth Bush, Jonathan Hall, Roland Kostic, Gerd

Nonneman, Jan Selby, Ashok Swain, Jonathan Tonge and Nicholas Van Hear. I am also indebted to colleagues and friends in the Center for Global Studies at George Mason University, especially Terence Lyons, Peter Mandaville and other researchers associated with the Global Migration and Transnational Politics project, funded by the John D. and Catherine T. MacArthur Foundation. This project provided me with generous financial assistance for fieldwork in New York in 2008, which is greatly appreciated. A number of scholars and friends associated with the project helped me to refine my thoughts and revise my arguments during the course of completing the book. They include Fiona Adamson, Jennifer Brinkerhoff, David FitzGerald, Kristian Harpviken, Jóse Itzigsohn, Randa Kayyali, Ken Menkhaus, Camilla Orjuela, Eva Østergaard-Nielsen, Peter Spiro and Heather Williams.

Lisa Hyde and everyone at Irish Academic Press provided me with great encouragement and have steered the project smoothly through the writing and production process, for which I am extremely grateful. I would especially like to thank my wife, Professor Rosaleen Duffy, for her constant encouragement during the writing of the book and also for conducting some of the interviews in New York. I particularly want to thank Rosaleen for accompanying me into countless Irish theme bars around the world in the name of research and for the purposes of some much needed participant observation. I would also like to thank my mother and father, Roisín and Gerry Cochrane, and the rest of my family; Niall, Geraldine, Éamonn, Peter and Seán, for all their love and support.

Finally, the usual academic health warning applies, in that notwithstanding the references to friends and colleagues supplied above, there is no guilt by association. All errors of fact and analysis are mine alone. The book is dedicated to the Irish people in all of its variety, whoever and wherever they are.

The End of Irish-America?
Globalisation and the Irish Diaspora

It is true that we are born, we live and we die ... but living, the place we are at in the present, is a condition of in-be-tweenness, a crossroads of various real and imagined comings and goings.[1]

This is a book about the changing relationship between Ireland and America. Its main themes examine the shifting patterns of Irish migration over time and the implications of these changes for the relationship between the two countries. The central argument made in the book is that the historic relationship between Ireland and America is in flux and while Irish-America is not disappearing completely, it is changing in fundamental ways, mediated by the forces of globalisation and modernity.

For a small country on the edge of Europe, emigration has been a constant companion for those who have lived in Ireland over many generations. During the mid-nineteenth century, waves of Irish people were forced to leave post-Famine Ireland out of desperation in order to survive, and they were the lucky ones who could scrape the fare together to get to England, Europe or board a 'coffin-ship' in search of salvation in the New World. Ireland's great dispersal followed its Great Hunger, though there have been regular waves of migration before and since the 1850s. On one level, Irish migration represents a national tragedy for those involved, and a failure at the policy level to protect, feed, employ and nourish its own people. However, within the wider context, the Irish diaspora have helped to make Ireland what it is today, and while initially discarded and forgotten by the state, the Irish abroad have come full circle and are now seen as being critical partners in Ireland's economic, political and cultural rejuvenation over recent years. Over time, therefore, this dispersal sowed the seeds for a de-territorialised nation.

These have long since germinated and grown into organic networks that have provided political support, economic resources and cultural enrichment. Irish-America has been at the forefront of much of this story and is synonymous with the idea of the Irish diaspora, connecting the disparate strands of history, politics, economics and culture together.

The relationship between Ireland and America has been an important one for both countries in historical, political, economic and cultural terms for at least the last 150 years. The periodic waves of Irish migration from the mid-eighteenth century onwards gave the modern United States soldiers, labourers, presidents and an array of cultural icons. At the same time, America became the land of opportunity for generations of Irish migrants, a chance to escape political oppression, economic destitution and something of a dreamscape for those left behind in Ireland, who wondered about the chance of a better life overseas. The relationship has produced a stream of individuals (from de Valera to the Kennedys, the Clancy brothers to Michael Flatley) who have cumulatively built political, economic and cultural connections between the two countries. Beyond the individual level, the regular waves of Irish migration, sustained over a period of time, witnessed the development of a group mentality. This collective consciousness led to the emergence of an ethnically based civil society as the Irish organised themselves through the Catholic Church, the Gaelic Athletic Association (GAA) and new groups, such as the Ancient Order of Hibernians (AOH). Many of the Irish migrants initially felt the need to connect into ethnic networks from home, which produced a desire to maintain their Irish identity (or even their county identity) rather than trying to integrate into their new environment. The exception to this rule was provided by the Irish Protestants and Scotch-Irish (or Scots-Irish) Presbyterians who migrated to America before the Famine and were significantly different from their Catholic compatriots. They found it easier to connect into WASP society and, as a consequence, over time these migrants and their descendents became less visible, until they became indistinguishable from American-Americans.

Consequently, while some Irish migrants integrated and disappeared into the American mainstream, others maintained a strong ethnic consciousness and organised around this in political, social and cultural terms. The picture of how the Irish have come to terms with living in

America is a complicated one and continues to be so. This book seeks to illustrate and explain this complexity, between Irish-born and American-born, young and old, and between liberals and conservatives, within the context of the political, economic and cultural evolution of both countries in recent years. The main aim of the book, therefore, is to explore the dramatic changes that have taken place within Irish-America, focusing in particular on the changing patterns of contemporary migration from Ireland to the US and on how this has affected the cultural, political and economic relationship between the two countries.

The book explains these changes in the context of wider global trends and pressures in the twenty-first century that are ironically serving to both facilitate and undermine the Irish diaspora. On one level, modern mobility and communications technology allow the Irish abroad to keep in touch with 'home' relatively easily today, yet on another level, this also frees up the modern migrant from the need to hang onto ethnic networks and patterns of behaviour while living overseas.

The central argument presented in the book suggests that a paradigm shift has taken place within Irish-America and in the wider relationship between the two countries, caused by three separate though inter-relating factors connected to the push and pull nature of migration trends. Firstly, the process of globalisation has allowed potential migrants to live simultaneously in a multiplicity of locations rather than having to choose one geographical, political or cultural space. Secondly, the reasons for Irish migration have changed significantly between the nineteenth and twenty-first centuries and this has had a substantial impact on the type of people who leave Ireland for America in the twenty-first century and how they behave when they arrive in the US. Thirdly, the 9/11 attacks and the response of the Bush administration in tightening its immigration laws and targeting a 'global war on terror' soured the relationship between Ireland and America and made life difficult for many Irish people within the US. While the Obama presidency may offset some of the problems this has created, the issue of immigration reform for the undocumented remains a major fault line in the Irish-American political psyche.

For all of these reasons, the Irish-American relationship is in flux today and the subsequent chapters of this book seek to explain why and how this is happening.

A METHODOLOGICAL NOTE

Diaspora research lends itself to an interdisciplinary approach as such people, by definition, flow over borders and move beyond traditional categories. As a result, this book seeks to combine and connect literatures across a number of academic areas, chiefly political science and sociology but also incorporating work in anthropology, political geography, cultural studies and international relations. The research carried out has tried to be open to this range of secondary literatures in the expectation that these connect some of the conceptual and empirical synapses together and help to advance key academic debates surrounding diasporas, globalisation and contemporary migration, beyond the Irish case.

In addition to the range of secondary literature used, the book takes advantage of the many column inches written in the print media about Ireland in general and its migrant population in particular. The analysis is also informed by a series of qualitative semi-structured interviews carried out with informed stakeholders in the Irish and Irish-American communities between 2004 and 2008. These include contributions from a wide range of individuals and organisations within the Irish and Irish-American communities, including journalists, academics, political activists, immigration lawyers, members of the New York Police Department (NYPD) as well as a number of NGOs active within the Irish community, including the Emerald Isle Immigration Center (EIIC) and the Aisling Center. Leading journalists such as Niall O'Dowd, publisher of the *Irish Voice*, Ray O'Hanlon, senior editor of the *Irish Echo* and Niall Stanage, author of a book on the Obama presidential election campaign, were also interviewed,[2] as was a member of former Governor George Pataki's administration in New York and representatives from the Irish consulate in New York.

In empirical terms, the book does not attempt to survey all of Irish-America, nor does it claim to have gathered a representative sample of views from across the whole geographic or demographic universe within Irish-America. It focuses instead on New York as one vibrant and historic locus of Irish-American opinion, and as an important junction for the intersection of those born in Ireland and Americans with Irish ancestry. New York is an appropriate location for a qualitative litmus test of the Irish-American relationship for a number of reasons.

Firstly, due to its historical importance as the point of entry for many

Irish emigrants during the nineteenth and twentieth centuries, together with the large Irish community that continues to be located there. In the wake of the Famine in the mid-nineteenth century, New York quickly became established as America's most heavily populated city in terms of Irish immigrants. 'Between 1845 and 1851 New York housed 12 per cent of America's Irish population. The US census of 1850 counted 133,730 people (26 per cent of the city's total population) born in Ireland, while the New York State census of 1855 reported 175,735 (27.9 per cent of the city's population) born there.'[3] This historical legacy continues to have a contemporary political resonance in New York's civic and political life and can be seen in its public sector organisations and in the realm of arts and culture.

Secondly, as one of the main sites of the attacks of 11 September 2001, New York City is emblematic of the new security climate in the US post-9/11 which has played an important role in relations between Ireland and the United States, at least until the election of President Barack Obama to the White House in 2008.

Thirdly, in cultural terms, New York is one of the clearest examples of the hyper-real expression of 'Irishness' with the St Patrick's Day parade in Manhattan. For all of these reasons, New York City brings together many of the core themes that will be explored in the book, from historical patterns of migration to modern trends in global mobility, communication and security.

STRUCTURE OF THE BOOK

Each of the chapters that follows addresses in different ways the changing relationship between Ireland and America in political, social, economic and cultural terms, arguing that we are on the threshold of a new beginning between the two countries mediated by the forces of globalisation and modern communication.

Chapter 2 sets out to provide a theoretical foundation for the book by exploring the meaning of diaspora and connecting this to the history of Irish migration and the impact of globalisation in the modern world. The argument made in this chapter is that while it is possible to define what a diaspora community is, this fails to fully explain the condition of the modern migrant, in the Irish context at least. In other words, the Irish have extended the traditional view of diaspora communities as being in an uneasy relationship with their homelands where they are torn between their past and present, historically, culturally and politically. In the Irish case, the diaspora have become increasingly transient, mobile and pragmatic. Decisions about migration are often taken *post hoc* rather than before the physical act of leaving, and this has had an important impact on behaviour. It is argued here that migrants who leave home because they *choose* to are radically different in terms of their behaviour in the 'host' country to migrants who leave because they *have* to. This chapter argues, therefore, that there is a major difference between defining yourself as having emigrated to another country and defining yourself as someone who is merely living and working in another country for an undefined period. Many of the Irish who are living in America today would place themselves in the second of these categories and have a mindset that is characterised by mobile, fluid and hybrid forms of communication that are capable of transcending geographical boundaries. This has been summed up by Ulrick Beck, in an ugly but useful phrase, as constituting 'transnational place polygamy', where people can belong in several places simultaneously.[4] This notion of being at ease with living in multiple locations is a theme that flows throughout several of the chapters in the book and is central to the arguments within it. Modernity has facilitated our ability to live in several places at the one time, to fuse cultures, cuisines, economies and even political allegiances, and the Irish abroad have skilfully adapted to this twenty-first century condition.

Chapter 2 also examines the historical pattern of Irish migration and looks at how the forces of globalisation have impacted on traditional notions of the Irish diaspora. Globalisation has empowered the Irish and other diaspora communities seeking to communicate with their home countries, yet at the same time the chapter illustrates how the forces of globalisation lie at the heart of the reason why Irish-America is in transition, namely it is resulting in many people forestalling (or avoiding altogether) questions surrounding emigration. In the short term, the digital revolution in communications technology such as the internet, e-mail, Skype and satellite television has revolutionised life for diaspora communities in ways that would have been unimaginable to those who left their home country during the 1850s or 1950s. In this sense, globalisation has liberated diaspora communities and allowed them to live simultaneously at home while being away from home, and even to blend and twist notions of where 'home' is located. Global communications have given Irish migrants the best of both worlds and have allowed many of them to inhabit Atvar Brah's hybrid 'diaspora space' where they can tap into a menu of cultural options from both Ireland and the US as they desire.[5] This resort to global communication to mediate between the country of birth and the place of residence is typical of many other accounts from the Irish community in America and among diaspora communities in other parts of the world. As a result of cheap air travel, e-mail, internet and satellite television, it is possible to live in two (or more) places at once in the twenty-first century, both geographically and psychologically. While the process of globalisation has been accompanied by economic and social costs, it has liberated diaspora communities around the world from the restrictions on mobility imposed by geographical distance and separation.[6]

However, Chapter 2 argues that in the longer term globalisation is undermining the Irish diaspora, as those who travel from Ireland to the US are economically mobile, transient and pragmatic individuals who often seek to integrate within American society rather than retain their Irish cultural associations. Such people do not feel the need to 'hang on to home' because home is still available to them though modern technology and economic mobility, compared with their predecessors in the nineteenth and twentieth centuries.[7] This chapter will therefore illustrate how these trends in globalisation are on the one hand acting to liberate the Irish diaspora while on the other are helping to undermine it.

Chapter 3 moves on from this conceptual discussion to examine the political role of Irish-America, especially within the context of the Northern Ireland conflict. The narrative explores the roles played by various US administrations, from the Carter era through the Clinton presidency up to the current Obama administration. Throughout the course of the current conflict in Northern Ireland, several Irish-American pressure groups have played a prominent role in lobbying the US government over Northern Ireland, with varying degrees of success. This interest was a direct result of the flow of Irish migrants to America over several centuries.

While very few of these people held on to the day-to-day details of politics in Northern Ireland, many harboured romantic notions about Ireland and rather less positive images of Britain's role in the political conflict. This chapter illustrates the twists and turns that took place in efforts to get the White House involved in what was technically a matter of British domestic policy. The fact that US administrations from the Carter presidency onwards were prepared to recognise a foreign policy angle to the Northern Ireland conflict was testament to the activity and power of the Irish-American lobby, which was itself moulded by previous patterns of Irish migration. Chapter 3 explains the evolution of this lobbying activity and the reasons why these activists managed to transform themselves from political outsiders to policy insiders during the Clinton presidency during the 1990s.

Chapter 3 finishes by exploring the way in which Irish-American voting patterns have become more diffused within US politics. While Irish-America has historically been close to the Democratic Party, this allegiance has been weakening since the Reagan presidency. As Irish migrants moved up through the economic and social gears in the US, they also became more conservative politically. Irish-America has become much less politically cohesive over the last twenty years, with many Catholic Irish-Americans preferring President George W. Bush's conservative social programme during the 2004 presidential election, regardless of the fact that the Democratic nominee, John Kerry, was a practising Catholic and would have been the first Catholic since John F. Kennedy to win the US presidency. This argument was reflected by the New York-based *Irish Voice* newspaper during the run up to the 2004 election. While the paper endorsed the Kerry/Edwards ticket, it suggested that the connection between the Irish vote, the Catholic vote and the Democratic Party was itself in flux.

> The latest exit polling data had the Catholic vote going to Bush, 52% to 47% … Kerry's performance is troubling for the Democrats. Kerry, after all, is Catholic himself. In addition, Democrats, according to most statistics, had actually won the Catholic vote in the last three elections. Both times he ran, Bill Clinton won the Catholic vote by more than 10%.[8]

During the 2008 election, meanwhile, candidate Obama saw little electoral advantage in connecting into Irish-America and was quite willing to keep the Irish lobby at arm's length from his campaign, both in the democratic primaries and in his subsequent contest with John McCain. Trina Vargo, Obama's spokesperson on Irish issues during the campaign, enraged sections of Irish-America with an article published in the *Irish*

Times in November 2007. In her article, entitled 'Irish illegals are not a special case', Vargo, president of the US–Ireland Alliance, claimed that Irish lobby groups were seeking a special deal with the US government over legislative reform for the Irish undocumented following the failure of the McCain–Kennedy bill in Congress. While Vargo's policy position was regarded as being unhelpful by groups such as the Irish Lobby for Immigration Reform (ILIR), some of the language used was less than diplomatic.

> To support a special deal … would single out illegal Irish immigrants for preferential treatment, would be morally wrong, could harm the US-Ireland relationship, damage the high regard in which Irish-Americans are held, and lead to a divisive debate in the US between the Hispanic community and the Irish-American community.
>
> … There is also talk of trying to mask a 'special deal' by cloaking it in innocuous immigration provisions but this is just an attempt to, as they say on Wall Street, 'put lipstick on that pig'.[9]

This article began a war of words with various constituencies within the Irish-American community and within the polarised sides over the issue of immigration reform. AOH national vice-president Séamus Boyle responded to the article by claiming that Vargo's view was not shared by his organisation. 'It is very obvious to the membership of the AOH in America that the recent article by Trina Vargo delivers a message that she is out of touch with the real situation for the undocumented Irish immigrants living in the USA and their families back home in Ireland.'[10] Regardless of the various perspectives on this issue, it was clear that candidate Obama did not feel the need to smooth ruffled feathers in order to gain Irish-American votes. Niall Stanage, who has written authoritatively about the Obama election campaign in his book *Redemption Song*, encapsulates the peripheral nature of Irish-America to the internal politics of the Democratic Party and to the presidential election more generally during the 2008 campaign.

> The single most persistent myth that I grappled with was the belief that Irish-America plays an important role in American electoral politics. That may have been true half a century ago, when John F. Kennedy became president, but it had been a fantasy for at least 20 years … For an ethnic group to hold genuine sway in

American politics, it needs at least two of three things: serious nu-
merical strength; a capacity to deliver some semblance of a bloc
vote; and a set of issues, discrete from the mainstream political
debate, that play a pivotal role in determining where those votes
go. African-Americans, Hispanic-Americans and Jewish-Americans
meet those criteria. Most other ethnic groups, including the Irish,
do not.[11]

The breakdown between the Irish-American vote and the Democratic
Party links into one of the over-arching themes of the book, namely
that the contemporary Irish-American community is a fluid and
mobile, rather than a fixed and static, category. Its political bedrock is
shifting as it has become more affluent and as it has moved from the
beleaguered migrant society of the mid-nineteenth century to the
corporate, moneyed, hegemonic elite of the twenty-first.

Chapter 4 moves on to explore the impact of the 9/11 attacks and their
aftermath on the Irish community living in America. This chapter examines the ways in which the US administration's zero tolerance policy
towards international terrorism impacted directly upon the Irish
migrant community. This has particularly affected those who emigrated
from Ireland to the US during the 1980s and 1990s and who either did
so illegally or who overstayed their visas to work in the US and remain
undocumented. The enforcement of immigration law has been tightened up considerably since 2001 and has been used by the Department
of Homeland Security, among other US government agencies, to
deport those who have overstayed their visas and are found to be working illegally within the US. New anti-terrorist legislation introduced
since 9/11, most notoriously the Patriot Act and Homeland Securities
Act, were resisted by Irish-American groups who lobbied vigorously
against them, while others have focused on lobbying for immigration
reform legislation that would allow the undocumented to regularise
their status. This chapter illustrates the ways in which the post-9/11
environment is squeezing the Irish community in America to the point
where it has started to threaten the futures of many who live there.

While the United States has traditionally been seen as a country that
has welcomed immigration and celebrated its multicultural makeup,
the post-9/11 environment has called this into question, with some
well-placed observers claiming that this is now little more than a latent
memory or empty rhetorical flourish that is out of step with present-day

experience. As a result of the post-9/11 enforcement of US immigration regulations, Irish NGOs in New York such as the EIIC and the Aisling Center have been advising the Irish community to become American citizens as soon as they qualify to do so, even if they are in possession of a green card. Those who are undocumented face a bleaker future, searching for the means to become legal, continuing their shadowy existence as illegal migrants, or by leaving the country altogether. This story intersects with the overall theme of the book that Irish-America is in flux through a combination of long- and short-term factors. The post-9/11 environment for Irish migrants in the US and the inability of the undocumented Irish to legalise their status has been seen by many as one of several push factors that has seen growing numbers of Irish people leaving the US to return to Ireland.

Chapters 5 and 6 move from an examination of global *political* impacts on Irish-America to an exploration of the changing *cultural and economic* representations of Irishness in the twenty-first century. The over-arching theme of these chapters concerns the construction of Irishness as a cultural commodity and globalised identity. Conceptually, the chapters examine the notions of cultural hybridity and what has been referred to as the hyper-real expression of identity.[12] In other words, the extent to which external constructions of the Irish identity have been magnified and distorted until they have become more Irish than the Irish themselves.

To assess this external branding of Irishness in the twenty-first century, the chapters look at two separate illustrations of the marketing of Irish culture within the context of American life. These two case studies are linked to wider debates on the impact of globalisation on identity formation. Firstly, the development of the St Patrick's Day parade in New York is examined in Chapter 5, as an emblem of both old and new representations of Irishness. The particular focus is on the disagreement about how the main St Patrick's Day parade in Manhattan depicts 'Irishness', and how this parade has been choreographed by the AOH. In short, the official parade is white, Catholic and heterosexual with more than a tinge of traditional Irish nationalism. This official AOH version of Irishness is increasingly at odds with more inclusive constructions of Irish culture and, in particular, the exclusion of the gay, lesbian, bisexual and transgender (GLBT) communities from the official parade. This chapter highlights the political and cultural debate surrounding the St Patrick's Day parade in New York, charting the evolution of new pressure groups such as the St Pat's for All Society and the Lavender and Green Alliance. Brendan Fay, an Irish-born New York-based gay rights activist and founder of the Lavender and Green Alliance, epitomises the tension between the official and alternative St Patrick's Day celebrations and the reasons for establishing an alternative to the official AOH parade. 'We want it [the St Pat's for All parade] to challenge discrimination and not let everyone think that the Fifth Avenue parade is the only expression of Irishness. It is the biggest expression of Irishness because it is controlled by people with power in the Irish community [the AOH].'[13] Chapter 5 explores the conflicting narratives surrounding this struggle for the memory of St Patrick within New York City and how St Patrick's Day has become embroiled in contemporary arguments about the construction of Irish culture in the twenty-first century and who has the right to act as gatekeeper of the Irish identity.

Chapter 6 develops the debate over cultural authenticity and the hyper-real by examining the growth of the Irish theme bar and its branding of a particular globalised version of Irishness, sponsored and facilitated by large multinational corporations such as Guinness. Irish theme bars have become synonymous with the global branding of Irishness, stretching across the world like a perverse form of cultural imperialism. Tom Inglis has observed that 'Most major global cities now have an Irish pub; Shanghai has three.'[14] There are Irish theme bars in Bangkok, Afghanistan and in Dubai airport, complete with Gaelic inscriptions and rusty bicycles on the ceilings. Yet these bear little resemblance to bars in Ireland and have a homogenous quality to their physical composition and cultural ambience. Ironically they tend to be frequented by British tourists eager to catch the latest English Premiership games during their holiday, largely oblivious to the subliminal messages of armed resistance to their colonial past that surround them on the walls.

The main point made in this chapter is that the marketing of the Irish theme bar is anything but haphazard or authentic, with large drinks manufacturers supplying the *paraphernalia* of Irishness to many of these bars, importing much of the physical surroundings (1916 proclamations of the Irish Republic, revolutionary posters of Sinn Féin leaders such as Arthur Griffith and Michael Collins, and even autographed Irish football shirts) from Ireland. These careful cultural constructions link into everything, from the name of the bar, the physical surroundings within it, the type of drink that is served and even the music that is played. The chapter finishes by pointing out how even some of the Irish theme bars in the US are evolving in the twenty-first century.

While much of the book focuses upon America and the changing political and cultural behaviour of the Irish community living there, Chapter 7 switches attention to the other end of the telescope, examining the region that Irish people are leaving rather than the country they are going to. Ireland has changed radically over the last forty years. In social, cultural and economic terms, Ireland is a different country to the one that many emigrants left during the 1950s. Chapter 7 seeks to outline how these changes have impacted upon the dynamics of Irish migration patterns. The Ireland of Éamon de Valera has largely vanished; his 1937 constitution has been reformed to reflect contemporary Irish social views and to take account of the denouement of the political conflict in Northern Ireland. In addition, the influence of the Catholic Church on public policy has diminished dramatically over recent years due to social trends such as urbanisation, a youthful population and the exposure of human frailties within the Catholic clergy with several *causes célèbres* of the sexual abuse of children by paedophile priests during the 1990s. Over the last thirty years Ireland has slowly woken up to the hypocritical morality where it was impossible to buy a condom over the counter in a state where abortion was illegal under the constitution. Much better to export the 'problem' to England, incarcerate young women in 'Magdalene Laundries' to protect them from their shame, or let them die during childbirth in the ditches of Ireland due to the social stigma invented, fostered and promoted by the state in conjunction with the Catholic Church. A stern judgement perhaps, borne of contemporary values, but not as harsh as the behaviour, laws and social norms constructed by Ireland's political and religious gatekeepers until relatively recently. Tom Garvin's assessment of the theocratic authoritarian cruelty that took place during this period within the Irish education system does not overstate the charge that faces the Catholic Church in Ireland and the abuses it carried out on the country's young and vulnerable population, with the tacit consent of the political elite.

It is also now established, and it was fairly well known at the time through personal experience and grapevine rumour, that physical abuse and sexual assault frequently occurred in the school system generally, and such abuse and assaults were apparently particularly common and particularly uninhibited in the industrial schools [borstals] and orphanages. Children were sometimes, in effect, legally or otherwise stolen from their parents by clerics. Pregnant girls, or girls who had been raped and were brave enough to talk about it in public, were effectively imprisoned in 'Magdalene Laundries' run in a fantastically authoritarian fashion. This imprisonment was also illegal, but police and judicial authorities were either afraid to intervene or were themselves complicit.[15]

The Commission to Inquire into Child Abuse which was established in 2000 to determine the scale of physical, mental and sexual abuse of children within state institutions within the Republic of Ireland from 1930 to the 1970s issued its report in May 2009. Its findings were damning, both for the egregious acts carried out by religious orders and their lay associates and for the state itself, which had a duty of care for the children who were abused during the period.

More than 90% of all witnesses who gave evidence to the Confidential Committee reported being physically abused while in schools or out-of-home care. Physical abuse was a component of the vast majority of abuse reported in all decades and institutions and witnesses described pervasive abuse as part of their daily lives. They frequently described casual, random physical abuse but many wished to report only the times when the frequency and severity were such that they were injured or in fear for their lives. In addition to being hit and beaten, witnesses described other forms of abuse such as being flogged, kicked and otherwise physically assaulted, scalded, burned and held under water … Sexual abuse was reported by approximately half of all the Confidential Committee witnesses. Acute and chronic contact and non-contact sexual abuse was reported, including vaginal and anal rape, molestation and voyeurism in both isolated assaults and on a regular basis over long periods of time. The secret nature of sexual abuse was repeatedly emphasised as facilitating its occurrence.[16]

While the contemporary narrative has branded 'Irishness' as a literate, fun-loving and independently minded (if unpredictable) national consciousness, this was certainly not the experience of independent Ireland from the 1930s to the 1980s. While Tourism Ireland might not emphasise such factors in its advertising campaigns, the *céad míle fáilte* of 100,000 welcomes was certainly not extended to its own people during this period, and while the abuses may have been eradicated from day-to-day life, they have still left an imprint on the national psyche.

While a degree of caution is necessary when judging yesterday's Ireland by today's standards, as this risks misinterpreting important aspects of historical and social context, there can be little debate that Irish society has changed utterly in political, social, economic and cultural terms. For better or worse (and this book believes the former) Ireland is no longer an insular Catholic state, idealised by de Valera in his 1943 St Patrick's Day radio address as a land of 'cosy homesteads' which was 'joyous with the sounds of industry' and where 'comely maidens' would dispense 'the wisdom of serene old age'.[17] This point was reflected upon by Brendan Fay, who emigrated from Ireland to New York in 1984 in search of a more tolerant society.

> I learned to come out here, I learned to speak gay. New York changed me. When I left Ireland it was still under an old British Law that made it a criminal offence to be gay. But Mary Robinson changed all that from 1990 ... Ireland has changed. It is a different country to the one I left.[18]

It is recognised by many Irish people, both at home and abroad, that the Republic of Ireland has moved from being a peripheral state on the edge of Europe to being an EU success story despite its recent economic recession. That Ireland has changed dramatically (both North and South) in recent years is not a matter of great debate. However, the impact of these changes for Ireland politically, socially and culturally is more hotly contested. Chapter 7 assesses the changes that have taken place in Ireland and their impact upon the numbers of Irish people emigrating to America at the beginning of the twenty-first century.

This theme links the chapter into the wider argument at the core of the book, namely that the Irish who arrive in the US in the twenty-first century are fundamentally different to their predecessors. They are a younger, more confident and more transient community who, contrary to many of those who left Ireland in the 1850s, 1950s or even the

1980s, do not feel the same need to 'hang on to home' and thus are not immediately driven to organisations such as the GAA, the AOH or the Catholic Church. Added to this is the fact that in the wake of the Celtic Tiger revolution that has taken place at home, Ireland and America do not appear to be such different worlds in the twenty-first century as they might have done in the twentieth. This view was expressed pithily by Fintan O'Toole, a Dublin-based journalist who epitomises the Irish middle-class cultural revisionism which has tried to map Ireland's reinvention of itself over the last thirty years.

> We brought America down to size by becoming America. We made ourselves sexy and cool. We got tans. We got Porsches. We built Nevada-style ranch houses in Connemara. Some of us got pools, though the weather being what it is, they soon succumbed to dank weeds and wind-blown detritus. We went to work making Viagra in Cork and microchips in Maynooth. We got so used to living an American life that it ceased to be such a big deal ... We are no longer tormented by the illusion, because it is, for us, no longer an illusion but our mundane reality. And if we sometimes feel the tectonic plates shifting beneath us and wonder where we are, it is simply because America is the ground on which we now stand.[19]

Chapter 7 also looks at the post-conflict relationship between corporate Irish-America and the modern Irish state, and the way in which economic and political relationships have evolved from philanthropy to commerce between the two countries. This has witnessed a shift from a patron–client model to one based on corporate equality, mediated by the growing strength of the euro against the US dollar. It also stems from economic necessity as both the Irish and US economies suffered significantly during the global financial difficulties which emerged during 2008.

The chapter finishes by arguing that, alongside the impacts of globalisation, the changing nature of Ireland itself provides a structural explanation for the paradigm shift in relations between Ireland and America. Put simply, the Irish no longer need to leave the country of their birth to escape political oppression or economic destitution. Despite the recession which took hold of Ireland in 2008, most of those who leave Ireland today seeking work have a return ticket. More immediately, many find it harder to get into an America that no longer wants the world's 'huddled masses' or to avoid detection if they overstay their visas. At the same time, it is argued here that the new economic relationship between Ireland and the US is built on a model that is as much paper tiger as it is Celtic Tiger. Much of the 'economic miracle' in Ireland experienced during the 1990s was based on foreign direct investment (FDI), which has made the country especially vulnerable to outside conditions. Ireland may have excelled as a large-scale manufacturing plant for high-tech US companies, but it occupied the status of employee rather than shareholder, and many of the profits made by these companies were exported from the country. Thus the Irish economy is just as reliant on external actors in the twenty-first century who own the companies and their profits as it was during previous generations. Louis MacNeice's critique of the Northern Ireland economy in the inter-war years, published in his 1939 poem 'Autumn Journal', possesses an eerie resonance with the political economy of contemporary Ireland:

> The smoking chimneys hint
> At prosperity round the corner
> But they make their Ulster linen from foreign lint
> And the money that comes in goes out to make more money.
> A city built upon mud;
> A culture built upon profit;
> Free speech nipped in the bud,
> The minority always guilty.[20]

In the final chapter, the main arguments are drawn together to address the central theme, namely that the relationship between Ireland and America is in transition in a way that threatens the critical mass of Irish-America in the longer term. This relates to the reasons why people are leaving Ireland, the political and economic conditions under which they do so, and the impact of modernity upon their behaviour after they arrive in America. The book concludes that the ethnographic map of Irish migration has become more complex than it was in the nineteenth or twentieth centuries. Crucially, the vast majority who travel from Ireland to America today do not make the psychological decision to emigrate at the point of their departure from Ireland. This is having a major impact on their behaviour after they arrive in America as there is less demand today for traditional Irish cultural support groups than there was in previous generations. Organisations such as the AOH are suffering as a consequence of this; their numbers are dwindling and they are losing critical mass, particularly in urban areas. AOH Divisions are merging or disappearing altogether, as their officers and members get old together. A similar trend can be observed in sporting organisations such as the GAA, whose numbers are also in decline.

This change in the character and behaviour of the Irish immigrant community has been aided and abetted by the forces of globalisation. On the one hand it has brought American culture and politics closer to Ireland, while on the other, global communications have allowed the Irish emigrant to maintain existing social and cultural ties with Ireland and travel between the place of birth and place of residence much faster, much cheaper and thus much more frequently than was possible in the past. Globalisation has liberated the Irish abroad and allowed those who want to, to live in two places (or more) at the same time, both home and away from home, practising what Ulf Hannerz has termed 'long-distance interconnectedness'.[21] While this global mobility is not without its costs, it does result in allowing people to prevaricate upon the central question for the migrant, namely 'where is my home?' Pragmatism seems to be the *modus operandi* of the Irish community living in America today. There remains the option, perhaps the intention, to return to Ireland if things do not work out well. However, the days when Irish emigrants boarded ships to the New World with a one-way ticket to an uncertain future are gone.

The book concludes with the recognition that the relationship between Ireland and America is in flux because the supply of migrants is drying up, the United States is becoming less interested in welcoming migrant labour, and global trends are changing the behaviour of many of the Irish people who do arrive. Hanging on to home is simply unnecessary in the era of twenty-first century mobility, communication and global interconnectedness. This is damaging social and cultural cohesion within the new wave of Irish migrants who are, in the main, transient, pragmatic and optimistic, and as a result are happy to integrate within US society rather than remain within their indigenous ethnic community. We are entering a new phase in the relationship between Ireland and America which is simultaneously exciting and unsettling. In political terms, Ireland has come of age as a modern European state and its developing relations with America will emerge within that context. Irish-American novelist Peter Quinn concluded in 2000 that a fundamental transformation has taken place within Irish-America.

> The unique American subculture that the Irish created in the wake of the Famine – the culture I grew up in, a culture that cohered around the Catholic Church and the Democratic Party, with a working class base and widespread aspirations to lace-curtain propriety, a culture deeply skeptical about WASP institutions and pretensions, and suspicious and resentful of the mainline tradition of Protestant moral reform and economic self-determination – is dead and gone ... it's as doomed as the dodo, and no amount of humpty-dumpty yearning for the way things were – or the way some like to imagine they were – will bring it back.[22]

The chapters that follow seek to examine the changing relationship between Ireland and America and assess the implications of previous patterns for the future of the political, cultural and economic ties between the two countries.

NOTES

1. Dawson, A. and Johnson, M. 'Migration, Exile and Landscapes of the Imagination', in B. Bender and M. Winer (eds), *Contested Landscapes: Movement, Exile and Place* (Oxford: Berg, 2001), p.330.
2. Stanage, N. *Redemption Song* (Dublin: Liberties Press, 2008).
3. Diner, H.R. '"The Most Irish City in the Union": The Era of the Great Migration 1844–1877', in R.H. Bayor and T.J. Meagher (eds), *The New York Irish* (Baltimore, MD: Johns Hopkins University Press, 1997), p.91.
4. Beck, U. *What Is Globalization?* (Cambridge: Polity Press, 2000), p.73.
5. Brah, A. *Cartographies of Diaspora: Contesting Identities* (London: Routledge, 1996), p.209.
6. Giddens, A. *Beyond Left and Right: The Future of Radical Politics* (Cambridge: Polity Press, 1994).
7. Basu, P. 'Hunting Down Home: Reflections on Homeland and the Search for Identity in the Scottish Diaspora', in Bender and Winer (eds), *Contested Landscapes*, p.333.
8. *Irish Voice*, 11 November 2004, www.irishabroad.com.
9. *Irish Echo*, 10–16 December 2007, www.irishecho.com.
10. Ibid.
11. Stanage, *Redemption Song*, p.170.
12. Featherstone, M., Lash S. and Robertson, R. (eds), *Global Modernities* (London: Sage, 1995), p.9.
13. Brendan Fay, Lavender and Green Alliance/St Pat's for All, interviewed by Professor Rosaleen Duffy on 22 September 2004.
14. Inglis, T. *Global Ireland* (London: Routledge, 2008), p.99.
15. Garvin, T. *Preventing the Future: Why Was Ireland So Poor for So Long?* (Dublin: Gill and Macmillan, 2005), p.190.
16. The Commission to Inquire into Child Abuse (CICA), *Executive Summary* (Dublin: CICA, 2009), pp.12, 13.

17. Éamon de Valera provided this iconic view of Ireland in a radio broadcast on St Patrick's Day, 1943.
18. Brendan Fay, interviewed by Professor Rosaleen Duffy on 22 September 2004.
19. O'Toole, F. 'What We Think of America', *Granta* (Spring 2002).
20. MacNeice, L. 'Autumn Journal', in *Collected Poems* (London: Faber & Faber, 1998).
21. Hannerz, U. *Transnational Connections: Culture, People, Places* (London: Routledge, 1996), p.17.
22. Quinn, P. 'The Future of Irish America', in J.J. Lee and M. Casey (eds), *Making the Irish American* (New York: New York University Press, 2006), p.680.

2

Patterns of Irish Migration and the Impact of Globalisation

Migration has been a constant and influential feature of human history. It has supported the process of global economic growth, contributed to the evolution of states and societies and enriched many cultures and civilizations. Migrants have often been amongst the most dynamic and entrepreneurial members of society, people who are prepared to venture beyond the confines of their own community and country in order to create new opportunities for themselves and their children.[1]

Decisions over migration relate to a combination of push and pull factors and, as Nicholas Van Hear points out, are the products of both compulsion and choice.[2] This chapter focuses on how questions of migration have changed within the context of global modernity, and the way in which modern patterns of Irish migration differ dramatically from those of past generations.

The main argument presented in this chapter is that the reasons for migration are directly linked to the experience and behaviour of those who travelled from Ireland to America during this period. In other words, that there is a cause and effect relationship between the circumstances under which people have left Ireland and their behaviour after they have arrived in America. More specifically, this chapter suggests that the motivations for migration are increasingly related to choice rather than compulsion in the twenty-first century and that this is changing the nature of the Irish diaspora in fundamental ways. The fact that the Irish are coming to America out of preference rather than desperation is having an important impact on their outlook and behaviour when they arrive. Firstly, many may not even view themselves as having left Ireland at all (other than for a temporary or clearly defined period) and would not categorise themselves as migrants or members of the Irish diaspora. Unlike many of their predecessors in the nineteenth and twentieth centuries, most of the Irish community living in America today have the economic means to return and find that decisions relating to migration only begin to creep up on them as they put down roots within the US. Thus, decisions relating to migration are taken long after the act of travelling itself has occurred. This obviates the need for today's Irish to go through the mental process of leaving one geographical and cultural reality for another, with all of the psychological trauma that often accompanies such decisions, for the migrants themselves and their families. In the twenty-first century, the majority of Irish people entering the US for anything other than an extended vacation do so either to work (whether legally or illegally) or with a pragmatic view about the length of time they will stay. The vast majority have the economic means to return to Ireland if their experience in America is a negative one, and hardly anyone today is forced to leave Ireland and travel to the US because of economic destitution or political oppression at home.

This issue of *choice* rather than *compulsion* is crucial to understanding today's Irish diaspora. The ability to physically and psychologically return to their country of origin is what distinguishes the member of the diaspora from the refugee. Because many of today's diaspora community feel that they are going to return to Ireland (and often do so regularly, while living in the US) there is less need to group together along ethnic lines while they are in America. The fact that they are more economically mobile and connected to 'home' has reduced their motivation to seek out their co-nationals and join socio-political or cultural support networks.

This chapter demonstrates the way in which the contemporary Irish community living in New York have evolved beyond traditional typologies of diaspora that seem more relevant to the nineteenth and twentieth centuries than they do to the twenty-first.

Today, diaspora communities are emblems of global modernity, capable of inhabiting hybrid spaces where their mobility is psychological as well as physical and where their attachments are fluid and decentred, simultaneously being home and away from home. The main argument here is one that flows through the other chapters of the book, namely that traditional definitions of diaspora and ethnicity no longer apply as neatly as they once did within Irish-America and that the desire of migrants to join ethnically defined cultural, social and political support groups or to engage in the process of 'hunting down home' is less apparent today than it was in the past.[3] After all, why bother to hunt down home if you feel that it will continue to be readily available to you?

LOCATING THE IRISH DIASPORA

Defining the precise limits of diaspora communities is an inexact science. The word 'diaspora' is often used with negative connotations, to denote those displaced, banished, exiled or otherwise removed, however accidentally, from their native place. Robin Cohen has provided a useful taxonomy for diaspora communities, suggesting a combination of the following features:

- Dispersal (often traumatic) from the homeland;
- Self-exiles in search of work, trade or colonial ambitions;
- A collective memory and myth concerning the homeland;
- An idealisation of the homeland;
- A return movement;
- A strong ethnic group consciousness sustained over a period of time;
- An uneasy relationship with the 'host' society;
- A sense of solidarity with diaspora communities in other countries;
- The possibility of a positive experience in tolerant host countries.[4]

A similar typology has also been put forward by William Safran.[5] Referring to the creation of transnational communities, Nicholas Van Hear suggests that the types of dispersal required for the creation of diaspora communities may emerge from a combination of cumulative processes and specific crises.[6] While these categorisations neatly encapsulate past patterns of migration, the argument here is that such typologies are more relevant to past patterns of migration (certainly in the Irish case), where compulsion rather than choice was a dominant factor, than to the transnational mobility of the twenty-first century.

Cohen points out that the concept of diaspora varies widely and can include the active coloniser, the banished exile and others who inhabit a space between these two extremes.[7] A note of caution has been introduced into this conceptual debate by Rogers Brubaker with his observation that the term 'diaspora' has become so diffused that it risks being rendered irrelevant.

> The dixie diaspora, the yankee diaspora, the white diaspora, the liberal diaspora, the conservative diaspora, the gay diaspora, the deaf diaspora, the queer diaspora, the redneck diaspora, the digital diaspora, the fundamentalist diaspora and the terrorist diaspora ... The problem with this latitudinarian, 'let-a- thousand-diasporas bloom' approach is that the category becomes stretched to the point of uselessness. If everyone is diasporic, then no one is distinctively so. The term loses its discriminating power – its ability to pick out phenomena, to make distinctions. The universalization of diaspora, paradoxically, means the disappearance of diaspora.[8]

Despite this conceptual health warning, what diaspora communities share is an 'inescapable link with their past migration history and a sense of co-ethnicity with others of a similar background'.[9] While notions of this inheritance may vary greatly in strength and be expressed positively or negatively, this ancestral genealogy exerts some emotional pull upon members of that diaspora community.

The contention here is that while this was perhaps true in the past, modern migration trends from Ireland to America bring very little of this baggage to bear on the behaviour or socio-cultural outlook of today's Irish community in the US. Going back to Cohen's typology:

- Contemporary patterns of Irish migration are rarely defined by a traumatic dispersal from the homeland;
- Those who have migrated have done so on their own terms and would not define themselves primarily as economic or political exiles;
- Many of these people have been happy to immerse themselves in the cultural iconography of America rather than preserving memories and myths from their homeland;
- There is evidence that such people have a pragmatic rather than a romantic outlook and do not idealise their country of origin or necessarily coalesce along ethnic lines.

In other words, existing theoretical models relating to diaspora communities require updating to take account of contemporary political and economic forces defined by global mobility and digital technologies.

Diaspora communities today (including the Irish) are the embodiment of the processes of globalisation, where transnational links and relationships are impacting on economies, political systems, social spaces and national cultures. In line with global trends in politics and economics, the sense of 'belonging' of diaspora communities is not confined today within national borders but is characterised by mobile, fluid and hybrid forms of communication that are capable of transcending geographical boundaries. Jan Art Scholte neatly summarises this point by arguing that globalisation has encouraged a growth of hybrid identities and overlapping communities in the twenty-first century which have compelled the individual 'to negotiate several national and/or non-territorial affiliations with the self'.[10]

Within the Irish context, Richard Kearney has remarked that the imagined community has spilled over the geographical limitations of the state, connecting those who live within its physical borders to those who live beyond them. 'When we speak of the Irish community today, we mean not only the national community but also our international communities abroad and our subnational communities at home ... Whatever one's linguistic or geometrical preference, one thing is clear: the Irish sense of belonging is no longer predetermined by the map lines on our island.'[11]

THE IRISH DIASPORA

The Irish are just all over the bloody planet, either digging holes in it, or drinking in it or putting up buildings in it, but basically we are all over the planet, and by and large, I think we contribute and we help to make it spin.[12]

We are either in a transitional moment when some new sense of Irish-America is going forward over the next few years, or we are at a point where it is really dissolving basically.[13]

Within the Irish context, the largest waves of emigration came from traumatic experiences such as the potato famine of the 1840s, forced exile during periods of British administration and economic hardship during the twentieth century (caused by Irish rather than British misrule) where people left Ireland (a de facto migration for many) in search of employment and better opportunities. Sizeable numbers also emigrated through more gradual migratory processes both before and after the Famine, connecting up with the larger waves of forced migrants and helping to form a critical mass of what today would be referred to as civil society. The statistics on emigration during these periods are dramatic for a small and relatively developed nation on the edge of Europe and indicate that the history of migration during this period is fundamental to understanding Ireland's self-image and its relationship with the outside world. Irish emigration was not purely a Famine phenomenon as up to a quarter of a million Ulster Scots sailed to colonial America during the eighteenth century. However, the trickle became a flood during the famine years of the mid-nineteenth century and the profile of those emigrating shifted from the relatively mobile economic entrepreneurs seeking to make their fortunes beyond Ireland's shores in the other British colonies to famine victims desperate to get out of Ireland in order to survive. Historian Christine Kinealy charts the rise in Irish emigration during the famine years and connects this to the formation of the diaspora network that subsequently emerged.

> One to one-and-a-half million people left Ireland between 1845 and 1851 and as many as a further two million in the subsequent twenty years ... Even when the famine was over, the high level of emigration continued and, in the following sixty years, an additional six million persons left. As a consequence, by the end of the nineteenth century, an international network of Irish communities had been established. The prime destination of the emigrants was overwhelmingly the United States, with approximately 80 per cent choosing to go there.[14]

The Irish sociologist Tom Inglis has argued that this regular pattern of migration sent out a sonic boom which continues to reverberate today, and he makes the point that the contemporary image of Ireland owes more to the country's diaspora than to those who currently live there.

> If Ireland has a global reputation it has less to do with the 6 million people who inhabit the island today and more to do with the influence of the Irish diaspora around the world ... Like many other things, it is not that the Irish are unique in the way they emigrated. It is just that the Irish started early and lasted longer. Between 1801 and 1921, approximately 8 million people left Ireland. Although the flow of people from Europe was high – 44

million migrated between 1821 and 1914 – the contribution of
the Irish to this flow was, relative to its size, larger than any other
country's.[15]

These sizeable and relatively regular flows out of Ireland to Britain,
America and elsewhere provided the raw material for the creation of
ethnic networks to be formed and for voluntary associational groupings
to become established, some of which are still going today. These networks were aided and abetted by the unifying power of the Catholic
Church and its socio-economic agencies such as the St Vincent de Paul
society and the county identification, which remained strong in many
of the Irish emigrants of the time. The one caveat to this, but an important one nonetheless, is that not all of these people formed ethnic
associations or conceived of themselves as part of the Irish diaspora as
it is now termed. The sizeable numbers of Irish Protestants and Scotch-
Irish Presbyterians integrated more easily into WASP hegemonic American society and did not feel the same need to form ethnic associations
as their Catholic compatriots. This group can lay some claim to being
the forgotten diaspora, as they melted relatively easily into American
society and wanted to emphasise their similarities to their host society
rather than their differences from it. This had the added advantage of
distinguishing them further from the Irish Catholic migrants who felt
more vulnerable in their new location and adopted a policy of 'putting
the wagons in a circle', clustering together physically, socially, culturally
and politically. Despite the retrospective stereotyping of popular culture
provided by films such as Martin Scorsese's *Gangs of New York* (2002),
the post-Famine wave of Irish migrants co-operated together out of
necessity and organised themselves along ethnic lines. The motivations
for this behaviour came out of the radicalising experience of the Land
War in Ireland, the trauma and grievance caused by the Famine itself,
and Daniel O'Connell's campaigns for Catholic emancipation and subsequent demands for political and economic reform. Motivation also
came through the bitter taste of discrimination, exclusion and racism in
America in the nineteenth century from the WASP majority. Professor
Joe Lee suggests that this experience helped to cement the Irish
Catholic community together politically and socially, producing strategic alliances and sublimating petty differences in the face of the wider
external threat.

A common enemy, particularly one already familiar from home, provides an enormous incentive to pull together. And the hostility and derision they met from the anti-Catholic, anti-immigration Know-Nothing movement, in particular, recycled over later generations by the American Protestant Association in the 1890s and by the Ku Klux Klan in the 1920s, provided just the incentive to provide a united front. Apart from African Americans, who endured a unique horror, they were the most frequent Americans to be regularly mocked as sub-hominid, as apes and monkeys, in the pages of 'respectable' intellectual periodicals.[16]

This has surrounded the Irish diaspora with a sense of loss and of endurance against heavy odds, yet paradoxically, the survival and success of this emigrant community and its descendants has transformed over time into a more positive narrative. 'Forced migrants may opportunistically make the best of a migration crisis; they are not simply victims, but are active within the circumstances in which they find themselves.'[17] Journalist and author Tim Pat Coogan sounds a typically pugnacious tone in his popular book on the Irish diaspora, *Wherever Green is Worn*, where he points out that the Irish diaspora have prevailed despite the hardships they have endured.

> Abroad, the history of Irish emigration is one of the success stories of the world. Dispossessed and ravaged by war, famine and centuries of economic decline, the Irish nevertheless managed to battle their way to pinnacles of political and economic success, epitomised by the entry to the White House of John FitzGerald Kennedy, the descendent of a Famine emigrant from County Wexford. Success was not achieved without great suffering and loss, both in terms of life and human happiness.[18]

Their survival and growing prosperity as a migrant community slowly changed their victimhood from a political reality to a cultural remembrance. Thus, to be a member of the Irish diaspora is, for many, a bitter-sweet cocktail of endurance and displacement that has been reflected in social cohesion and group solidarity, producing a whole genre of Irish literature and music lamenting and celebrating the plight of the émigré. The musician and academic Mick Moloney produced a CD in 2002 entitled 'Far From the Shamrock Shore', which sought to connect the disparate elements of the Irish-American experience in song. In the accompanying sleeve notes, Moloney encapsulates the interwoven fabric of the Irish-American story and sets out the objective of the musical anthology.

> The songs tell of leaving, arriving and surviving in the New World: of working on the railroads, on the canals, and in mining, construction, and factories. They tell of the discrimination the immigrants faced and their fight for fair treatment and fair pay. They tell of sacrifices made by Irishmen and of young lives lost in the revolutionary and civil wars. They speak of the accomplishments of the Irish in politics and the success that they ultimately achieved in all walks of American life. And they speak of an attachment to the homeland that seemed to grow stronger with the passing years even as the Emerald Isle itself became a romanticized and idealized paradise in the popular culture.[19]

Moving the focus from America to Britain, Christy Moore, one of Ireland's most celebrated contemporary folk musicians, popularised the Jimmy McCarthy song 'Missing You' and its cautionary tale of emigration to England in search of work and better opportunities during the Irish recession of the 1980s. The song became a staple of Moore's live performances from the mid-1990s. 'I wear the song like an old donkey jacket,'[20] he says in his autobiography, and explains how it connects with the Irish migrant experience.

> It contains some elements that would only apply to a tiny number of people, but as a whole it has something for everyone. It is also two-sided in that it simultaneously embraces the emigrants and the ones left behind in the home place. It has elements of the old emigrant songs, along with the harsh realities of modern building site life, the racism of police, the comfort of the bottle and the terrible realism of the immigrant at rock bottom gazing into the shop window reflection and knowing how far away home really is.[21]

Migration became nothing less than a leitmotif of the Irish experience, as powerful and binding within the national psyche as famine, British colonial oppression and Catholicism. Many of these themes were of course connected and combined with each other to produce a collective sense of self and community. Yet simultaneously, this experience has produced a sense of pride about being Irish, frequent cultural celebrations, most notably St Patrick's Day, and, until relatively recently, political extremism related to ethno-national conflict within Northern Ireland. There is a clear connection here between notions of the cultural and the political as illustrated by the abundance of emigration songs which have become an important part of the Irish folk music tradition. The lyrics of such songs neatly capture the contradictory tensions that have surrounded previous waves of Irish migrants combining pain, death and suffering with resistance, hope and action. They also mask the stark fact that those who made this journey to America were, relatively speaking, the more affluent within Irish society who managed to survive famine in the first place, and scrape together the fare to get beyond Britain.

Inglis makes an important distinction between Irish migrants to Britain and America before and after the Famine.

> Before 1841, when mass migration had already seen an annual exodus of 50,000 from Ireland, Britain was the main destination, ahead of Canada and the United States. This began to change around the Famine. Between 1845 and 1855, 1.5 million sailed to the United States, another 340,000 embarked for British North America, and about 250,000 went to Britain. ... Many of the Irish who went to Britain in the nineteenth century were the poorest of the poor. They were emigrants of despair, the unskilled poor and without property who inhabited the slums and scrublands of the cities and countryside. They were distinguished from the 'emigrants of hope' who could afford the fare to America.[22]

The distinct circumstances whereby these two groups within the Irish diaspora left their homeland were underlined by the alternative political cultures that resulted from their experiences of living in Britain and Ireland, which continue into the present. Over time, Irish-Americans have been able to embrace both parts of their hyphenated identity in a way that those who emigrated to Britain have not managed to do quite so easily. The reasons for this are complex and cross-cut history, politics and culture. Irish-Americans were removed from the colonial presence of their erstwhile oppressors and, more recently, from those held chiefly responsible for the political conflict in Northern Ireland. In the early years of the union, many Irish-Americans embraced their new nationality as a means of sticking two fingers up to the empire and demonstrating that they were talented, hard-working and law-abiding citizens. The Irish who went to live in Manchester, Liverpool or London did not have the same alternative nationality to grasp onto, trapped as they were within the 'belly of the beast'. Thus Irish-Americans were able to celebrate both aspects of their citizenship and national identity, while the 'Irish-British' clung desperately to the first part of the hyphen and surrounded their Scouse, Cockney and Brummie offspring with Irish iconography in the hope that some of it would stick. Christina McIlwaine, former press officer in the Irish consulate in New York, made a similar point when comparing Irish-Americans with those emigrants who settled in Britain.

> The one thing that you will find striking if you went to an Irish-American event here, the AOH … or an immigration dinner dance, is that they always play the Irish national anthem but they always play the American national anthem as well. You would never get that in England. I worked in London in our embassy and I'm struck to this day about the difference between the two communities … They are equally proud [of being Irish and American]; I mean the two ideas aren't mutually exclusive, whereas you are either Irish or British living in Britain. You are not Anglo-Irish in that sense … People here are very open about their identity and are very comfortable with a dual identity.[23]

The phrase 'Irish diaspora' is normally used in conjunction with Irish-America, and is often accompanied by stereotypical assumptions about the cultural and political outlook of what is assumed to be a relatively cohesive group of people. Officially at least, the United States accounts for somewhere in the region of 30–40 million Irish-Americans. The 1980 and 1990 census in the United States showed that 43.7 million Americans (19 per cent of the total population) defined themselves as Irish-American;[24] the 2000 census suggests the figure has fallen to around 34 million.[25] Nearly half of all the presidents of the United States have been (or have claimed to be) of Irish or Scotch-Irish extraction; the list includes figures such as James Monroe, Andrew Jackson, James Buchanan, Ulysses S. Grant, John F. Kennedy, Ronald Reagan and Bill Clinton. Kennedy was the descendent of a famine emigrant from County Wexford. At a more surreal level, Barack Obama found Irish ancestry during his presidential campaign in 2008. 'Muhammad Ali, Victor Mooney, Alex Haley, Billie Holiday, Ella Fitzgerald, Alice Walker, Ishmael Reed are not the only African Americans with Irish roots. It emerged in 2007 during the Democratic primaries that Barack Obama's third great-grandfather on his mother's side, Fulmuth Kearney, had emigrated from Moneygall in County Offaly to the United States in 1850.'[26]

However, while the basic numbers seem impressive at first glance, it is important not to overstate their significance and to recognise that the quantity masks a lack of quality in terms of any depth of political or cultural engagement with Ireland. Kevin Cullen of the *Boston Globe* newspaper makes the point pithily: 'However impressive it sounds to say that there are, according to the 1990 US census, some 40 million Irish-Americans, the reality is that most of them think IRA stands for an Individual Retirement Account.'[27] In his book on Barack Obama's presidential election campaign, Irish-born journalist Niall Stanage argues that this is largely a chimera which obscures the fact that the vast majority of this number 'are now, culturally and politically, indistinguishable from the American mainstream'.[28] Irish historian Joe Lee is equally sceptical of the headline numbers, whether they are put at 43 or 34 million, and his suggested differentiation between 'active' and 'passive' categories of Irish-American seems judicious.

> What then is Irish America? One must distinguish sharply between the ancestral association and the active identification. The idea of forty million hearts, or even thirty million, beating as one, begs basic questions. The essential one is how many of them allow their lives to be influenced by the fact. Only when that can be determined – and no scholarly estimates exist of the number – can any serious conclusions be deduced from census returns.[29]

The government of the Irish Republic has recognised the importance of the diaspora's political, economic and cultural role by commissioning a 'task force' report on issues surrounding emigration in 2002. This report, entitled *Ireland and the Irish Abroad: Report of the Task Force on Policy Regarding Emigrants*, notes that: 'Despite increasing levels of prosperity in more recent times, some 20,000 people continue to emigrate every year ... It is also estimated that of the 3 million or so Irish citizens abroad, almost 1.2 million were born in Ireland, the equivalent of approximately 30% of the present population.'[30]

Mary Robinson became Ireland's first female president in 1990 and made the Irish diaspora a key theme of her office. Symbolically, she kept a lighted candle in her official residence to commemorate the Irish abroad and as a physical symbol of the connection between those remaining on the island of Ireland and those who had left for foreign shores. In 1995, Robinson addressed the Irish parliament in a speech entitled 'Cherishing the Irish Diaspora'.

> At my inauguration I spoke of the seventy million people world-wide who can claim Irish descent. I also committed my presidency to cherishing them – even though at the time I was thinking of doing so in a purely symbolic way. Nevertheless the simple emblem of a light in the window, for me, and I hope for them, signifies the inextinguishable nature of our love and remembrance on this island for those who leave it behind ... In places as far apart as Calcutta and Toronto, on a number of visits to Britain and the United States, in cities in Tanzania and Hungary and Australia, I have met young people from throughout the island of Ireland who felt they had no choice but to emigrate. I have also met men and women who may never have seen this island but whose identity with it is part of their own self-definition ... The more I know of these stories the more it seems to me an added richness of our heritage that Irishness is not simply territorial ... In fact, I have become more convinced each year that this great narrative of dispossession and belonging, which so often had its origins in sorrow and leave-taking, has become – with a certain amount of historic irony – one of the treasures of our society.[31]

The election of Mary Robinson to the Irish presidency in 1990 has often been seen as the starting point for a new phase of modernity in Irish politics, and her focus on the diaspora was emblematic of a period where Ireland looked outwards at Europe and the rest of the world as well as inwards at its own society. This theme has been continued by her successor, President Mary McAleese, who has been eager to position the issue of the diaspora at the centre of her tenure as president and as a signifier of Ireland's arrival as a modern European state. A speech in the US in May 2003 indicated how the issue of Irish migration has evolved to the point where it can function as a non-threatening (almost non-political) uniting part of the national consciousness that allows Ireland to simultaneously look back to its past and forwards to a more prosperous future. This was overlaid with a sense of historical and spiritual self-justification (perhaps even to the point of self-satisfaction) in a 'what doesn't kill you makes you stronger' type of way. 'No other nation holds on to its children and its children's children like we do ... We are a connecting people. It is our strength, and our global Irish family is today one of our greatest resources, feeding our culture, expanding its imagination, opening doors, keeping faith with our intriguing homeland.'[32]

More generally, diaspora groups (including the Irish) have become emblems of multi-locality within the twenty-first century, occupying supranational spaces within creolised communities.[33] Creolised communities are understood here as being the synthesis of the migrant and indigenous populations, the 'third way' version of transnational movements – neither entirely host nor migrant society, but a combined socio-cultural space with the capacity to bridge across the host/migrant community divide in response to the multiple interactions and transactions between the population.

Put simply, it is much easier and cheaper to travel from one side of the world to the other in the twenty-first century. Perhaps more importantly, it is just as easy to get back to where we came from as it is to get outside our country of origin. These forces and trends challenge traditionally understood twentieth-century definitions of nation, community, identity and ethnicity. Today we are more mobile than our predecessors were in the nineteenth or twentieth centuries. This geographical mobility is impacting on issues relating to our ethnicity and notions of nationality and belonging within contemporary society. Until relatively recently, the state dominated our notions of nationhood. It was the state that had the power to declare and end wars, pass and enforce laws, control the media, shape economic conditions, collect taxes and, ultimately, coerce its citizens. However, in recent years all of these factors have been subject to an erosion of state supremacy.

The point here is that due to the processes of political, economic and technological globalisation, notions of political or cultural identity are no longer defined by the geographical limitations of the state but have overflowed beyond it, where those who live outside the state inhabit a 'diaspora space'[34] located somewhere between the local and the global. The remainder of this chapter examines this notion of the 'diaspora space', with particular reference to the Irish living in New York City.

THE IMPACT OF GLOBALISATION ON PATTERNS OF IRISH MIGRATION

The point was made earlier in this chapter that the nature of many diaspora communities is changing, and this is certainly true in relation to the Irish and Irish-American communities living in New York.[35] Unlike patterns of forced migration in the nineteenth or twentieth centuries, emigration is now a lifestyle choice for most migrants at the beginning of the twenty-first century, rather than an economic or political necessity. Many of those who leave do not have to decide when (or even if) they will return to their homeland. Today we live in the era of gap years, backpacking and low-cost air travel. Those who travel are younger, it is cheaper, and it is often done before or in between periods of employment. While travelling, people can stay in touch with home through their mobile phones, e-mail, Skype technology and the internet. While their ancestors may have picked them from the hedgerows of rural Ireland, today's migrants have an altogether different relationship with blackberries, and can use them to keep in touch with friends and family regardless of geographical location. As a consequence, the stresses, costs and sacrifices of travelling abroad are much lower today than they were in the past. The story of Barry Doyle, who emigrated from Limerick to New Zealand in the 1950s, emphasises the finality of emigration in the past and the link between the process of migration itself and the mindset of the individual concerned.

> When I was 17 and decided to make the step [to emigrate], it was a big step but I also made a determination that I would succeed and I would not regret it. So I made a whole lot of mental steps which made it easier ... I came out on a ship. That was the mode of transport, so to go back was a very, very big issue. I would say that for the first twenty years here it was almost unthinkable to go back. Aircraft then started to kick in and especially with the jumbo [jet]. That made a fantastic difference. One of the greatest inventions of the twentieth century was the jumbo jet so far as the emigrant was concerned ... There has been a dramatic reduction in the cost of travel so it has become easier as a consequence, and in recent years I have been back.[36]

Ironically, Barry Doyle found that globalisation caught up with him and facilitated what he thought was impossible when he left Ireland in the 1950s, namely frequent contact and communication with his homeland. The arrival of cheap airfares and digital communications saw him reconnect with his Irish culture to the point that he became involved in organising the Wellington St Patrick's Day Festival in New Zealand.

Doyle's story is typical of many tales of migration from the twentieth century and before. It was a difficult process, often undertaken with a sense of foreboding and finality. The act of leaving was preceded by a party colloquially referred to as the 'American wake', mimicking the death of the emigrant, and the prevailing sentiment was that those leaving were going into exile rather than temporarily relocating.

More than this, such events were also poignant reminders of social and community disintegration in rural parts of Ireland. They provided a connection with a dark past where starvation, death and political oppression stalked the land, and a reminder that (regardless of the reasons) the country was incapable of sustaining the people who lived there. These were often emotional events where families and friends said their farewells and where those who were leaving and those staying behind resigned themselves to the fact that they were unlikely to see one another again. This is markedly different from the twenty-first century experience of the Irish diaspora. Here, emigration has increasingly become a question of pragmatism rather than necessity, where both the decision to emigrate and the behaviour of the potential migrant are often taken long after the act of travelling has occurred. This of course is directly related to the cost and availability of long-distance travel in the twenty-first century. This changing profile is in turn having a direct impact upon the behaviour of the Irish community living in New York. The Irish who enter New York in the twenty-first century are not doing so out of economic or political desperation. While the recession that gripped Ireland in 2008 due to the worldwide financial crisis may have longer-term impacts in terms of Irish migration trends, unemployment is not the same as starvation and disillusionment is not the same as destitution. Crucially, most of today's migrant community have the means (if not an immediate intention) to return to Ireland if they do not like living abroad. Siobhán Dennehy, executive director of the Emerald Isle Immigration Center in New York, claimed in 2004 that fewer Irish people had been arriving since 2001 and that those who did saw the US as one of a number of possible options rather than an all-or-nothing chance to be grasped with both hands.

> Less people are arriving. They are certainly not arriving in the droves they arrived in the early 1990s, mid-1990s ... I think it is a calculated risk before they get here [New York]. They know they are coming here to overstay ... that's a risk that they are willing to take, that upon exiting they will be told that they will be barred for three to ten years, and that's no big deal to them. It's like 'well I don't need America now' ... there is the one to three or one to five-year plan in most of their minds, that this is something they are *absolutely* doing on a temporary basis.[37]

In other words, decisions relating to emigration do not have to be faced at the outset of the journey, with all the psychological trauma that would normally accompany such a momentous change of lifestyle. None of the Irish-born people interviewed in New York for this research who were under fifty years of age said that they had decided to emigrate at the time they actually *left* Ireland. They all either drifted into the decision over time as they put roots down in America or they have avoided the decision altogether. Éamonn Dornan, a lawyer originally from County Down in Northern Ireland, who is now a New York-based attorney specialising in Irish extradition and immigration law, epitomised this trend.

> I'll have been here eleven years in a couple of weeks ... We had a five-year plan that turned into a ten-year plan! How that pans out is that for the first few years when you go back [to Ireland] you feel obliged to tell people when you are asked 'when are you coming back?' 'Ah it will be four or five years.' I've just given up doing that now. There are a couple of points where you have to bite the psychological bullet [over emigration]. One is when you buy a piece of property, then you are tied down for a certain length of time. The second is if you are married and you have kids.[38]

Dornan's response suggests that definitions of diaspora crept up on him gradually as he put social and economic roots down in the US, but belie a pragmatism about the future. Niall Stanage, a journalist from Northern Ireland who has lived and worked in New York for six years, epitomises this trend. 'I would never say to somebody "I've emigrated", I would say "I live in America" ... I came over to cover the 2004 presidential election actually, a year before that election happened, and the plan was to give it a year and see how it went. After a year it was not that my career was particularly spectacular but it was good enough to stick with it and then you just keep going down that road.'[39] Unlike Barry Doyle, Stanage, Dornan and many others like them who have left Ireland in recent years did not give much thought to the issue of migration at the point of their departure but have come to terms with its reality after the fact. In other words, Stanage and Dornan are living within the 'diaspora space' available to many contemporary migrants and playing out Beck's notion of 'transnational place polygamy'. While Barry Doyle's lifestyle choices were initially confined to some degree by the limitations of geographical space, Dornan and Stanage have been able to mediate between their places of birth and residence due to the enabling aspects of global mobility and the digital communications revolution.

The key issue here is that both the circumstances and profile of the Irish emigrant have changed fundamentally at the beginning of the twenty-first century from the type of people who left Ireland in the 1850s and 1950s. To use terms such as emigrant or diaspora to describe these people is itself problematic. Many of the Irish who live and work abroad would not define themselves as emigrants in the traditional sense, while others would have a very clearly defined notion that they are temporarily resident in the host country and a determination to return to their country of origin in the short to medium term. Many others, like Éamonn Dornan, find that definitions of emigration and diaspora creep up on them unexpectedly after they begin to put roots down in the host country, while psychological decisions about whether they have emigrated can be avoided altogether. A good example of this is provided by the issue of taking out American citizenship. As the Irish community in the US can hold duel citizenship, they are able to become American citizens when they meet the qualifying criteria *without* giving up their Irish citizenship. This greatly reduces the need to bite the psychological bullets described above and enables the pragmatic incrementalism of contemporary migrant behaviour.

The Irish diaspora therefore masks a complex array of individuals who have left Ireland for a variety of reasons, from the long-term emigrant to the gap year student or backpacker. This issue of transience is important, as it affects the behaviour of the Irish community and in particular their desire to seek out and join Irish social and cultural associations that help to provide cultural cohesion and critical mass to diaspora populations. Organisations such as the AOH, a mainstay of the Irish-American political lobby throughout the 1970s and 1980s, are suffering as a consequence. According to AOH activists themselves, their numbers are dwindling dramatically, particularly in urban areas where AOH Divisions with increasingly elderly demographic profiles and a dearth of younger members are merging or disappearing altogether.[40]

The taxonomy for defining diaspora communities outlined at the beginning of the chapter does not apply as neatly therefore to these twenty-first century patterns of Irish mobility as it did to their predecessors. Among the Irish community in New York, the timeline between the old and new versions of Ireland is very apparent. Niall O'Leary, an Irish dancing instructor who has settled in New York, commented that the Irish people who arrive in New York today 'are coming from an Americanised Ireland in the first place ... someone told me a great statistic that most of the traditional Irish music bought in Ireland today is bought by Americans.'[41] O'Leary claimed that most of his Irish dancing classes were populated by Chinese and Korean children who had seen 'Riverdance' (disembodied from any notion of Irishness), with Irish participants being few and far between. Liz Kenny, director of the Fáilte Irish Center in Long Island city, New York, commented that Irish-born people were less likely to come to their cultural events than other groups and nationalities.

> There is a Chinese gentleman who comes here who is a fluent Irish speaker and an excellent Irish dancer. The guy who helps us out – he volunteers his time and he drives to pick up food for the seniors [lunch] every Wednesday – he just started the Irish [language] class last night and he's Moroccan ... There's a lot less direct Irish people [taking Irish dancing classes] than Irish-American and that's because it is mostly younger people that do Irish dancing and the people who now come over here from Ireland are now in their twenties or thirties or forties and have gone a little bit past [the age of] learning Irish dancing from scratch.[42]

Globalisation has in effect reduced the distance between Ireland and America to the point that it has enabled the sort of cultural hybridity outlined above and has facilitated people who want to take a pragmatic outlook over what Professor David FitzGerald has termed 'citizenship à la carte'. While remaining sceptical of the view that globalisation was the harbinger of the end of the Westphalian state, where national boundaries were being trampled under the feet of transnational movements of labour and culture, he argues that traditional models of state power have certainly been altered by the intersection of migration and globalisation.

> The territoriality of political power is being reconfigured through the embrace of citizens abroad – a condition I have called *emigrant citizenship* (or *extra-territorial* citizenship when extended more broadly to include the ancestral citizenship of emigrants' descendents). While resident citizens can make only narrow choices about the share of their resources they are willing to exchange for benefits from a monopolistic state, emigrants have more choices. Emigrants can take their business elsewhere and vote with their feet, giving them leverage to demand new terms of exchange with the state. The leviathan becomes a supplicant. Consequently, emigrants and the governments of their countries of origin are negotiating citizenship à la carte based on voluntarism, citizen rights over obligations, and multiple affiliations.[43]

Thanks to global technology, therefore, we can take advantage of electronic banking beyond the borders of our nation-state, download our print and broadcast media via the internet (within certain limits), own multiple passports, cast our postal votes and even import ethnic foodstuffs via specialist suppliers. This can be consumed within the context of virtual dinner parties where we can see and talk to other friends and family members in 'real time' who are eating the same meal in different parts of the world. In this sense, global technology has functioned as a cultural wormhole, shortening the distances imposed by geographical space and blending national distinctiveness into new forms of cultural creolisation. While it would be unwise to exaggerate this trend, as not everyone eats their dinner with a Skype headset on in a culinary conference call with their loved ones, it is still fair to suggest that globalisation has brought America closer to Ireland and vice versa and has enabled people to access an international menu of cultural options.

Many of those interviewed during the course of writing this book made the similar point that at both the cultural and the economic levels, Ireland and America are less distinct from one another today than they were in the past. In relative terms, Ireland has caught up with the US economically and fused with it at some point culturally, given America's impact on global cultural trends. In other words, the US dominance of popular culture has Americanised Ireland at some level to the point that those who leave Ireland to work in the US are already inculcated with American cultural iconography and are keen to experience more of it rather than hang on to their Irish ethnic consciousness which can always be returned to at a later date.

This fact was reflected upon with great disappointment by Martin Kelly, who had emigrated to America from County Galway in 1964. 'They are not the same type of people who came out here forty years ago in the '50s and '60s … and Ireland has gone to the dogs. Ireland is not the country I left, I don't know what they think they are up to.'[44] Kelly, a former state past president of the AOH, lamented that very few of the Irish who came to New York in recent years had joined cultural organisations such as the AOH or Irish sporting groups such as the GAA.

One reason for this is because the Irish who arrive in America in the twenty-first century are fundamentally different to their predecessors. They are a younger, more confident, more digitally connected and more pragmatic community who, contrary to many of those who left/escaped from Ireland in the 1850s and 1950s, do not have the same desire to 'hang on to home' and thus are not immediately driven towards organisations such as the GAA or the AOH. Professor Larry McCarthy, secretary of the New York GAA Board, substantiated this view when speaking about the fall-off in GAA membership in 2008. He makes the point that the drop in numbers is partly explained by the changing profile of contemporary Irish migrants from construction workers to professional white-collar graduates. This connects back into the changing nature of the global economy and its impact on Irish migration patterns and behaviour.

> I would see that the type of guy who is coming over is different as well [from past waves of emigration]. There's a lot more transience in them, in so much as a lot of people are not coming to be in the construction business … which is traditionally a place where a lot of our [GAA] guys work. That has changed and we've ended

up getting more professionals [coming] over, and so finding the engineer or the banker on Wall Street – who might be a GAA player at home but is not dependent upon Gaelic Park – is a little more difficult for the clubs, you know. Now they are there and they are quite willing to play, but the GAA is not the be-all and end-all of their lives as it was for the previous generation.[45]

New York-based journalist Niall Stanage remarked that the effects of this more pragmatic, individualistic and transient Irish migrant were being felt in the publishing industry in recent years.

I know that the [*Irish*] *Echo* a couple of years ago was thinking to reorientate itself towards newer arrivals, but whether those newer arrivals, who are typically of my generation or younger – who are making the choice to come to the United States as opposed to feeling obliged or exiled to the United States – whether those people are keen to cling to an Irish identity is debatable. I think those people have chosen to come and have the American experience.[46]

As several of the subsequent chapters in this book will illustrate, living as an Irish person in America in the twenty-first century is a vastly different experience than it was for past generations. Social and economic change at home has radically altered the balance between compulsion and choice that often provides the dynamic to leave.

Globalisation and in particular digital communications and the availability of relatively cheap air travel have changed the rules dramatically and have empowered the Irish diaspora and other migrant communities seeking to communicate with their home countries. The digital revolution has helped diaspora communities transcend geographical space and has in some cases functioned to reconnect emigrants to a cultural past that they thought had been surrendered at the point of their emigration. In this sense, the forces of globalisation have liberated diaspora communities and allowed them to live simultaneously at home while being away from home, and even to blend and twist notions of where 'home' is located.

While the revolution in global communications has allowed some Irish emigrants to rediscover their cultural roots, it has also allowed many of today's Irish migrant community to forestall questions and decisions concerning emigration and allowed them to avoid making this fundamental psychological choice for longer. In other words, they can put off deciding whether to emigrate until long after they have arrived in their country of residence. Global communication has given diasporic communities, including the Irish migrant, the best of both worlds and has allowed many of them to live both home and away from home, inhabiting this 'diaspora space' where they can tap into a menu of cultural options from both Ireland and America as they so choose. This trend was epitomised by Pauline Turley, a native of Northern Ireland, who has lived in New York for thirteen years and is director of the Irish Arts Center in Hell's Kitchen. Speaking in 2004, Turley explained how modernity had impacted on issues of migration:

> At the minute, my boyfriend is Irish and he spends half of his time over there … now my boyfriend has so many frequent flyer [air] miles that it has completely changed my notion of living here, because now I can go home and do go home every other month and my boyfriend commutes, he is in Ireland for two weeks and then he is here [New York] for two weeks and for him it is just like getting on the bus to go from Dublin to Cork! So we have a home in Ireland now as well, so having a place in Ireland has changed my notion, and my parents' notion [of where home is]. The question of being 'at home' is complicated by the internet and e-mail. I would go home to the North of Ireland and stay there an extra day and work from there and do a bit of business … with the internet and with technology too it [Ireland] is not as far away as it used to be.[47]

This resort to global communications to mediate between the place of birth and the place of residence is typical of many other accounts from the Irish community in New York and among diaspora communities in other parts of the world. As a result of cheap air travel, e-mail, internet and satellite television, it is possible to live in two (or more) places at once in the twenty-first century, both geographically and psychologically. Going back to David FitzGerald's phrase, we can now all be 'citizens à la carte' if we want to be, which complicates our notions of belonging, nationality, ethnicity and allegiance. Home might still be where the hearth is but, finances and schedules permitting, we can now have many hearths, in many homes, scattered across multiple locations.

CONCLUSION

It has been argued here that the nature of the Irish migrant is changing fundamentally. The very use of the terms emigrant or diaspora to describe the Irish community arriving in America in the twenty-first century is itself problematic. The ethnographic map has become more complex than it was in the twentieth century; many of those who arrive in New York from Ireland today are young, economically mobile and transient. Some, such as backpackers and gap year students, place a very clearly defined time limit on their stay, while others drift into migration by default or for reasons of pragmatism (buying property, getting married and due to career opportunities). Crucially, the vast majority who travel today do not make the psychological decision to emigrate at the point of their departure from Ireland. This is having a major impact on their attitudes and behaviour within New York as there is less demand for traditional Irish cultural support groups than was evident in the past. Organisations such as the AOH are suffering as a consequence of this as their numbers are dwindling, particularly in urban areas of New York. The Irish who are arriving in 'the big apple' today are as interested in sampling American culture as they are in playing out traditional notions of Irishness as portrayed by the AOH or the GAA. One of the reasons for this is because, for better or worse, Ireland has become more like America in economic and cultural terms, especially in its urban centres where the majority of the Irish population now lives. Professor Larry McCarthy commented, in the context of the GAA, that the different mindset of those arriving was having a negative impact on numbers within the organisation in New York:

> It's a different immigrant. It's not coming for life or it doesn't see itself coming for life … But that comment you said about younger people not saying that they've emigrated would be true still, very very true I would suggest, and the GAA doesn't seem to be as important to them as it was to people of the [19]50s and [19]60s, because there was a huge social side to going to Gaelic Park in those days … Our crowds are down hugely. It would have been at around 4-5,000 at its height way back in the '40s and '50s consistently. We fill the place now once a year for a Connaught championship game. And we get 3,000 people at it and that's a very good crowd for us. We are averaging at the moment about $4,000 a Sunday, at $10 a

head, so around 400 people and you are talking around 300–400 people consistently throughout the summer.[48]

This change in the character and behaviour of the Irish community in New York has been aided and abetted by the forces of globalisation. On the one hand it has brought American culture and politics closer to Ireland, while on the other, global communications have allowed the Irish emigrant to maintain existing social and cultural ties with Ireland and to travel between the place of birth and place of residence much faster, much cheaper and thus much more frequently than was possible in the past. Technology such as the internet has also allowed new forms of media to emerge which bridge the geographical and cultural gap between Ireland and America. An internet radio station called RadioIrish.com began broadcasting at the beginning of 2008, marketing itself as the only Irish radio station in the New York area. This digital venture was started by Irish journalists Seán McCarthy and Bob Gallico, both of whom had previously worked for Irish commercial radio stations such as Radio Nova in Dublin. McCarthy, a colourful character whose activities in addition to being a DJ encompass journalism, Hollywood acting and voiceover advertising, commented that RadioIrish.com had a unique selling point in that it was the only Irish radio station actually on the ground in New York. He claimed that this provided the Irish in New York with a more relevant and tailor-made connection than was available by simply listening to RTÉ over the internet.

> We're here on the ground, you know? I can walk in anywhere in Manhattan with a microphone, now who else is doing that? You don't find any [other journalists] out and about with microphones bringing the news of the Irish community to the rest of the world. Now there are programmes, there's 'Irish Radio' and Adrian Flannelly who's a historic figure here in New York ... He has had his radio show in New York for decades so he's an institution ... There's only two of us now, there's RadioIrish and Adrian Flannelly, and Adrian does an hour every week and we are on 24/7.[49]

Ventures such as RadioIrish.com illustrate the ways in which internet technology can be used to break down traditional barriers connecting national cultures with territorial spaces, facilitating what Ulf Hannerz has termed 'long distance interconnectedness'.[50]

In addition, the Irish diaspora is a declining category in the twenty-first century. The tap of Irish emigration is being turned off as Ireland's economy has accelerated and the political crisis in Northern Ireland has declined. Going back to the beginning of this chapter, the suggestion here is that traditional typologies of diaspora that emphasise group cohesion do not accurately reflect the condition of Irish migration patterns in the twenty-first century. Today there is an absence of compulsion and an absence of *decision* at the point of people's departure from Ireland. Most have a return rather than a one-way ticket to America, and an open mind about how long they will remain. They do not need to coalesce along ethnic lines or hang on to home, because they do not believe they are giving anything up at their point of entry into the US. The subsequent chapters will illustrate the changing patterns of Irish migration and the ways in which the Irish in America have evolved beyond traditional twentieth-century theorisations of diaspora and migration.

Before examining contemporary patterns of migration any further however, it is necessary to explore one of the central planks of the Irish-American narrative, namely its political analysis of Britain's role in Ireland and subsequently its critique of British government policy with regard to the conflict in Northern Ireland.

NOTES

1. Global Commission on International Migration (GCIM), *Migration in an Interconnected World: New Directions for Action* (Geneva: GCIM, 2005), p.5.
2. Van Hear, N. *New Diasporas: The Mass Exodus, Dispersal and Regrouping of Migrant Communities* (London: UCL Press, 1998), p.47.
3. Basu, P. 'Hunting Down Home: Reflections on Homeland and the Search for Identity in the Scottish Diaspora', in B. Bender and M. Winer (eds), *Contested Landscapes: Movement, Exile and Place* (Oxford: Berg, 2001), p.333.
4. Cohen, R. *Global Diasporas: An Introduction* (London: UCL Press, 1997), p.180.
5. Safran, W. 'Diasporas in Modern Societies: Myths of Homeland and Return', *Diaspora: A Journal of Transnational Studies*, 1, 1 (1991), pp.83–99.
6. Van Hear, *New Diasporas*, p.47.
7. Cohen, *Global Diasporas*, p.180.
8. Brubaker, R. 'The "Diaspora" Diaspora', *Ethnic and Racial Studies*, 28, 1 (2005), p.3.
9. Cohen, *Global Diasporas*, p.ix.
10. Scholte, J.A. *Globalization: A Critical Introduction* (Basingstoke: Palgrave, 2000), p.161.
11. Kearney, R. 'The Fifth Province: Between the Global and the Local', in R. Kearney (ed.), *Migrations: The Irish At Home and Abroad* (Dublin: Wolfhound Press, 1990), p.109.
12. Barry Doyle, organiser of the Wellington St Patrick's Day Festival, Wellington, New Zealand, interviewed by author, 15 December 2003.

13. Niall Stanage, journalist, interviewed by author, 13 September 2008.
14. Kinealy, C. *This Great Calamity: The Irish Famine 1845–52* (Dublin: Gill and Macmillan, 2006), p.297.
15. Inglis, T. *Global Ireland* (London: Routledge, 2008), p.88.
16. Lee, J.J. and Casey, M.R. (eds), *Making the Irish American* (New York: New York University Press, 2007), p.25.
17. Van Hear, *New Diasporas*, p.47.
18. Coogan, T.P. *Wherever Green is Worn: The Story of the Irish Diaspora* (London: Hutchinson, 2000), pp.x–xi.
19. Moloney, M. 'Far From the Shamrock Shore: The Irish-American Experience in Song' (Shanachie Entertainment Corp., 2002 – sleeve notes).
20. Moore, C. *One Voice: My Life in Song* (London: Hodder and Stoughton, 2000), p.99.
21. Ibid.
22. Inglis, *Global Ireland*, p.89.
23. Christina McIlwaine, interviewed by author, 3 September 2004.
24. See Arthur, P. *Special Relationships: Britain, Ireland and the Northern Ireland Problem* (Belfast: Blackstaff Press, 2000), p.136; O'Hanlon, R. *The New Irish Americans* (New York: Roberts Reinhart, 1998), p.13.
25. See http://www.census.gov/Press-Release/www/releases/archives/facts_for_features_special_editions/003581.html.
26. See Irish-Americans for Obama at: http://www.irishamericansforobama.com. This tenuous connection led to the song 'There's No-one as Irish as Barack Obama' by spoof band Hardy Drew and the Nancy Boys, which became a YouTube phenomenon during the election campaign.
27. Cullen, K. 'America and the Conflict', *Frontline*, June 1998, http://www.pbs.org/wgbh/pages/frontline/shows/ira/reports/america.html.
28. Stanage, N. *Redemption Song* (Dublin: Liberties Press, 2008), p.171.
29. Lee and Casey (eds), *Making the Irish American*, p.38.
30. Task Force on Policy Regarding Emigrants, *Ireland and the Irish Abroad* (Dublin, 2002), p.5.
31. President Mary Robinson, 'Cherishing the Irish Diaspora', address to the Houses of the Oireachtas, 2 February 1995. See http://www.oireachtas.ie/viewdoc.asp?fn=/documents/addresses/2Feb1995.html.
32. President McAleese, quoted in Inglis, *Global Ireland*, p. 92.
33. Augé, M. *Non-Places: Introduction to an Anthropology of Supermodernity* (London: Verso, 1995).
34. Brah, A. *Cartographies of Diaspora: Contesting Identities* (London and New York: Routledge, 1996), p.209.
35. The demarcation lines between Irish and Irish-American are also blurred and to some extent depend upon individual choice. These terms are used here to distinguish between those born on the island of Ireland and those born in America of Irish ancestry.
36. Barry Doyle, interviewed by author, 15 December 2003.
37. Siobhán Dennehy, director, Emerald Isle Immigration Center, New York, interviewed by author, 20 September 2004.
38. Éamonn Dornan, formerly of Smith, Dornan and O'Shea Attorneys, interviewed by author, 3 September 2004.
39. Niall Stanage, journalist, interviewed by author, 13 September 2008.
40. Martin Kelly, former AOH state president, interviewed by author, 9 September 2004.
41. Niall O'Leary, interviewed by author 2004.
42. Liz Kenny, director, Fáilte Irish Center, Long Island City, New York, interviewed by author, 10 September 2008.
43. FitzGerald, D. *Citizenship à la Carte: Global Migration and Transnational Politics*, Working Paper No. 3 (March 2008), Center for Global Studies, George Mason University, Fairfax, Virginia.
44. Martin Kelly, interviewed by author, 9 September 2004.
45. Professor Larry McCarthy, secretary, New York GAA, interviewed by author, 9 September 2008.

46. Niall Stanage, interviewed by author, 13 September 2008.
47. Pauline Turley, Director of the Irish Arts Center, New York, interviewed by author, 2 September 2004.
48. Professor Larry McCarthy, interviewed by author, 9 September 2008.
49. Seán McCarthy, Radio-Irish.com, interviewed by author, 11 September 2008.
50. Hannerz, U. *Transnational Connections: Culture, People, Places* (London: Routledge, 1996).

3

Becoming Political: Irish-America and the Northern Ireland Conflict

The leadership of Óglaigh na hÉireann has formally ordered an end to the armed campaign. All IRA units have been ordered to dump arms. All volunteers have been instructed to assist the development of purely political and democratic programmes through exclusively peaceful means. Volunteers must not engage in any other activities whatsoever.[1]

There is no doubt, whatsoever, that without Irish America this could never have succeeded.[2]

We are regularly engaged with the Irish diaspora. And if you move outside the diaspora and talk to anyone, they will tell you – and I defy anyone to contradict this – that most people who know anything about Ireland know the British government should have no claim or jurisdiction. What we have to do is galvanise that.[3]

When Irish-America is mentioned, images of lobbying over the political conflict in Northern Ireland are often not far behind. At particular spikes in the conflict such as Bloody Sunday in 1972 or the republican hunger strikes in 1981, Irish-American attitudes towards Northern Ireland came across to many on the outside as being crude and extreme, to the point of sharing sympathy for the Provisional IRA's 'armed struggle'. This was perhaps true of the 1970s and 1980s, but was less pronounced during the 1990s as a new wave of powerful and well-networked Irish-American activists emerged, who focused on process rather than outcomes. In more recent years, Northern Ireland has effectively disappeared as a lobbying issue for all but the most radical within the Irish-American community.

This chapter looks at the role of Irish-America from a political perspective and explains the evolution of the Irish-American lobby within the context of its impact on the Northern Ireland conflict and subsequent peace process in the 1990s. This focuses in particular on the evolution of political lobbying activities by Irish-America and on how these changes have mirrored modernising trends within the Irish diaspora more generally. The chapter explains the way in which the decision of the Provisional IRA to end its campaign of violence in July 2005 was influenced considerably by three separate but interrelated factors. Firstly, the internationalisation of Northern Ireland as a policy issue by successive US governments, from President Carter onwards, beyond being merely a matter of domestic UK politics. Secondly, the evolution of the Irish-American political lobby during the 1990s and its shift from outcome-driven objectives to process-driven and attainable goals. Thirdly, the response of the Irish republican movement to the political and social changes taking place within Irish-America (especially after 9/11) helps explain why PIRA strategy led to a final decision to end its 'armed struggle'. An important caveat to bear in mind here is that none of these factors, either on their own or in combination, were causal factors in bringing political violence to an end in Northern Ireland. They were, however, vital building blocks in enabling such change to take place and served to help reconfigure the issues at the heart of the Northern Ireland conflict, up to and beyond the Good Friday Agreement in 1998.

At a more general level, the evolution of the Irish-American political lobby mirrors the central conceptual argument explored within the other chapters of this book, namely that the nature of Ireland's relationship with America is undergoing a significant change. This has been fashioned by long-term factors such as rates of migration from Ireland and the impacts of globalisation, and short-term factors linked to political developments in both regions, chiefly the Northern Ireland peace process and the 9/11 attacks. One of the main arguments made in this chapter is that the peace process in Northern Ireland would not have taken place in the 1990s without American involvement and that the nature of the US intervention illustrates the revolution that has taken place within Irish-American political lobbying. This transformation, from those referred to by Ray O'Hanlon of the *Irish Echo* newspaper as the New Irish Americans, was itself a product of the wider social and political development of the Irish diaspora in the United States.[4]

In a precursor to the IRA statement of July 2005, Sinn Féin president Gerry Adams summarised the logic of the republican position in a high-profile speech on 6 April which laid the foundations for the later announcement by the IRA. Essentially, this claimed that 'armed struggle' had in the past been the only means of resistance available to Irish republicans but that circumstances had changed such that their objectives could now be pursued through purely political methods.

> For over 30 years, the IRA showed that the British government could not rule Ireland on its own terms ... That struggle can now be taken forward by other means ... Now there is an alternative [to armed struggle]. I have clearly set out my view of what that alternative is. The way forward is by building political support for republican and democratic objectives across Ireland and by winning support for these goals internationally.[5]

Within another political context, Professor Joseph Nye, a leading commentator on US foreign policy, has developed the theory of 'soft power' (persuasion, encouragement co-option) as opposed to 'hard power' (force, pressure, coercion).[6] This concept provides a useful framework for analysing the relationship between the American government and the Northern Ireland conflict. In essence, Irish-America's 'soft power' was a vital factor in leading Irish republicans towards the view that democratic politics (rather than paramilitary violence) was the way forward. It is also argued here that the evolution of Northern Ireland during the early 1990s from UK domestic issue to an aspect of US foreign policy was fundamental to the changing political strategy of Irish republicanism during the period. Given the relative failure of the IRA's military campaign by the beginning of the 1990s, the international angle stressed by Adams was the means by which republicans could achieve political change. This provided them with the belief (or excuse) that the unionist veto on political change could be overcome indirectly via American involvement. The engagement with Irish-Americans and, through them, to the US administration itself as 'soft power' actors *outside of* the domestic UK policy context was crucial to the IRA's decision to end its armed campaign.

This chapter examines the internationalisation of the Northern Ireland conflict from the Carter administration through to that of Barack Obama, arguing that the evolution of the Irish-American lobby, from its initial demands in the 1970s for immediate British withdrawal from Northern Ireland to cheerleader and core funder of incremental peaceful change, facilitated a constructive engagement with the US administration.[7] The capacity of the Irish-American political lobby to open (and close) doors for Irish republicanism at the highest levels of the US administration altered the structure of a predominantly internal ethno-national conflict, which in turn provided the dynamic for change that lies at the heart of the IRA statement of July 2005. While Irish-America could not use 'hard power' strategies of force or compulsion to achieve this, it was able to use constituent elements of its 'soft power', namely credibility, influence, encouragement and persuasion.

BACKGROUND TO INVOLVEMENT

The political relationship between Ireland and America is an unusual one, mediated by generations of migration from Ireland that has created an organic link between the two countries, yet it is located firmly within the context of modern international relations and dominated by America's more important diplomatic relationship with the government of the United Kingdom.[8] Within the modern era (at least until 9/11), the central issue connecting successive administrations in Washington, London and Dublin has been the political conflict in Northern Ireland. Formally, the US has treated Northern Ireland as a constituent part of the United Kingdom and, therefore, as a purely internal matter for the UK government rather than as an independent foreign policy issue.[9] As a former US diplomat put it: 'That the conflict involved two countries with each of whom the US had traditionally friendly relations reinforced our desire to stay out of it. Our policy could best be described as abstentionist neutrality. In this it was similar to our policy on Gibraltar.'[10] However, informally US administrations have periodically (both at the height of the conflict and while on the cusp of the peace process) taken an unusual degree of interest in Northern Ireland and have not treated it as being purely a matter of UK domestic concern.

The reasons for this level of interest are both historical and political, linked in particular to regular waves of Irish migration to the US during the nineteenth and twentieth centuries. This produced a tight network of Irish-Americans in the twentieth century who steadily grew in power and influence within civil society, not just within the police force and the construction industry but increasingly within labour unions, major business enterprises, NGOs and the public sector. They formed their own political and cultural support mechanisms such as the AOH and the GAA, while the Catholic Church functioned as another element of the social glue that allowed Irish-Americans to coalesce. Today, the United States accounts for somewhere in the region of 35–40 million Irish-Americans.[11] However, as explained previously, a large health warning needs to be applied to this figure as it masks an extremely varied and diverse community. New York-based journalist Niall Stanage (a native of Belfast) was sceptical of the census evidence. 'A lot of so-called Irish-Americans are really indistinguishable from Americans! The notion that there is an Irish-American vote, for example, I mean I just don't accept that that is true ... The notion that those people are Irish in any everyday sense is absurd. It just doesn't happen that way.'[12]

Nevertheless, while erratic and inconsistent, the presence of Irish-America as a periodic issue-based political lobby helps explain why US governments have taken such an interest in Northern Ireland and have not always treated it as being purely a matter of UK domestic politics. While the political impact of Irish-America on US policy towards Northern Ireland should not be overstated, the seeds of its periodic political interest lie in the existence of an Irish-American lobby which, during particular pressure points in the conflict and during the peace process, has had an impact upon US government policy. The existence of this lobby is a direct result of patterns of emigration to the US since the Famine in the mid-nineteenth century. The post-Famine wave of Irish emigrants had a well-defined political view which persisted until very recently in the US.

> The post-Famine migration from Ireland brought to the United States those who felt that they were not making a free choice to seek a new life in the new world but rather were in exile from their homeland as a result of British policy. American Irish thus bore a deep and enduring hatred for the British that was in no way ameliorated by the events of the latter half of the nineteenth and early part of the twentieth century when Britain reneged on the Home Rule Bill of 1912, crushed the rebellion of 1916 and attempted to defeat Sinn Féin in the war from 1918–1921.[13]

The economic success of Irish-Americans during the twentieth century, particularly following the Second World War, together with a long-lasting irritation at the Irish Republic's neutrality during the war and the strengthened alliance between the US and Britain in its aftermath, contributed to Irish-Americans losing interest in Ireland and stressing the second part of their hyphenated identity rather than the former during the post-war period. However, the post-Famine sentiments within Irish-America outlined above reconnected with Irish politics when ethno-national political conflict reignited in Northern Ireland in 1968–9 and when the British government attempted to control and defeat paramilitary violence by military means.

IRISH-AMERICA AND THE NORTHERN IRELAND CONFLICT

Irish Americans held their nationalist myths antiseptically intact. That basically republican image of Ireland – Green, Gaelic, Catholic, and subject to British imperial exploitation – was preserved in older Irish neighbourhoods, social clubs and civil service unions.[14]

One of the reasons why Irish-America reconnected politically when ethno-nationalist violence erupted in the late 1960s in Northern Ireland was because Irish-American civil society existed structurally, in the form of the AOH, together with other politico-cultural NGOs that had grown up around Irish neighbourhoods in the US such as the GAA. Equally importantly, this matrix of civil society organisations was relatively coherent in the early 1970s, viewing Ireland as an unfortunate victim of malign British interference.[15]

The Irish Northern Aid Committee (known colloquially as Noraid) formed in 1970 and was openly supportive of the IRA's armed campaign. Brian Hanley claims that Noraid 'was the best-known and most important Irish-American republican support group during the course of the Northern Ireland conflict'.[16] However, Noraid's support and influence was episodic rather than consistent and relied heavily on events within Northern Ireland itself, with its major boost coming during the republican hunger strikes of 1981.[17] According to Adrian Guelke, 'between its founding [1970] and 1991 – when it ceased to report remittances – it officially remitted approximately $3.5 million to Ireland to a Sinn Féin-controlled charity that assisted the families of republican prisoners.'[18] While this was not a huge sum, it was supplemented

with less official activities not given to careful auditing and vital publicity and support for the Irish republican cause on the international
stage. In a high profile court case in 1982, Noraid's founder, Michael
Flannery, admitted his role in a gun-running scheme to the IRA, but in
a surreal turn of events managed to convince the jury to acquit him on
the grounds that he believed the shipment of arms to have been autho-
rised by the CIA.[19] Kevin Kenny argues that Noraid quickly became the
leading political voice within Irish-America. 'By 1972 Noraid claimed
one hundred chapters and eighty thousand members and had established
itself as the dominant Irish-American nationalist organization.'[20] While
estimates of Noraid's membership vary (e.g. Linda Dowling Almedia puts
the figure at between 7,000 and 10,000 at its peak),[21] the wider point is
that the organisation had effectively established itself as the mouthpiece
of Irish-American nationalism in the early 1970s and gave the Provisional
IRA a degree of international legitimacy in the process.

The Irish National Caucus (INC), which formed in 1974, was less
militant than Noraid though equally energetic in critiquing British policy in Northern Ireland. The INC succeeded in lobbying support for
the MacBride Principles throughout the 1980s. These were designed
to promote fair employment in Northern Ireland and specifically targeted US investment in the region, requesting US companies to engage
in non-discriminatory employment practices to offset what they argued
was a systematic pattern of anti-Catholic discrimination in Northern
Ireland. Fr Seán MacManus, for many years president of the INC, outlines the way in which Irish-America was attempting to use economic
muscle as a form of political leverage.

> The MacBride Principles have been the most effective American
> campaign on Ireland since Partition. It has provided Irish-Ameri-
> cans with a direct, meaningful and non-violent means of address-
> ing discrimination in Northern Ireland. No longer does one hear
> the British Government or others telling Irish-Americans to 'mind
> their own business'. It is our business to mind what our invest-
> ment dollars and foreign aid are doing in Northern Ireland. The
> MacBride Principles are non-violent, morally correct, politically
> effective and our duty as responsible investors.[22]

While the INC claimed that the MacBride Principles were fair and
equitable, they were not uncontroversial within Northern Ireland, with

unionists claiming that they represented reverse discrimination against the Protestant community. The British government also opposed their introduction as this was an implicit admission of *their* responsibility in patterns of discrimination that would require reform. Despite such opposition, several states in the US adopted the MacBride Principles during the 1980s (Massachusetts in 1985, New York and New Jersey in 1986 and many others in subsequent years) and passed legislation requiring US companies to comply with them. This forced the British government to bring forward new legislation of its own, in the form of the Fair Employment Act of 1989 and a Fair Employment Commission (FEC) to tackle discrimination.[23] Bill Clinton had also indicated his support for the MacBride Principles during his 1992 presidential campaign but was reluctant to bring them forward as legislation due to British government and unionist opposition.[24] Clinton felt that the need for the MacBride Principles had been overtaken by events, given the British government's introduction of the FEC and its own legislation. He was also worried that the MacBride Principles were tainted by their association with the INC and would paint his own administration as pro-Irish nationalist at the very time he was trying to make overtures to unionist politicians in Northern Ireland. What followed was an unedifying wrangle between the White House and the INC over the tying of the MacBride Principles to US funding. This was particularly the case with the International Fund for Ireland (IFI) in the mid-1980s, which was an initiative for US funding put together in the wake of the Anglo-Irish Agreement of 1985. As Andrew Wilson explains, this legislation was watered down so that applications to the International Fund for Ireland (IFI) '*should* rather than *shall* adhere to the MacBride Principles' and the requirement for quotas to reverse discrimination was also removed.[25] Notwithstanding these objections, the MacBride Principles were eventually signed into law (in watered-down form) by President Clinton in October 1998.

The relative success of the INC promotion of the MacBride Principles in the face of determined opposition from both the UK government and unionist politicians within Northern Ireland in the 1980s illustrates the impact of Irish-American civil society on Northern Ireland. According to Ray O'Hanlon, senior editor of the *Irish Echo* in New York, the MacBride Principles 'were to draw support from a far wider spectrum of Irish America than just about any other single issue in the 1980s and 1990s'.[26]

GETTING ON THE WASHINGTON POLICY AGENDA

In the early 1970s, influential Irish-American politicians such as Senator Edward Kennedy and Speaker Tip O'Neill frequently adopted public positions critical of the British government. However, these rarely impacted on US policy towards Northern Ireland, which was viewed then as a purely UK domestic matter. As T.J. Lynch remarks: 'The heightened political, anti-British policy rhetoric that Kennedy employed raised the profile of the [NI] Troubles in the United States whilst simultaneously complicating the response of the American government to the conflict ... Despite Kennedy's best efforts to internationalize the issue, Northern Ireland remained a domestic British problem.'[27] These interventions were often striking in their simplicity, with Kennedy introducing a Senate Resolution in 1971 that called for a united Ireland and the immediate withdrawal of British troops from Northern Ireland. In a further illustration of the Irish-American political temperature at the time, Congressman (later Governor) Hugh Carey of New York called the British army 'thugs' in 1971.[28] In 1973 Kennedy wrote an article in *Foreign Policy* which declared the conflict in Northern Ireland to be beyond the domestic jurisdiction of the UK government and a matter for intervention by the international community.[29] Kennedy also made a parallel between British security policy in Northern Ireland and failed US involvement in Vietnam, which presented a striking alternative to official narratives which were reluctant to concede that a political conflict was taking place in Northern Ireland or that the British government was failing to manage it effectively. In other words, during the 1970s the narratives of the Irish-American lobby and the US government were poles apart, with the former having little available 'soft power' to use against the latter.

While these interventions, both by NGOs and well-connected individuals within the Washington political elite, found little purchase within US policy circles, they were nevertheless an important source of political support for republicans in Northern Ireland. High profile politicians such as Edward Kennedy, Tip O'Neill, Hugh Carey and Daniel Moynihan[30] were careful to avoid making comments in support of violence, but their vocal opposition to British policy was used nevertheless by Irish republicans to justify the IRA's armed campaign. This in turn helped them internationalise the political conflict in Northern Ireland to a global audience and frame the 'armed struggle' as a war of liberation rather than domestic criminality.

This Irish-American consensus over the Northern Ireland conflict (and Britain's role in it) only began to fracture after the mid-1970s. By this point, John Hume, the leader of the SDLP, and Seán Donlon, then Irish ambassador to Washington, began to convince both O'Neill and Kennedy of the importance of separating out constitutional Irish nationalism, as represented by the SDLP and the Irish government, from the militant Irish republicanism of Sinn Féin and the IRA. Hume and Donlon argued that by supporting achievable reformist objectives and by helping to cut off support from republicans in Northern Ireland, Irish-America would have a better chance of challenging British policy through their own administration. The Irish government, together with Hume, led a charm offensive in Washington to reduce funding, publicity and political support from groups such as Noraid and the INC. 'This process, referred to as the "greening of the White House", was remarkably successful: the US is now an important partic-ipant in the peace process in Northern Ireland.'[31] As a consequence of the arguments of the Irish government in association with the SDLP, together with the worsening levels of IRA violence, attitudes among Irish-American elites to Northern Ireland began to deviate sharply in the latter stages of the 1970s away from those of Noraid and other radical NGOs who supported the republican analysis and what they regarded as the IRA's legitimate physical resistance against a British army of occupation.

While it is important to stress that the Irish-American lobby had no sustained impact on US foreign policy, there were nevertheless specific occasions when their moderate stance paid dividends. At Tip O'Neill's encouragement, President Jimmy Carter made a statement on North-ern Ireland in August 1977. While the content of Carter's statement lacked any real substance, beyond calling for a form of government 'acceptable to both communities' and other well-worn platitudes and non-controversial aims, its importance was that it was made at all rather than what it contained. This was the beginning of the internationalisation of the Northern Ireland conflict that concluded with the hands-on involvement of President Clinton in the peace process of the 1990s. The Carter statement gave Northern Ireland a diplomatic identity that belied its status as an integral part of the UK and a political presence that took it beyond a matter of purely British domestic concern. 'This was a fundamental shift from abstention to involvement.'[32]

Periodically within the Carter administration, the 'Four Horsemen' acted as a buffer between the government and more radical NGOs with more demanding policy agendas. As Brian Hanley comments: 'By the 1980s influential figures such as Ted Kennedy, Tip O'Neill, Hugh Carey and Patrick Moynihan were supporters of the Irish government's thinking on the north. Their joint 1977 St Patrick's Day statement ... when they called on Irish-Americans to refuse to contribute to Noraid was a watershed in terms of mainstream Irish-American politics.'[33]

As a consequence of its moderation (in comparison to Noraid or the INC) the Irish-American political elite was (on occasions) able to prize policy changes out of the US administration in return for controlling the more radical agendas of the INC and other high-profile republican supporters. Carter risked embarrassing London by including the United Kingdom on a register of states deemed to have violated human rights standards, due to the British government's treatment of prisoners in Northern Ireland. The State Department, meanwhile, suspended the sale of weapons to the Royal Ulster Constabulary in July 1979 in response to pressure from Irish-America and as the price for Tip O'Neill squashing efforts by more radical activists to convene congressional hearings on Northern Ireland. These hearings would have dragged the British government into a public defence of damaging reports from Amnesty International and the European Court of Human Rights over its treatment of prisoners in Northern Ireland.

While the activities of Irish-America had an irritating rather than a fundamental impact upon US policy towards Northern Ireland, the process of internationalising the conflict had begun by the late 1970s which, in combination with other factors, led to the 1994 paramilitary ceasefires, the 1998 Good Friday Agreement and the statement of July 2005 by the Provisional IRA. Firstly, the Irish-American lobby was activated by the outbreak of violent conflict in Northern Ireland, with Britain playing the role that Irish-America had scripted for it through generations of mythology. Secondly, the divergence of the Irish-American political elites from the more radical NGOs that took place during the 1970s, and in particular their denunciations of IRA violence and connection to constitutional sources in Irish politics (including John Hume and the Irish government), led to more moderate statements and policy demands. This in turn led to small, though significant, impacts on US government policy. Thirdly, the presence of the Irish-American political elites acting as a moderating influence on more radical groups encouraged the Carter administration to lift Northern Ireland out of the position that the political conflict in the region was purely a matter for British domestic policy-making. This began the process of internationalising the conflict that was seen more tangibly in the peace process of the 1990s.

This was a very gradual process however, and was barely perceptible at the time. The Carter intervention was not a major break with the State Department domination of US policy towards Northern Ireland which characterised the post-war period. Both the Carter and Reagan administrations continued to look at the political conflict in Northern Ireland through Anglophile spectacles and within the context of this more important Cold War alliance. Nevertheless, a precedent had been set by Carter that was periodically revived by Reagan before becoming a mainstay of the Clinton presidency, when officials at the National Security Council wrenched control of Northern Ireland policy away from the State Department. This precedent was that US administrations felt able, on occasions, to use their 'soft power' in relation to Northern Ireland (i.e. their influence and persuasion rather than coercion or force) when they considered that this was necessary.

President Reagan used such soft power with his close ally Margaret Thatcher when she was British prime minister, encouraging her to forge a closer alliance with the government of the Irish Republic as a means of achieving greater security and managing the Northern Ireland conflict more effectively. This influence contributed to British–Irish diplomatic initiatives in the 1980s and most notably the signing of the Anglo-Irish Agreement by the British and Irish governments in November 1985.

THE IMPACT OF IRISH-AMERICA ON THE PEACE PROCESS

While the political identity of Irish-America seemed relatively cohesive during the 1970s, campaigning for Irish national self-determination and critiquing British government policy in Northern Ireland, this has been changing significantly since the mid-1980s and accelerated with Clinton's election as US president in 1992.[34] During the Clinton candidacy for the US presidency, a new lobby group emerged called Americans for a New Irish Agenda (ANIA), itself a more formalised manifestation of a previous group, Irish-Americans for Clinton/Gore.[35] ANIA was a coalition of influential Irish-Americans, including journalists, lawyers, labour and corporate business leaders, who epitomised the twentieth-century evolution of Irish-America from refugee/immigrant community to an integrated, moneyed and highly networked sector of the indigenous population.[36] 'ANIA was a potent configuration of well-funded, business-orientated Irish-American opinion: geared towards constitutional nationalism, concerned that Washington should abandon the traditional non-involvement, and also prepared to woo moderate loyalists.'[37] ANIA lobbied Clinton before he became US president, focusing on *process* rather than any particular *outcomes*, and presented him with practical and non-partisan policy options rather than a platform that would embarrass the UK. As Adrian Guelke concludes, ANIA moved away from the traditional demands of Irish-America for a 'united Ireland' to a more sophisticated discourse that urged the need for conflict resolution and peace-building while being less prescriptive about the precise shape that should take.[38]

In April 1992, while still governor of Arkansas, Clinton was invited to speak at an Irish-American forum and was as surprised by the intensity of his audience as they were by his candour. Clinton later remarked of this meeting: 'I was exhausted. It was late at night and it was almost like I was being put through an oral exam for a PhD in Irish politics.'[39] At this meeting, Clinton was pressed as to whether, if elected to the presidency, he would grant Sinn Féin president Gerry Adams a visa to enter the United States. Clinton's direct answer surprised many of the delegates, who were used to more anodyne and non-committal responses from their national politicians. 'I want to give you a precise answer to the question. I would support a visa for Gerry Adams. I think it would be totally harmless to our national security interests, and it might be enlightening to the political debate in this country.'[40]

Corporate Irish-America wanted to engage with the Clinton White House rather than confront it, a strategy that soon paid dividends when ANIA helped secure Clinton's decision to grant a forty-eight hour visa to Gerry Adams to attend a conference on Northern Ireland in the United States. This was before the IRA ceasefire of August 1994, went against advice from the State Department, the Department of Justice and the CIA, and provoked an angry reaction from the British government. According to Andrew Wilson, this initiative by Clinton 'was an important element in the IRA's decision to declare its first ceasefire in

August 1994'.[41] Veteran Irish journalist Déaglán de Breadún suggested that: 'The [British] Prime Minister's annoyance must have been all the greater when the Sinn Fein leader became the darling of the US media during his brief visit, but whether London liked it or not there had been a fundamental shift in US policy which would have huge effects further down the road.'[42]

ANIA placed Northern Ireland onto the foreign policy agenda of the Clinton administration by focusing on *process*– rather than *outcome*-driven goals. In parallel with the profile of ANIA activists, an important link was made between politics and economics, with Clinton buying into a twin-track process of economic rejuvenation as well as the promotion of political dialogue.

The wider ideological point here is that the Clinton administration sold an essentially neo-liberal political and economic strategy to a supposedly neo-Marxist paramilitary movement that had in the past identified itself with the ANC in South Africa and the PLO in the Middle East. By the 1990s, it was buying into a US-generated 'peace dividend' based on international capitalism and investment by the global hegemon. 'In a broader context, therefore, the Irish initiatives of the US administration were framed within a foreign policy that sought the resolution of regional conflicts as a means of accelerating the free movement of American capital and commodities through globalization.'[43]

The post-Cold War period also played a role in the success of ANIA, complicating the foreign policy environment and allowing Clinton to detach his initiatives on Northern Ireland from the traditionally Anglophile State Department and its arguments that any unilateral statements would carry an unacceptable risk of alienating the UK.[44]

To a degree, ANIA and the Clinton administration were taking advantage of the changes taking place in republican thinking at the beginning of the 1990s, with Sinn Féin and the IRA moving in a direction that made political engagement a possibility for Dublin and London, as well as Washington. The new phase in the politics of Sinn Féin had interesting side-effects upon their connection to their Irish-American allies. In particular, the relationship between Noraid and Sinn Féin became increasingly strained as the peace process developed into the 1990s. The erstwhile cheerleader for the IRA's armed struggle was effectively sidelined in 1995 with the formation of the Friends of Sinn Féin group, formed in the aftermath of Gerry Adams' visit. This was followed by Sinn Féin opening an office in Washington shortly after the IRA ceasefire in 1994, headed by Rita O'Hare, a republican from Northern Ireland and close ally of Adams. This move was partly financed by corporate Irish-America and Chuck Feeney of Atlantic Philanthropies, an Irish-American billionaire who was active within ANIA and part of the new wave of lobbyists who focused on the importance of US engagement in the *process* of conflict resolution rather than traditional pre-determined outcomes associated with Irish-American lobbying of the 1970s. Niall O'Dowd, a key figure within ANIA and one of the central fixers between Sinn Féin and corporate Irish-America, has commented on the importance of Feeney's role in bringing republicans in from the cold.

> Feeney also took the considerable risk for a man of his stature of coming to the aid of Sinn Féin, shortly after the 1994 IRA ceasefire, when the party desperately needed funding to establish its political agenda … Feeney [put] up more than a million dollars to ensure that the party was properly represented in America … What he was doing was helping ensure that politics, not violence took precedence in the republican movement. He succeeded in helping Sinn Féin establish their American presence, to build on their links to successive White House administrations and to fully staff an office in Washington for a time.[45]

From this point onwards, Sinn Féin controlled publicity and fundraising in the US and sidelined the activities of Noraid. As Brian Hanley argues: 'The IRA's ceasefires and the launch of Friends of Sinn Féin opened up avenues of funding which [would] never have been accessible to Noraid.'[46] The move away from Noraid towards Friends of Sinn Féin in the mid-1990s epitomised this new era and is consistent with the strengthening links between Sinn Féin, corporate Irish-America and the US administration.

This was in turn networked into an emerging White House strategy, where key officials, including Clinton, commerce secretary Ron Brown, national security adviser Anthony Lake and Nancy Soderberg, staff director at the NSC, looked at ways in which the US could underpin the peace process via an economic development package. While the feature event of this initiative was a major investment conference in the US, other elements of the strategy were perhaps more important in the longer term. Firstly, the US Department of Commerce organised a number of trade missions to Northern Ireland aimed at convincing American CEOs of the economic benefits of investing in the region. These were headed up by the charismatic Ron Brown, who brought an element of chutzpah to the strategy before his unfortunate death in an air crash over the Balkans in April 1996. Secondly, Clinton supported the development of the Walsh visa program, a scheme developed by New York congressman James Walsh which provided young unemployed Irish people with three-year working visas in the United States. The assumption was that this would imbue them with political tolerance and economic savvy that could be deployed usefully on their return to Ireland. In the words of Walsh himself: 'On an economic level, we want to nurture prosperity which leads to tolerance. On a social level, we want to share our multicultural experience and the lessons we've learned. This visa represents an American commitment to provide support for the peace process and all that it promises for the people of Ireland and Northern Ireland.'[47] Thirdly, in an effort to co-ordinate this strategy, Clinton appointed Senator George Mitchell as his special advisor for economic initiatives in Ireland, an involvement which gradually evolved into Mitchell's more central role in the multi-party negotiations from 1996 to 1998 leading to the Good Friday Agreement itself.

It was this triangle of contacts between Sinn Féin, corporate Irish-America and the Clinton White House that established a virtuous circle of relationships where influence was exercised and a degree of trust developed between the main actors on the nationalist side (though the importance of other key actors – Reynolds/Ahern, Blair/Mowlam and David Trimble, then leader of the Ulster Unionist Party (UUP) – was also vital to the wider peace process in the 1990s). This trust was put to the test with the breakdown of the Provisional IRA ceasefire in 1996, but the fact that Gerry Adams was able to lift the phone on 9 February 1996 and call US national security adviser Anthony Lake, minutes before the Canary Wharf bomb went off in London, to tell him that he was hearing 'some disturbing news' illustrates how far the soft power relationship between Sinn Féin and the Clinton administration had progressed. The attributes of trust and loyalty associated with soft power relations extended to the point that the White House was prepared to keep the lines of communication open with Sinn Féin and see the Canary Wharf bombing as a blip rather than a trend. Adams was to discover several years later in the post-9/11 environment that such access was not guaranteed and could just as easily be denied as granted.

During the heady days of the peace process, however, lines of communication between Sinn Féin and the White House were relatively open. During this period, it was corporate Irish-America that was the facilitator of movement by the IRA and it played a major part in the choreography of the peace process in the 1990s. A group of influential figures including Niall O'Dowd, publisher of the *Irish Voice* newspaper, Bill Flynn, former CEO of Mutual of America, and chair of the National Committee on American Foreign Policy, Bruce Morrison, co-chair of Irish-Americans for Clinton/Gore, Chuck Feeney, CEO of Atlantic Philanthropies and Tom Moran, then CEO of Mutual of America, visited Ireland in August/September 1993 to determine the possibilities for political progress. The IRA announced a seven-day ceasefire to coincide with their arrival and as evidence of their willingness to engage in the peace process.[48] This lobby linked up with the Irish-American political elite and in particular Edward Kennedy and his sister Jean Kennedy-Smith, who had been appointed by Clinton as US ambassador to Ireland. Having been convinced by ANIA and the Irish government that progress was possible, Clinton pushed the Northern Ireland peace process to the front of his foreign policy agenda. Following the announcement of the IRA ceasefire in 1994, Clinton granted Adams another visa in March 1995 to attend St Patrick's Day celebrations in the US and to conduct fundraising activities. This decision came at a point when the British government (under pressure from unionists at Westminster) was trying to delay allowing Sinn Féin into multi-party talks by arguing that as there was no guarantee of the ceasefire's permanence, Sinn Féin could not be fully trusted in the democratic process. The fact that the White House was much more upbeat about the *bone fides* of Sinn Féin and the IRA further angered the British government, as they saw this as undermining their strategy. British prime minister John Major was reportedly so incensed by Clinton's granting of a visa for Adams in 1995 that he refused to accept telephone calls from the US president for a week – a reaction which did not inflict any noticeable damage on the White House.

This revolution in American foreign policy towards Ireland was symbolised by Clinton's visit to Northern Ireland in December 1995. The first serving US president to visit Northern Ireland was treated to a hero's welcome in Belfast, Derry and Dublin with speeches and walk-abouts carefully choreographed to present the US administration as a neutral third party. While anxious not to embarrass the British government unduly – for example, his 1992 pre-election promise to appoint a 'peace envoy' to Northern Ireland was quietly dropped following advice from Dublin that this would antagonise the British government and jeopardise his macro-strategy[49] – Clinton pushed Northern Ireland to the top of the US foreign policy agenda and became personally involved in the multi-party talks that led to the Good Friday Agreement in April 1998. During the latter stages of the negotiations, Clinton was in regular contact with the British and Irish governments, as well as talks chairman George Mitchell, in an attempt to resolve sticking points and encourage the participants.[50]

In light of the third-party role of the US in Northern Ireland during the 1990s and the soft power relationships that evolved over time between the Clinton administration, corporate Irish-America and Sinn Féin, it is clear that these connections played an important role in the peace process and eventual political settlement reached in 1998.

IRISH-AMERICA IN THE TWENTY-FIRST CENTURY: DEMOGRAPHIC DECLINE AND DOMESTIC POLITICS

This section examines the broader patterns within which Irish-American lobbying takes place and argues that long-term social changes have altered the nature of the Irish diaspora in the US and the way in which Irish-American lobbying takes place. These shifts, combined with US domestic concerns post-11 September 2001, have focused the direction of Irish-America's lobbying activities and left little appetite within the US for anything that might come under the heading of 'terrorist' activity.

It is clear that the push and pull factors governing migration have altered significantly in the Irish case and that fewer people are leaving Ireland to begin a new life in America. Those who do so are generally pragmatic, economically mobile and young. Within the context of the Northern Ireland peace process, few of these people gravitate towards political lobbying activities linked to British government policies in Northern Ireland, as it is generally working in partnership with their own government. More broadly, few Irish people who arrive in the US today feel the need to establish political or social support networks in the manner of previous generations.

The Irish-American political lobby has evolved to reflect these more complex patterns of migration, as well as the changes taking place in the Northern Ireland peace process. Increasingly Irish-America is moving away from a broad-based consciousness-raising agenda (because there isn't one) into micro-campaigns for individual candidates considered to be helpful on Irish issues. Niall O'Dowd explained this evolution with the following remark in 2004.

> The Irish-American lobby, at the moment, what we do is we raise money for candidates and we are very good at that. We raised over a quarter of a million [$USD] for Hillary [Clinton] when she was running here [New York] for the Senate. More and more we are focused on that because there is no grassroots mass issue. So what we have become, really, is almost a fundraising arm of the Democratic Party.[51]

In this sense, the Irish-American lobby is no longer grievance-driven and finds it more difficult to mobilise its widely differing constituencies on issues relating to Northern Ireland in a way that will exert political muscle beyond the micro or regional level. The 2004 US presidential election was a case in point, as there was no concerted effort from Irish-America to launch an Irish-Americans for Kerry/Edwards or an ANIA-style pressure group. There were two reasons for this. Firstly, there was no defined set of issues/grievances that such a lobby could unite behind; the big idea of ANIA (that the US administration needed to engage with the Northern Ireland peace process) had been achieved. Secondly, the Irish-American community has become less politically cohesive since the early 1990s, with many Catholic Irish-Americans preferring Bush's conservative social programme regardless of the fact that Kerry himself is a practising Catholic. During the 2004 campaign, William Cobert, director of the American Irish Historical Society (AIHS) in New York, reflected on the fact that Irish-America had evolved economically and how this had led to a more diffused political environment.

> It's no longer just the meat and potatoes type of [culture]. Maybe there is wine and acquired tastes too. [Irish-America is no longer] just the blue-collar type of Irishness, it's also the white-collar

[type] and that's how it is. I think that's how the progression has been of the Irish in America. They've put in their dues and they've educated themselves and they want their children to be better off than they were. They are now in higher positions in all stretches of life and maybe that is also reflected in their politics, because their politics have gone more conservative. I don't know if that is purely an economic conservatism or a sense that they've gravitated to a conservative party, a Republican Party, in part because the Democratic Party isn't as they knew it.[52]

This economic and political evolution of Irish-America also served to illustrate the wider differences in political culture that exist between Ireland and America. New York-based journalist Niall Stanage pointed out that, in political and social terms, 'the centre of gravity within Irish-America is significantly to the right of the centre of political gravity amongst the Irish-born.'[53] Linda Dowling Almeida points out that this gulf in political outlook between the two groups is nothing new, as Bernadette Devlin discovered in 1969 when she toured the US to generate support for the civil rights movement in Northern Ireland. During this trip, Devlin's socialist rhetoric and the parallels she made between the militant civil rights groups in the US such as the Black Panthers and the cause of Irish nationalism in Northern Ireland alienated as much of her Irish-American audience as it attracted, including powerful constituencies such as the Catholic Church and the AOH. 'While Devlin's visit highlights the differences between American Irish groups, it also points up the gap that existed between the Irish and Irish Americans and each group's understanding of partition and the concept of nationalism. Clearly the Irish in America and the Irish in Ireland were not a monolithic group.'[54]

While the eight years of the Bush presidency highlighted the dissonance over social values between an increasingly liberal and secular Ireland (leaving aside the rampant racism towards its own immigrant community) and a growing social conservatism in America, this 'attitude-gap' between Ireland and America is likely to be a one-way street.

A similar trend to 2004 was apparent in the race for the Democratic nomination in 2008 between Senator Hillary Clinton and Senator Barack Obama. While there was a small group of Irish-Americans supporting Clinton's nomination, such as Niall O'Dowd and Bruce Morrison, this failed to mobilise Irish-American public opinion at any broad level. Indeed once Clinton was eclipsed in the Democratic primaries, several prominent Irish-Americans were rather under-whelming in their support of candidate Obama and at times flirted with support for John McCain. O'Dowd himself gave a personal donation to the McCain campaign (despite sitting on Hillary Clinton's finance committee) and there was no small degree of chagrin expressed over Obama's unwillingness to stroke the egos of corporate Irish-America or single the Irish out for special treatment over the immigration reform issue. 'Obama was not some kind of unbending idealist who floated above all political posturing: he was as likely to don a green tie on St Patrick's Day as any other candidate. But he seemed, at least at first, less keen than Clinton to go through the usual black-slapping and back-scratching with the various ethnic lobbies, including the Irish.'[55]

Major opinion formers within the Irish-American community such as Niall O'Dowd and Ray O'Hanlon (of the *Irish Voice* and *Irish Echo* respectively) suggested that a more pragmatic attitude was apparent in recent years in terms of Irish-American political allegiances. O'Dowd commented that while his newspaper had endorsed the Kerry presidential campaign in 2004, it had also lent support to the electoral campaigns of Congressman Peter King and New York Governor George Pataki (both prominent Republicans) because of their interest in Ireland:

> I would be a big supporter of George Pataki, and one of the main reasons is that he built the Irish famine memorial and that was something that had been promised and promised and promised, and this guy came in, and guess what, he delivered it. I think that was a seminal moment in commemorating who we are and where we came from. He is well disposed and has a lot of Irish people around him and even though I am a strong Democrat, at the last election I voted for him, no problem at all, because he is attuned to our issues.[56]

In addition, the evolution of the peace process in Northern Ireland made it very difficult for the Irish-American lobby to coalesce around a coherent agenda in the manner of ANIA, in either the 2004 or 2008 presidential elections. They had achieved their previous objectives of getting the administration to engage with the peace process, grant Gerry Adams a US visa and open dialogue with Sinn Féin.

This time there is nothing I could point to that would energise the base. There's peace in Ireland, relatively speaking, the issues of Sinn Féin speaking over here and raising money over here, I mean in a lot of that we were successful. In fairness to the Bush administration ... they have followed up on the North ... they've stayed involved. So, as an activist issue, Northern Ireland is still there, but in terms of how we deal with it politically it is not there, it is not the same issue at all [as it was in 1992]. Back in the eighties, we went heavy on immigration, we won that battle. In '92 we went heavy on the North, we won that battle. I don't see a battle this time [2004], I just don't see one.[57]

It has become more difficult to lobby around the complicated and often dull specifics of the Good Friday Agreement than it was about Bloody Sunday in the 1970s or the republican hunger strikes in the 1980s. In other words, there are less tangible issues of injustice (perceived or actual) for Irish-America to focus upon. While some groups such as the Irish American Unity Conference (IAUC) and the AOH actively critique British policy in the spirit of the INC, this makes few inroads at the policy level. The ceasefires have taken place, Sinn Féin leaders are regular visitors to the US, there are very few incidents involving British armed forces in Northern Ireland and there has been a 'cold peace' in existence since 1998.

This change in the social profile of Irish-America is important in terms of the evolution of republican politics in Ireland. The 'soft power' influence of Irish-America is today focused upon the process of conflict resolution and the continuing implementation of the Good Friday Agreement. Within the complicated environment of the peace process, it had become difficult for Irish republicans to articulate a coherent set of grievances that could only be addressed through violent means, when they were themselves central to the political process, thanks in no small part to the efforts of the Irish-American lobby and the Clinton administration.

DISSENTING VOICES

While this paints a relatively optimistic picture, it should not be assumed that militant republicanism has disappeared completely (from Ireland or America). Dissident republican groups such as the Real IRA, the Continuity IRA and the recently established Óglaigh na hÉireann (ONH) remain active in Northern Ireland and have proved their violent potential in recent years. In November 2008, the *Independent*'s Ireland correspondent David McKittrick reported on the shooting of a Catholic police officer by the Real IRA. In an article entitled 'The Afterlife of the IRA' he reported ominous warnings from the then PSNI chief constable Sir Hugh Orde, that despite the efforts of the security forces to reduce its threat, the constituency of militant republicanism was changing.

> So more than a decade of effort has not eradicated dissident activity; in fact it is clear that enough new recruits are joining up to keep the groups going. In the early days, seasoned ex-IRA operators formed the backbone of these organisations. But today, according to Sir Hugh: 'The people we are arresting are not 50- or 60-year-olds from the old world. These are young people who are being targeted by dissidents – disenfranchised, marginalised young people who they are now using to do their dirty work.'[58]

Evidence also emerged in 2009 that dissident republican groups were using new technologies to attract younger recruits and tap into a constituency that felt itself to be socially excluded, disadvantaged and disconnected from Sinn Féin or the post-Good Friday Agreement structures of government which they represented. Social networking sites such as Bebo had a number of Real IRA support groups which were being investigated by the police in April 2009 following an upsurge in violence by dissident republicans the previous month. One group on Bebo called 'Support the Dissidents' reportedly had a membership of 117 people in April 2009. One posting from this website indicated the extent to which some were prepared to go in voicing their antipathy towards the peace process and the leadership of Sinn Féin.

> The Republican cause has been betrayed by traitors such as Gerry Adams and Martin McGuiness. [They] are enemies of Irish republicanism. Traitors and sell outs … These men represent a British party. The Provisional IRA has disgraced themselves on a national and local level. The signing of the Good Friday Agreement is surrender to the British forces and a surrender of the beliefs the men of 1916 died for. Is this what our martyrs fought for?[59]

In an interesting throwback to the traditional republican mindset, militant micro-groups such as the Real IRA treat the Sinn Féin electoral mandate with the sort of contempt that the Provisionals used to display towards Dáil Éireann and the partitionist structures that followed the emergence of the Free State in 1921. The fact that Sinn Féin have a mandate from the people or that they are organised on an all-Ireland basis does not dissuade the dissidents because they, like the Provisional IRA before the peace process, believe in physical force rather than in democratic politics.

These groups also have supporters within Irish-America who regard Sinn Féin's support of the peace process as a betrayal of traditional Irish republicanism. Groups such as the Irish Freedom Committee, and contributions to the letters columns of Irish-American newspapers, are often unambiguous in their rejection of the peace process in general and the Good Friday Agreement in particular. This view regards Sinn Féin's strategy as a capitulation to British rule in Ireland, a recognition of partition and a betrayal of the goals of the republic declared in the 1916 Easter Rising. A small constituency remains which is aligned with the critique of Republican Sinn Féin (not to be confused with Provisional Sinn Féin), which does not believe that the Good Friday Agreement will ever lead to a united Ireland or even to an Ireland that will divest itself of British influence. Within this analysis, the Good Friday Agreement provides a cloak of respectability for Sinn Féin's participation in a British administration in Belfast. An example of this was provided in 2007 when the National Irish Freedom Committee (NIFC) criticised Sinn Féin for accepting new policing reforms that laid the groundwork for a deal with the DUP and a restoration of devolved government in Northern Ireland under the terms of the Good Friday Agreement. In a statement on its website, the NIFC provides a classic exposition of its position:

> The National Irish Freedom Committee (NIFC) condemns the decision of the Provisional Sinn Féin party to encourage republicans to join the British police force in Ireland. The British police force has and will continue to use violence, terror, intimidation and assassination to control republicans and maintain a British state in Ireland.
>
> For the price of a few minimum wage jobs, Provisional Sinn Féin has agreed to become part of that same police force in its

mission to uphold British rule in Ireland. Former Irish Republicans Adams and McGuinness are now no more than Members of the British Parliament and recruiting sergeants for the British police force in Ireland.[60]

The use of the term 'former Irish republicans' is an obvious attempt to criticise the Sinn Féin leadership and amounts to a form of ethnic outbidding for the hearts and minds of those with Irish republican sympathies. A letter in the *Irish Voice* newspaper in October 2008 presents a similar critique of Sinn Féin, ridiculing its alleged double standards for opposing a homecoming parade through Belfast for the Royal Irish Regiment, who had just returned from Iraq, while it supported the British presence in Ireland.

> Is this not the same party that signed away Ireland's claim to the six counties in the Belfast Agreement? Is this not the same party that now sits in Stormont as paid British MPs, administering British rule in the six Irish counties in the North? It is hypocritical of the Provos to protest against British aggression in Iraq and Afghanistan while supporting British rule in Ireland.[61]

While this view still persists within some sections of Irish-America, it is marginalised in the same way that militant republicanism lacks purchase in Northern Ireland. The vast majority of people in both places see these factions as peripheral obsessive groupings who feel more comfortable with the certainties of the past than with the challenges of the future. Some observers have even lampooned the most radical sections of Irish-American republicanism as being long-distance nationalists and part-time revolutionaries, whose resistance was more theatrical than actual. Perhaps the most scathing assessment of this brand of Irish-American political involvement has been provided by Pete McCarthy in his best-selling book *The Road to McCarthy*, when commenting on the Irish Freedom Committee's participation in the St Patrick's Day parade in New York.

> England get out of Ireland, says the County Derry Association banner, which is being carried by some polite looking ladies in sensible coats, and has all the more impact for it. Close behind come the self-proclaimed Irish Freedom Committee in their uniform of sunglasses, dark berets, black trousers, black leather gloves

and chunky cream sweaters with a cable pattern down the front. Andy Williams wore one on the cover of his Christmas album. The bizarre combination of paramilitary chic and yer granny's traditional hand-knit suggests bedroom revolutionaries whose mothers tolerate the black gear but won't let them out of the house unless they're dressed up smart in that nice jumper they got for Christmas.[62]

While there is no doubt that some poseurs were attracted by the paramilitary chic of such groups, it indicates nevertheless that some Irish-Americans remain committed to achieving their political goals through violent means. The activities of the dissident groups in Northern Ireland in 2008 and 2009 illustrate that while they may lack significant popular support for their violent campaign, they do have sufficient capacity to carry out lethal attacks. In terms of the wider political process in Northern Ireland, the most significant issue relates to whether dissident groups can sustain their violence over a period of time in such a way that the British government feels obliged to provide a security response. A re-militarisation of the conflict would endanger Sinn Féin's support of the police and its continuation in the post-Good Friday Agreement structures of government, and at the very least would increase disillusionment among its supporters who have, to date, bought into Sinn Féin's political analysis that the political process can provide gains for the republican community.

Within Irish-America, meanwhile, the vast majority believe that, despite its imperfections, the political process institutionalised by the Good Friday Agreement in 1998 is the only viable option for the Irish republican movement. In recent years Noraid has undergone something of a Sinn Féinesque ideological makeover, relaunching its website as Irish Northern Aid (INA) in 2009 with the tag line 'The Voice of Irish Republicanism in America'.[63] Today it offers unequivocal support to Sinn Féin and argues for the full implementation of the Good Friday Agreement.[64] While some radicals such as Irish Freedom Committee, Republican Sinn Féin and fringe elements within the AOH remain, they are relatively isolated, and few within Irish-America today are suggesting anything other than a constitutional path to peace in Northern Ireland.

IRISH REPUBLICAN STRATEGY AFTER 9/11

The relationship between Irish republicanism and Irish-America was changed significantly by the attacks of 11 September 2001. While few Irish-Americans made a direct link between Al Qaeda and the IRA, 9/11 and its aftermath reduced the number of people with any appetite for paramilitary violence. John T. Ridge, a noted historian of the AOH, commented in 2004 that the climate after the 9/11 attacks had required a totally new approach by the IRA and Sinn Féin.

> Before then [9/11] as far as the IRA was concerned, when IRA leaders came out here, they would be embraced by typical Irish-American society, and it was a case of loving the sinner, but condemning the sin. But now [2004] you are not going to have that at all. Anybody with any connections to a terrorist group is not going to be accepted at all. That's over with and Sinn Féin knows that if you are going to come to this country with the same [violent] programme, it would never be accepted in the same way.[65]

By the late 1990s the lack of any significant movement by the IRA on weapons decommissioning had become a source of growing tension between Sinn Féin, corporate Irish-America and the Bush administration. This was exacerbated by the 9/11 attacks, Gerry Adams' visit to Cuba in December 2001 and the arrest of three Irish republicans in Columbia in August 2001. The three men, who had been travelling on false passports, were charged by the Columbian government with training FARC guerrillas in bomb-making techniques. While they were eventually acquitted of these charges by a Columbian court in 2004, they were convicted on appeal and given sentences of seventeen years in jail. The men had since gone into hiding and only reappeared in the Republic of Ireland in the wake of the IRA statement of July 2005. Ironically, one of the men, Niall Connolly, was Sinn Féin's representative in Cuba. Finally, Gerry Adams' public denunciations of the US invasion of Iraq in 2003 further irritated the Bush administration and several high-profile Irish-American supporters, such as Peter King and Bill Flynn. While none of these events dealt a hammer blow to support for Sinn Féin within the US, they nonetheless increased doubts among some supporters about the commitment of the IRA to a peaceful settlement.

The relationship between Irish-America and Sinn Féin was damaged further at the end of 2004 following a £26 million robbery of the

Northern Bank in Belfast on 20 December. Responsibility for what was then the largest bank raid in UK history was laid at the door of the IRA by the Police Service of Northern Ireland (PSNI) and by leading politicians in Britain and Ireland. Hugh Orde, then chief constable of the PSNI, was quick to judgement: 'In my opinion the Provisional IRA were responsible for this crime and all main lines of inquiry currently undertaken are in that direction.'[66] Despite an IRA statement denying involvement, few were inclined to believe them, not least because the Irish prime minister, Bertie Ahern, seemed content to take the PSNI chief constable at his word: 'An operation of this magnitude ... has obviously been planned at a stage when I was in negotiations with those that would know the leadership of the Provisional movement.'[67]

The Northern Bank robbery was followed by the murder of Robert McCartney, (allegedly by members of the IRA) in Belfast on 30 January 2005. McCartney's murder put further pressure on Sinn Féin over allegations that republicans had attempted to cover up the murder scene and had pressurised witnesses from coming forward to the police. McCartney's sisters led a campaign to assist the PSNI investigation that involved an invitation to Washington to meet Senator Kennedy and President Bush on St Patrick's Day (17 March 2005). These meetings provided disastrous public relations for Sinn Féin, with Gerry Adams being publicly ignored by both Kennedy and Bush. The contrasting treatment of Adams and the McCartney sisters was a symbolic snub for the republican movement. While the IRA issued a statement threatening to shoot those responsible for McCartney's murder, this was rejected by the family. Given that the IRA was supposed to be on ceasefire and committed to the peace process, this offer to murder its own 'volunteers' was an alarming development to many Irish-Americans who had believed that the IRA was committed to pursuing its political objectives through non-violent means. While Sinn Féin denied any knowledge of the murder, the episode came close to alienating several key supporters in the US, notably Edward Kennedy and Peter King. According to Niall O'Dowd, King's wavering support was in part due to events in Northern Ireland but was also a product of the post-9/11 political environment within the US.

> Several key supporters in the US were wavering [in January 2005]. Congressman Peter King, for long the lynchpin of republican support in the United States, was the most prominent name. King had

been changed by the September 11 2001 attacks. He was now a dedicated partisan of the Bush position, a powerful voice for increased security measures and having no haven for terrorists. As part of his shift he became noticeably more critical of Sinn Féin.[68]

While there have been several arrests following the McCartney murder and the bank robbery, none has to date resulted in a successful prosecution.[69] Despite this, the IRA got the blame and Sinn Féin was considered to be guilty by association. As a consequence, doors began to close in the United States both in the White House and in the boardroom, with erstwhile allies such as Peter King and Edward Kennedy making their impatience clear. As a symbol of the new atmosphere at the beginning of 2005, Rita O'Hare, the director of Sinn Féin's Washington office, was denied a visa to enter the US. Peter King (former ally of Noraid), meanwhile, indicated how dramatically his position had changed when interviewed for the *New York Sun* by Ed Moloney (veteran Irish journalist and prominent critic of the IRA). Moloney traced King's volte-face on Sinn Féin to the combination of the 11 September attacks and the incongruity of a US-led 'global war on terror' in the presence of continuing criminality in Northern Ireland.

> The events of September 11, 2001, changed everything. The attacks made it untenable for an American politician to appear to be ambiguous about political violence ... The British and Irish governments criticized Mr Adams – Mr Bush cancelled the annual St Patrick's Day festivities at the White House as punishment – and Mr. King called on the IRA to disband ... 'I felt strongly that since the Good Friday Agreement, the political and military should be going to the finish line, and once you reached it, the military would disband ... There was no longer any rationale for the IRA.' ... What will he do if, as is now speculated in Ireland, the IRA refuses to disband? 'With the IRA, I will reconsider my relationship ... Whether they do it this week or next week, they have to do it pretty soon, and if they don't, I will consider speaking out against them.'[70]

It was partly as a result of the pressure placed on republicans from the US following these events, together with the necessity of maintaining the Irish-American lobby for Sinn Féin's wider project in terms of its electoral expansion in Ireland (North and South) that explains the republican movement over decommissioning, first with a public statement by Gerry Adams in April 2005 advocating it, followed by the IRA announcement of the end of its armed campaign in July 2005, which is quoted at the beginning of this chapter. Clancy points out that pressure from Irish-America (together with that of the Irish and US governments) combined with Sinn Féin's long-term electoral project on the island of Ireland explain the IRA decision to act in 2005. 'Adams's cold US reception – and perhaps the realisation that the loss of his international statesman image could negatively affect his party's electoral expansion in the Republic – brought home the need to act quickly. On 6 April Adams called upon the IRA to consider engaging in purely political and democratic activity.'[71] This also played a role in the IRA's eventual final acts of weapons decommissioning and Sinn Féin's acceptance of new policing structures in Northern Ireland, which precipitated a restoration of the structures of the Good Friday Agreement in May 2007. In other words, criticism from the White House and from Irish-America achieved what the British government and unionists had failed to do for over a generation in terms of helping to precipitate the IRA's announcement of the end of its armed campaign. In the wake of the IRA statement in 2005, King declared: 'I think the pressure from the US actually helped Gerry Adams and Martin McGuinness convince elements in the IRA that this had to be done.'[72]

An important caveat is worth restating here. While the soft power relationship between Irish-America and militant republicanism in Ireland encouraged movement towards democratic politics, it was not a causal factor of it. In other words, Irish-America played little part in the strategic and tactical reassessments by the paramilitary groups, constitutional politicians in Northern Ireland and the British government that a negotiated settlement was necessary. It is better seen as a facilitator, a critical enabler and catalyst for the birth of the peace process. To stretch the metaphor somewhat, Irish-America was the midwife to, rather than the mother of, the peace process in Northern Ireland.

CONCLUSION

This chapter has argued that the evolution of Irish-America played a pivotal role in the development of Irish republicanism during the peace process and in the decision of the Provisional IRA to announce the end of its armed campaign. In political terms, the internationalisation of Northern Ireland as an aspect of US foreign policy was crucial to this decision. This began slowly under the Carter administration, reached a peak during the Clinton presidency and has been continued at a lower level by George W. Bush. The presidency of Barack Obama is likely to focus (if only briefly) on Dublin rather than on Belfast. If President Obama ever has to deal with Northern Ireland, it will be through the eyes of the British and Irish governments and the leaders of the devolved administration in Northern Ireland rather than in response to the remnants of paramilitary organisations or their spokespeople.

In social terms, Irish-America has changed considerably over this period. There is little appetite today within Irish-America for 'armed struggle', while the Irish lobby in the US is changing for both demographic reasons and because it is difficult to pin political blame on the UK for failures in the Northern Ireland peace process. In addition, as the next chapter will explain in more detail, the post-9/11 political environment within the US has made it more difficult for Irish-Americans to separate out 'armed struggle' from 'international terrorism', especially in the absence of a coherent list of grievances over Ireland such as existed in the 1970s and 1980s. As Schmitt has observed, any resurgence in Irish republican violence would be viewed primarily through the lens of the war on terror.

> September 11 and the subsequent War on Terrorism have left vivid images in the minds of American citizens, from the sight of the twin towers collapsing in New York to the footage of the damage caused by attacks in Madrid, Bali and London. Americans, as well as most citizens of the modern democracies, now have an internalised view of terrorists as direct personal threats to their way of life. If the IRA were to launch another war or even engage in a few demonstration bombings, its actions would be roundly condemned.[73]

This post-9/11 context, together with the desire of the majority within Northern Ireland (including Sinn Féin and the DUP) to make a go of the peace process, helps to explain the public reaction within both Ireland and Irish-America to the outbreak of dissident republican violence which took place in March 2009. The Real IRA killing of two British soldiers on 7 March was attacked by Sinn Féin president Gerry Adams in rational rather than moralistic terms.

Last night's attack was an attack on the peace process. It was wrong and counter-productive. Those responsible have no support, no strategy to achieve a United Ireland ... Their intention is to bring British soldiers back onto the streets. They want to destroy the progress of recent times and to plunge Ireland back into conflict ... Irish republicans and democrats have a duty to oppose this and to defend the peace process.[74]

Following the murder of PSNI constable Paul Carroll by the republican dissident group the Continuity IRA, also in March 2009, the new political geometry was clearly outlined. Perhaps the greatest symbolism was provided by the joint photo shot of DUP leader and first minister Peter Robinson, deputy first minister and former IRA volunteer Martin McGuinness, and PSNI chief constable Sir Hugh Orde standing side by side at Stormont to condemn the murder. McGuinness's condemnation of the violent attack was unequivocal, as was his support for the police and the peace process. In his statement McGuinness called the Continuity IRA 'traitors' to the island of Ireland and asked the community to inform the PSNI if they knew anything that might bring the perpetrators to justice. Unsurprisingly perhaps, McGuinness was informed shortly after this by the PSNI that republican dissidents were actively targeting him for assassination.

This show of unity between Sinn Féin and the DUP is partly explained by the fact that the two sets of shootings in March 2009 had twice delayed Robinson and McGuinness from departing for a ten-day visit to the US which was to culminate with a meeting with President Obama in the White House on St Patrick's Day. President Obama did observe the traditional St Patrick's Day festivities on 17 March 2009, receiving a bowl of shamrock from Taoiseach Brian Cowen and meeting Peter Robinson and Martin McGuinness. These meetings were light-hearted in tone, with the fountains on the White House lawn being dyed green for the occasion, but once again provided the opportunity for Obama to emphasise US support for the Northern Ireland peace process in light of the recent killings by the Real IRA and Continuity IRA the previous week. Speaking in the Oval Office, he declared: 'Not all Americans are Irish but all Americans support those who stand on the side of peace and peace will prevail.'[75] Influential voices within Irish-America such as Fr Seán McManus, president of the INC, also condemned the killings. 'It is so wrong and so crazy to have that happen now, as if there were no peace process. There is certainly no support among Irish-Americans for this terrible development.'[76] Even INA publically attacked the actions of the republican dissidents and supported the position of Sinn Féin. In his condemnation of the killings, INA president Paul Doris echoed the remarks of Gerry Adams by connecting the murders to the wider context of the peace processs and the Good Friday Agreement.

> These killings are contrary to the wishes of the overwhelming majority of Irish people who voted for the Good Friday Agreement. The purpose of these attacks is to bring us all back into conflict and undermine the hard-won gains of the political process. Our sympathy extends to the families of the bereaved. INA reiterates our support for Sinn Féin and calls on Irish-Americans to stand firm behind the Peace Process.[77]

At the official level, the Obama administration is likely to continue the role of previous US governments by acting in a supporting role to the policy of the British and Irish governments. Tensions between Dublin and Washington are more likely to be caused by the impact of US economic policy than any US interventions with regard to Northern Ireland.

It is within this complex and organic evolution of Irish-America that the strategy of Irish republicanism in Northern Ireland is to be understood. Irish-America became the insider rather than the outsider in the political process and it did so incrementally via classic 'soft power' initiatives, by setting the agenda within which problems have been framed and by 'getting others to want what you want'.[78] This was the key that helped to unlock the US administration and it is through the 'internationalisation' of Northern Ireland and the triangle of relationships between Ireland, America and the UK that the leadership of the mainstream republican movement in Ireland sees its future. Within this context, Irish-America will continue to play an important role in the politics of Northern Ireland for the foreseeable future, but the impacts of this role will be to strengthen the fabric of a constitutional settlement rather than critique or attack the political status quo through violent means.

NOTES

1. Statement from the Provisional IRA Army Council, 28 July 2005.
2. McGuinness, M. quoted in Niall O'Dowd, 'Irish America Played Pivotal Northern Role', *Sunday Business Post*, 7 August 2005, p.4.
3. Adams, G. 'Irish Unity Campaign Can Tap into Diaspora, says Adams', *Irish Times*, 2 January 2009, p.6.
4. O'Hanlon, R. *The New Irish Americans* (New York: Roberts Reinhart, 1998).
5. http://news.bbc.co.uk/1/hi/northern_ireland/4417575.stm.
6. Joseph Nye has written extensively about 'soft' power. He developed the concept in *Bound to Lead: The Changing Nature of American Power* (New York: Basic, 1990). See also *Power in the Global Information Age: From Realism to Globalization* (London: Routledge, 2004); *Understanding International Conflicts: An Introduction to Theory and History* (New York: Longman, 2000); and *Soft Power: The Means to Success in World Politics* (New York: Public Affairs, 2004).
7. See Cox, M. 'Bringing in the "International": The IRA Ceasefire and the End of the Cold War' *International Affairs*, 73, 4 (October 1997), pp.671–93; Lynch, T.J. *Turf War: The Clinton Administration and Northern Ireland* (London: Ashgate, 2004), p.7; Dumbrell, J. "'Hope and History": The US and Peace in Northern Ireland', in M. Cox, A. Guelke and F. Stephen (eds), *A Farewell to Arms? From Long War to Long Peace in Northern Ireland* (Manchester: Manchester University Press, 2000), pp.214–22.
8. Lynch, *Turf War*, p.7.
9. Guelke, A. 'Northern Ireland: International and North/South Issues', in W. Crotty and D. Schmitt (eds), *Ireland and the Politics of Change* (London: Longman, 1998), p.201; see also Dumbrell, "'Hope and History"', p.215.
10. Dempsey, G.T. 'The American Role in the Northern Ireland Peace Process', *Irish Political Studies*, vol. 41 (1999), p.107.
11. See Arthur, P. *Special Relationships: Britain, Ireland and the Northern Ireland Problem* (Belfast: Blackstaff Press, 2000), p.136; O'Hanlon, *The New Irish Americans*, p.13.
12. Niall Stanage, journalist, interviewed by author, 13 September 2008.
13. Finnegan, R. 'Irish-American Relations', in W. Crotty and D. Schmitt (eds), *Ireland on the World Stage* (London: Longman, 2002), pp.95–110.
14. Ibid., p.98.
15. Dumbrell, "'Hope and History"', p.215.
16. Hanley, B. 'The Politics of Noraid', *Irish Political Studies*, 19, 1 (2004), p.1.
17. See Guelke, 'Northern Ireland: International and North/South Issues', p.203; Hanley, 'The Politics of Noraid', p.4.
18. Guelke, 'Northern Ireland: International and North/South Issues', p.203.
19. Ibid.
20. Kenny, K. 'American-Irish Nationalism', in J.J. Lee and M. Casey, *Making the Irish American* (New York: New York University Press, 2007), p.298.
21. Dowling Almeida, L. 'Irish America, 1940–2000', in Lee and Casey, *Making the Irish American*, p.558.
22. MacManus, Fr S. 'The MacBride Principles: The Essence', Irish National Caucus, 2001, http://www.irishnationalcaucus.org/pages/MacBride/MacBride%20Principles%20The%20Essence.html.
23. Guelke, 'Northern Ireland: International and North/South Issues', p.204.
24. Wilson, A.J. "'Doing the Business": Aspects of the Clinton Administration's Economic Support for the Northern Ireland Peace Process, 1994–2000', *The Journal of Conflict Studies*, XXIII, 1 (2003), p.11.
25. Ibid., p.12.
26. O'Hanlon, *The New Irish Americans*, p.207.
27. Lynch, *Turf War*, pp.15–16.
28. Finnegan, 'Irish-American Relations', p.99.
29. Ibid.
30. These four senior politicians became known collectively as the 'Four Horsemen'.

31. Laffan, B. and O'Donnell, R. 'Ireland and the Growth of International Governance', in Crotty and Schmitt (eds), *Ireland and the Politics of Change*, p.176.
32. Dempsey, 'The American Role in the Northern Ireland Peace Process', p.107.
33. Hanley, 'The Politics of Noraid', p.7.
34. Lynch, *Turf War*, p.114.
35. O'Hanlon, *The New Irish Americans*, p.202.
36. Arthur, *Special Relationships*, p.153.
37. Dumbrell, '"Hope and History"', p.216.
38. Guelke, 'Northern Ireland: International and North/South Issues', p.136.
39. Mallie, E. and McKittrick, D. *The Fight for Peace* (London: Hodder and Stoughton, 2001), p.150.
40. Ibid.
41. Wilson, '"Doing the Business"', p.1.
42. De Breadún, D. *The Far Side of Revenge* (Belfast: Blackstaff Press, 2001), p.11.
43. Wilson, '"Doing the Business"', p.14.
44. See Guelke, 'Northern Ireland: International and North/South Issues', p.208; Dumbrell, '"Hope and History"', p.220; Cox, 'Bringing in the "International"', p.677.
45. O'Dowd, N. 'Irish America Played Pivotal Northern Role', *Sunday Business Post*, 7 August 2005, p.4.
46. Hanley, 'The Politics of Noraid', p.15.
47. See Walsh Visa Programme at: http://usinfo.org/enus/government/forpolicy/walshvisa.html.
48. Dumbrell, '"Hope and History"', p.217.
49. O'Clery, C. *The Greening of the White House* (Dublin: Gill and Macmillan, 1997), p.40.
50. Mitchell, G. *Making Peace* (London: Hodder and Stoughton, 1999), p.178.
51. Niall O'Dowd, interviewed by author, 22 September 2004.
52. William Cobert, director, American Irish Historical Society, interviewed by author, 1 September 2004.
53. Niall Stanage, interviewed by author, 13 September 2008.
54. Dowling Almeida, 'Irish America, 1940–2000', pp.558–9.
55. Stanage, N. *Redemption Song: An Irish Reporter Inside the Obama Campaign* (Dublin: Liberties Press, 2008), p.174.
56. Niall O'Dowd, interviewed by author, 22 September 2004.
57. Ibid.
58. McKittrick, D. 'The Afterlife of the IRA: The Dissident Groups Bent on Shattering the Peace in Northern Ireland', *Independent*, 8 November 2008, p.3.
59. Corrigan, C. 'Real IRA, Other Dissidents Use Social Nets to Catch Teenagers', www.IrishCentral.com, 23 April 2009.
60. National Irish Freedom Committee website: http://www.irishfreedom.net/Statements/NIFC%20Statements.htm#Statement_by_Cumann_Na_Saoirse_Náisiúnta.
61. See *Irish Voice*, 22 October 2008, www.irishabroad.com.
62. McCarthy, P. *The Road to McCarthy* (London: Hodder and Stoughton, 2002), p.183.
63. INA website: http://irishnorthernaid.com.
64. Ibid.
65. John T. Ridge, interviewed by author, 9 September 2004.
66. http://news.bbc.co.uk/1/hi/northern_ireland/4154657.stm.
67. Ibid.
68. O'Dowd, N. 'Irish America Played Pivotal Northern Role', *Sunday Business Post*, 7 August 2005, p.4.
69. At the time of writing (June 2009) the only person tried for Robert McCartney's murder, Terence Davidson, was acquitted following his trial in June 2008 while two others were cleared of charges connected to the murder.
70. Moloney, E. *New York Sun*, 22 June 2005, http://www.nysun.com/article/15853.
71. Clancy, M.A. 'The United States and Post-Agreement Northern Ireland, 2001–2006', *Irish Studies in International Affairs*, vol. 18 (2007), pp.155–73.
72. http://news.bbc.co.uk/1/hi/northern_ireland/4725371.stm.

73. Schmitt, D. 'The US War on Terrorism and its Impact on the Politics of Accommodation in Northern Ireland', in C. Farrington (ed.), *Global Change, Civil Society and the Northern Ireland Peace Process* (London: Palgrave Macmillan, 2008), pp.56–7.
74. RTÉ News, 7 March 2009, http://www.rte.ie/news/2009/0308/massereene.html.
75. The mood of this press conference was lifted when Irish prime minister Brian Cowen inadvertently read out the same address that President Obama had delivered moments earlier due to a faulty teleprompter, only for President Obama to be caught out by the same fault seconds later and thanking himself for hosting the St Patrick's Day celebrations. See *Times* Online at: http://www.timesonline.co.uk/tol/news/world/us_and_americas/article5931422.ece.
76. Dee, J. 'Irish America Stunned by RIRA Attack', *Belfast Telegraph*, 10 March 2009, p.3.
77. Doris, P. 'INA Statement – Killings are Counter-productive to Peace Process', 10 March 2009, http://irishnorthernaid.com.
78. Nye, *Soft Power*, p.56.

Collateral Damage: Irish-America and the War on Terror

> The sepia-toned picture of huddled masses gazing at the Statue of Liberty remains front and central of the [American] national psyche. It's about as realistic these days as a donkey and cart postcard in microchip Ireland.

This comment by Ray O'Hanlon was written in an *Irish News* article entitled 'Illegals living on a dream and a prayer'[1] and sums up the fact that 9/11 changed the attitude of the US towards its migrants. Despite the fact that the 9/11 hijackers were not actually in the country illegally, the attacks on New York and Washington in 2001 and the response of President George W. Bush soured relations between America and its migrant communities. The fear, anger and insecurity experienced by many Americans after 9/11 translated easily into suspicion of recent arrivals and a belief among some that migrants represented a threat to the security of the United States. This securitisation of migration was nourished by the policies of the Bush administration which aggressively pursued its undocumented population and made a subliminal connection between these groups and terrorism.

This chapter examines the changing relationship between Ireland and America in the twenty-first century and the ways in which the new security climate within the US following the attacks of 11 September 2001 affected relations between the two countries. More specifically, the chapter charts the impact of the 'war on terror' on the Irish who were living in the US at the time, particularly those who were undocumented.

Following the 11 September attacks, President Bush made a powerful address to Congress and to the American nation where he announced that America was at war with terror. This was to be a new type of war fought in an unconventional way against loose transnational networks rather than America's traditional geopolitical enemies. This address left little political or moral room for neutrality and suggested that the war on terror amounted to a battle to uphold democratic freedoms and American values. These values were assumed to be universally shared by everyone who was not sympathetic to terrorism and even to have been ordained by God himself.

> Americans should not expect one battle, but a lengthy campaign, unlike any other we have ever seen. It may include dramatic strikes, visible on TV, and covert operations, secret even in success. We will starve terrorists of funding, turn them one against another, drive them from place to place, until there is no refuge or no rest. And we will pursue nations that provide aid or safe haven to terrorism. Every nation, in every region, now has a decision to make. Either you are with us, or you are with the terrorists. From this day forward, any nation that continues to harbor or support terrorism will be regarded by the United States as a hostile regime ... This is not, however, just America's fight. And what is at stake is not just America's freedom. This is the world's fight. This is civilization's fight. This is the fight of all who believe in progress and pluralism, tolerance and freedom ... The course of this conflict is not known, yet its outcome is certain. Freedom and fear, justice and cruelty, have always been at war, and we know that God is not neutral between them.[2]

This address set the tone for the focus of US foreign policy (and therefore the course of international politics) in the succeeding years and defined President Bush's two terms in the White House. However, not every country was comfortable with the black and white simplicities this speech (and subsequent speeches) outlined, or the scale of human devastation that the war on terror wrought, either at home or abroad. Ireland (despite its relatively compliant government) was one of those countries.

Officially, Ireland gave a muted two cheers for the US-led war on terror. However, beyond government and diplomatic circles, its predominantly young population – raised on a diet of neutrality in international politics and embarrassment at its own political conflict in the north of the island – gave a lot less than that, with large anti-war movements campaigning against the US invasion of Afghanistan and its 'liberation' of Iraq.

This chapter focuses on the ways in which 9/11 and its aftermath impacted politically on the Irish-American relationship. It also examines the extent to which this has sent a chill through the heart of Irish-America, to the point that some Irish-Americans have complained in recent years about their treatment when they visit Ireland on holiday, while others have alleged that Ireland has actually become anti-American, despite the organic and historical relationship between the two countries. The argument here is not that the global war on terror is irreparably damaging the Irish-American relationship, but that it is one factor among several others that is reducing the flow of Irish migration to the US and making America a 'cold house' for many of the Irish people who have settled there.

THE IMPACT OF 9/11 ON THE RELATIONSHIP BETWEEN IRELAND AND AMERICA

I moved to America some time ago from County Mayo and now eleven years later I can't wait to get out of this country.[3]

I think there is profound disappointment [among Irish-Americans] about what is going on in Ireland. It is threatening the American public's appreciation of Ireland. There was great sympathy and good will there, and it came through in fighting for Green Cards on up. But that goodwill is disappearing. The view in America now is becoming 'why are we for them when they are against us?'[4]

The first of these comments came from a disillusioned Irish emigrant whose view of the US while living there in the post-9/11 environment has soured considerably. The second comes from Bill Flynn, prominent Irish-American and leading light of Americans for a New Irish Agenda in the 1990s with a long record of involvement in the Northern Ireland peace process, voicing his frustration with Irish attitudes towards the US in the aftermath of the 9/11 attacks. While the Irish-American relationship remains strong, it was put under pressure during the war on terror and it remains to be seen whether this will be alleviated under the Obama administration.

Initially there was an outpouring of sympathy following the 9/11 attacks among the Irish community both inside the US and in Ireland, not least because of the Irish people who were killed but also due to the scale of the human tragedy involved. 'Long lines of people gathered outside the US Embassy in Dublin to express condolences. Their presence paid eloquent testimony to the almost familial relationship between Ireland and the United States.'[5] Pauline Turley, director of the Irish Arts Center in Hell's Kitchen, New York, commented: 'After September 11th particularly, I felt that my allegiance was to New York. I had been living here four or five years at that time and I felt more a New Yorker after it happened ... I felt that this was my city and how dare they come in and attack it.'[6] However, this wave of sympathy waned within the Irish community (both in New York and within Ireland itself) as a result of the response of the Bush administration to the attacks. An editorial in the *Irish Voice* epitomises the gradual shift that took place after 2001, as Irish opinion inside and outside the US gradually changed to reflect more divided and complex feelings as America pursued a 'war on terror' in Afghanistan, and more controversially in Iraq. 'In the immediate aftermath of September 11 there was a tidal wave of sentiment and sympathy encapsulated in *Le Monde*, the French paper, whose headline screamed "we are all Americans now". If another September 11 happened now, the prevailing opinion abroad might well be, "well, what did you expect?"'[7]

The self-proclaimed zero-tolerance policy of the Bush administration towards international terrorism had a dramatic impact upon the Irish community living in America, especially among those who emigrated from Ireland to the US illegally during the 1980s and 1990s and remain undocumented. The enforcement of immigration law has been tightened up considerably since 2001 and has been used by the Department of Homeland Security, among other agencies, to deport or imprison those whose legal papers are not considered to be satisfactory. New anti-terrorist legislation introduced since 11 September, most notoriously the Patriot Act, has been viewed by Irish-American groups such as the AOH and the Irish American Unity Conference as being harmful to the interests of the Irish community across the US, and such groups lobbied vigorously against such laws. Christina McElwaine, former press officer for the Irish consulate in New York, stated in 2004 that: 'The Patriot Act has galvanised already organised groups like the AOH and there is a very big campaign going on [against it]. It is their big issue at the moment.'[8] While the revolution in communications technology has had a lot of benefits for the Irish community abroad, it has also had a downside since 9/11, with the increased use of surveillance by the US federal government in its quest to improve intelligence against future attacks on the US and monitor human traffic across its national borders. This was reflected institutionally when the Immigration and Naturalization Service (INS) was placed within the orbit of the Department for Homeland Security. 'That in itself is enough to have anyone thinking seriously.'[9] Within a year of 9/11, different rules were introduced governing the exit procedures for those leaving the US, specifically the electronic scanning of passports, to ensure that there would be a record of every person entering and leaving the country.

> The US were mandating airlines to provide detailed information about everybody on the flights, down to credit card [information], down to next of kin, and that information technically goes to the Department of Homeland Security as soon as the plane is in the air. They know who is on that plane so that if they want to intercept anybody who they may think is a terrorist, they can do it by the time the plane lands in the US ... and this is the other factor along with the driver's licence that I think people are being driven out by. For people who are on Visa Waivers, where you don't have to get a visa, will now be biometrically scanned. They are going to have your fingerprint and they are going to have your iris. There is no way out ... So there are huge effects since 9/11.[10]

In recent years this surveillance has increased rather than reduced. By the end of 2008, all passengers flying into the US were required to upload their personal details online at least forty-eight hours before flying, to provide more time for background checks of passenger lists to be made. Evidence of this surveillance culture within the US was provided by the interception of British Muslim and former pop singer Yusuf Islam, formerly known as Cat Stevens, in September 2004. The plane that Islam was on from London to Washington was diverted, mid-flight, to Maine, when US officials realised that his name was on a 'watch list'. He was subsequently deported back to the UK following questioning by US immigration officials. Former Homeland Security secretary Tom Ridge accused Islam 'of having some unspecified relationship with terrorist activity'.[11] Regardless of the case itself, this event became emblematic of the political climate over immigration in the US in the wake of the 9/11 attacks.

The Department of Homeland Security's Bureau of Customs and Border Protection (CBP) expanded its 'expedited removal' procedures on 11 August 2004, introducing what became known as the '100 mile rule'. This represents an extension of 1996 immigration legislation and in essence allows for the removal of non-US citizens from the country without a hearing by an immigration judge. This allowed CBP officers to conduct spot-checks and invoke the expedited removal procedure against any non-US national with visa irregularities, if such people were encountered within 100 miles of a US land border within fourteen days of their arrival in the country.[12] While this legislation was not specifically targeted at the Irish community, those Irish who were undocumented or who had overstayed their tourist visas were inevitably caught up in the crossfire. Alan and Cliff Whelan, two cousins from County Waterford, were arrested by CBP officers on 26 November 2004 while on a train from Montana to Seattle. The '100 mile rule' was enforced by police doing a spot-check for visa irregularities and they were arrested for overstaying their holiday visas by three months. The cousins 'were held at gunpoint, clapped in irons and brought to a penitentiary where they were placed with hardened criminals including murderers and rapists'.[13] Their local Fine Gael TD John Deasy took up their plight with the Irish government, arguing that their continued detention in prison without trial was an over-reaction by the US authorities which was damaging the relationship between Ireland and the United States. 'This is causing resentment among the Irish community and it is not acceptable. I argued that it is not right to jail Irish people with general criminals when they haven't committed a real crime.'[14]

There have been several other cases where Irish people have either been arrested or immediately turned around at their point of entry under the terms of the Visa Waiver scheme, which people frequently use to enter the United States. Irish anti-war campaigner Damian Moran was refused entry into the US at Chicago's O'Hare airport by officials from the Department of Homeland Security on 6 April 2008. This decision was based on the fact that Moran had stood trial in Ireland in 2003 accused of causing €2 million criminal damage to a US military plane at Shannon airport in protest against the war in Iraq, a charge from which he was subsequently acquitted. Moran believed his deportation from the US was due to his anti-war activities and was indicative of the intolerance of the American government towards free speech.

My mobile phone was seized and I was interrogated about the purpose of my trip and why I had damaged US military property. I had been invited to speak at a university in Colorado Springs and at a conference in Omaha on US militarism in Poland and Ireland. I also had tickets to visit my brother and his family in Virginia. Homeland Security's unjustified refusal to allow me to enter the US is just another example of how quasi-fascist the US State apparatus has become ... I was barred from entering due to my act of dissent at Shannon 5 years ago against their disastrous militaristic policies at home and abroad. There is no room for dissenters' perspectives in America today.[15]

Several years earlier, immigration officials at O'Hare airport in Chicago apprehended the former civil rights activist Bernadette McAliskey, who was refused entry into the US in February 2003 on grounds of 'national security' while on her way to a relative's christening. McAliskey had a conviction for riotous behaviour in 1969 but had entered the US on many previous occasions without difficulty and was the recipient of several honours from the US in conjunction with her civil rights activism in the 1970s and 1980s. McAliskey complained about the manner of her treatment by US immigration officials and said that she intended to pursue the matter with the Irish government. 'The guy was treating me as if I was some sort of Al-Qaeda suspect ... They said [that] a person called Bernadette McAliskey had boarded the Chicago flight, was a person who, under the new security rules, was ineligible for entry to America and should be dealt with and deported.'[16] The legal reality, however, was that McAliskey had entered the US under the Visa Waiver scheme, in which individuals waive many of their rights regarding deportation and can be turned around at their point of entry by US immigration officials if they so choose, without reasons being given. Éamonn Dornan, an Irish lawyer working in New York who specialises in immigration law, pointed out that the McAliskey episode was one of several cases since 9/11 where Irish citizens had been refused entry to the US and had either been turned around and deported under the terms of the Visa Waiver scheme or had been arrested for providing false information on their forms.

A group of guys came from Derry through to Boston and three of them were arrested for giving false statements on their form. The question is 'have you been convicted of the crime of moral turpitude for which you have served five years [in jail]?' That depends on what your interpretation of moral turpitude is. It is an amorphous term. Is drunk driving moral turpitude? No. Is drunk driving where you hit and injure someone moral turpitude? Maybe. So it is interchangeable. In any event they arrested and prosecuted these guys who ended up spending several months in detention.[17]

Dornan was a legal representative for several *causes célèbres* relating to the detention or deportation of Irish republicans in the US, including Ciarán Ferry, John McNicholl and Malachy McAllister. Dornan's view was that the Department of Homeland Security and other agencies involved in issues related to immigration had applied existing legal mechanisms such as the Visa Waiver scheme to extraordinary and punitive levels because the post-9/11 security environment in the US had provided the space and motivation for them to do so. In other words, while they were empowered to turn people around at the point of entry as they did in the McAliskey case, they were instead choosing to detain, arrest and prosecute people for providing false information.

> Here's the deal. In all those cases they could have done exactly the same [as in the McAliskey case]. They could have said 'we know that you have been convicted. We are refusing you entry. If you want to come back to the United States, go to the embassy.' They could have done that very easily. But no, they had to go over the top and detain them, prosecute them, for the most innocuous of offences which is ticking the wrong box ... So it is over the top and it is outrageous. So that is the effect of 9/11. They are clearly prepared to go to greater lengths than they have done before and greater lengths than they need to.[18]

Beyond the Irish case, the statistics for the numbers deported from the US across all ethnic groups would suggest an upward trend since 2001, as both the techniques for detection and levels of enforcement of immigration violations increased. Official figures from the Department of Homeland Security itself '... show a dramatic rise in deportations since 2001. That year there were 116,460 "removals". By October of this year [2008] there were 349,041, an increase of more than 20 per cent from 2007.'[19] These figures provide at least some empirical support for the views of critical voices within the Irish-American community, human rights observers and immigration lawyers such as Éamonn Dornan, who has provided legal representation to several Irish clients facing arrest and deportation from the United States. Speaking in 2004, Dornan warned that, from his experience, the Department of Homeland Security had been over-zealous in enforcing immigration regulations and that this was a political reaction to the post-9/11 security environment.

> My feeling on the subject ... is that the Department of Homeland Security has been, if you like, let off the leash and they are going to push the envelope. They are going to do things that may not be strictly legal and they are going to [adopt the following position] 'we are just going to do it now and we'll take the consequences later. If the court tells us in four or five years' time that this was an unlawful arrest, [then] fair enough, but we are going to do this now and we're going to enforce this' ... That's the sort of message that they are sending out and that message is coming directly from the top. 'Just go out there, get numbers, arrest people, deport them, if you get it wrong once or twice [then] we'll deal with it.'[20]

For the undocumented Irish, meanwhile, even apparently mundane matters such as renewing a driving licence can cause a great deal of insecurity over whether they will be detected as being undocumented and thus lose their jobs and livelihoods. The reason for this is that, following the 9/11 attacks, the Department of Motor Vehicles (DMV) in New York and in other US States have been processing new applications for driving licences through their computer system and checking the authenticity of each social security number. Those who have invalid social security numbers have been refused driving licences and, given the necessity of owning a car in the US for employment purposes, many have lost their jobs as a consequence. Ray O'Hanlon, senior editor of the *Irish Echo*, said that the checking of social security numbers through driving licence renewal applications was having a major effect on the Irish community living in New York and elsewhere across the US. 'It is not directly linked to people leaving the country, because that comes down to passports, but it just means that staying in the country becomes that much more difficult, and I think that it is inspiring some [Irish] people to actually leave the country ... it is the straw that broke the camel's back.'[21] This concern about the Irish who had entered the US illegally but have subsequently put down roots, bought property and started families in the country was reflected upon in 2004 by Jack Irwin, assistant to the governor of New York, George Pataki, with special responsibility for Irish affairs.

> It is a big problem, because so many of these people now need the car for their jobs. So they come to us and we have to say, 'wait a minute, we didn't make this law, the federal government put it in place.' People are up in arms and the Emerald Isle Emigration Center is at the forefront of trying to do something about it. Hopefully it will be squared away because you have a tonne of people affected by it, there could be 100,000, it is not just the Irish, it is every ethnic group ... Letters have been going out to these people and obviously they are in a panic. 'What do we do now? If it doesn't come up with a new licence for us, how are we going to live, how are we going to work?' And they haven't been able to get around that as yet.[22]

The administration of former governor George Pataki had assiduously cultivated the Irish-American community. While he was governor, Pataki gave public support to several campaigns associated with Irish lobbying activity, notably providing several million dollars of public money for the establishment of the Irish Famine memorial, An Gorta Mór. Pataki also supported the case of Malachy McAllister against deportation and has in return received support from influential figures within the Irish-American community.[23] However, the new security environment following 9/11 made it difficult for the Pataki administration to support cases such as that of McAllister (who was convicted in Northern Ireland of membership of the Irish National Liberation Army (INLA) in the 1980s) while retaining his credentials with the federal government's zero-tolerance policy on terrorism.

Siobhán Dennehy, executive director of the Emerald Isle Immigration Center, claimed that the aftermath of 9/11 was making life more difficult for the undocumented Irish living in New York and that the driving licence issue was undermining the confidence of many Irish people who previously thought that their future lay in the US.

> I know that the fact that you cannot get a driver's licence in this state anymore [if you are undocumented], and you certainly can't renew one, has become a huge issue for people moving home [to Ireland]. It has become the driving excuse ... for people moving

back home. Because if you can't drive, you can't get your US-born child to school, you can't go shopping [the car] is everything.[24]

The Irish government has taken up the issue of the undocumented Irish in the US and has been lobbying the US administration to support draft legislation that may ameliorate the situation. In 2007, then Irish minister for foreign affairs Dermot Ahern commented on RTÉ's 'Morning Ireland' that:

> This is an issue we are concerned about; there are, we estimate, about 25,000 undocumented Irish (in America) ... Some people say there's only 5,000; the Americans say there's only 5,000, the Irish emigrant centres would say there's about 50,000 ... The Taoiseach and myself raised this with President Bush back on the 17th of March [2005] when we visited the White House in relation to, particularly in the post-September 11 situation. There are families in Ireland, if they have a bereavement, a wedding or whatever, if a relative is sick, their loved ones in America can't come back over to Ireland because of the fear that they may not be able to get back into America because they are undocumented.[25]

The driving licences issue briefly made an appearance during the 2008 presidential election when, during the Democratic primaries, Senator Hillary Clinton appeared to first support and then oppose a plan to provide licences to the undocumented, during a televised debate with Obama. Her apparent vacillation on the issue became characteristic of her general campaign and led to criticism that she lacked consistency and therefore credibility as a candidate for the US presidency. The confusion created by Clinton's performance in the debate and her apparently simultaneous support *and* rejection for giving undocumented workers driving licences required clarification. A subsequent statement after the debate disappointed many of her Irish-American supporters but indicated how toxic the immigration issue had become for politicians seeking the highest public office. Niall Stanage has pointed out that, following this debacle, 'Clinton was faced with a choice. She could follow through on the positive noises she had made to the liberal reformist lobby or she could throw the illegals over the side. To no one's great surprise, she chose the latter course. "As President I will not support drivers' licences for undocumented people."'[26]

While few people interviewed for this book suggested that the problems facing the undocumented were specifically targeted at the Irish community, the consensus was that they became collateral damage in the post-9/11 security environment in the United States and the Bush administration's pursuit of the 'war on terror'. There were, nevertheless, more sinister events linked to the treatment of the undocumented Irish by US law enforcement agencies, with allegations that federal authorities have been using the undocumented as leverage with intelligence gathering activities. The *Irish Voice* reported in October 2005 that the FBI had attempted to get an Irish construction worker to inform on the movements of three Irish republicans living in New York. 'The young man was warned [by the FBI] that his father, who is undocumented, would be deported and was being arrested at that moment unless the young man co-operated. He refused to do so.'[27] Ironically, Congressman Peter King, a key ally of Sinn Féin in the US and chair of the House Homeland Security Committee, condemned the actions of the FBI. 'I know all these three and can vouch for them ... they have been instrumental in the great strides made towards peace in Ireland such as we witnessed last week with decommissioning. They are 100% behind the process.'[28] King himself might be said to be something of a 'poacher turned gamekeeper', as he had been a vocal supporter of Sinn Féin and Noraid before the IRA ceasefire in 1994.

The issue of the zero tolerance policy over invalid social security numbers affecting the undocumented Irish community was seen by many as emblematic of a wider malaise, and an indication that the US attitude towards its immigrants was itself in a state of flux. Ray O'Hanlon of the *Irish Echo* suggested that the aftermath of 9/11 had accelerated a philosophical change in the attitude of the United States to immigration.

> It still officially lives in this world of sepia-toned old movies of the Statue of Liberty and boat loads of Europeans arriving. Those days have gone, but it won't say that. It won't turn to the world and say 'sorry, the golden doors are closed, we take certain selected amounts [of immigrants] based on very strict criteria now and we are no longer a nation based on what you would understand as regular immigration.'[29]

The view of many Irish people living in New York who were interviewed for this book was that immigrant communities have been looked upon with new eyes by the US state since 9/11. There was a widespread belief that legislation such as the Patriot Act was being enforced rigorously by the federal government and post-9/11 agencies such as the Department of Homeland Security, and that existing immigration law was being applied to the letter in an attempt to get rid of illegal immigrants and dissuade others from entering the country.

The following comment of an Irish-American Republican and gay activist was typical of the view that migration and security had become integrally connected since 9/11 and that a climate of fear had infected the freedom of America's immigrant communities.

> Overall those interested in staying here have become more patriotic towards America, not because they *are* more patriotic but because they feel they have to be otherwise they might get deported under the Patriot Act ... There is fear in this country. And people are told to be afraid all the time. In a group people don't feel vulnerable, but still they worry about deportation so we had fewer people willing to protest at the Republican Convention because they fear getting arrested, found out to be illegal, and deported. So there has been a subtle form of change in activism. It was easier before 9/11; now people are just more hesitant.[30]

This point was underlined by the case of Seán Devine, a native of County Derry in Northern Ireland. Devine was deported from the US in November 2005 on the grounds that he had engaged in fundraising activities for the Irish Republican Prisoners Welfare Association (IRPWA), which the US administration believes to be a front organisation for the Real IRA. The IRPWA is on the administration's list of foreign terrorist groups and Devine found himself being deported for providing it with 'material support'.

Professor Eileen Reilly, an academic at Glucksman Ireland House in New York University, observed that people were being held for several months in effective incarceration while their appeals against deportation were being considered and that while this was not unknown before 9/11, it had intensified since. 'People were in holding places for a year or a year and a half while their case was decided, but they didn't need to be and they were basically being interned ... So there is a very dark underside to that INS activity and it has just intensified now [since 9/11].'[31] Éamonn Dornan suggested that the US government was seeking to deport former Irish paramilitaries from the US by applying its immigration legislation to the letter of the law, despite the fact that these individuals were not being sought by the British government. 'I don't think the British [government] are interested in any of the deportees ... There are no outstanding warrants. They [the British government] are not seeking their extradition ... What it is instead is [US] law enforcement taken to its extremes.'[32] Dornan's view was that the aftermath of 9/11 and the creation of the Department of Homeland Security had provided the excuse for agencies of the federal government to use the full force of law against immigrant communities (including Irish citizens) in the United States.

As a result of the post-9/11 enforcement of US immigration regulations, Irish NGOs such as the EIIC and the Aisling Center in New York advised the Irish community to become American citizens as soon as they qualified to do so, to protect themselves from being deported on spurious grounds or for minor infringements of the law. This drive to become a US citizen resulted in some unexpected collateral impacts, given that 'right now, the quickest path available to anybody to adjust their status is through marriage to a US citizen. Love is in the air!'[33] Some of those who can do so are becoming US citizens today because of the extra legal protection from deportation this affords them, and because they are able to do so without giving up their Irish citizenship. Those who are undocumented in the US face a bleaker future, either searching for the means to become legal, continuing their shadow existence as illegal migrants until new legislation comes into force[34] or deciding to jump before they are pushed, either by moving on to another country with less stringent immigration controls or by returning to Ireland.

While there has been a lot of outward sympathy expressed towards the Irish undocumented, less charitable feelings have also been expressed by some within the Irish community who feel that the illegals were creating a bad impression of the wider Irish community. Mary McGlynn, an associate professor of English literature at Baruch College, City University of New York (CUNY), commented in 2004 that there was a sense in which, despite the public rhetoric, some people felt that the undocumented were tarnishing the image of the Irish community within mainstream American society.

> There's been a real shift in the last few years. In the '80s, to be an
> illegal Irish [person] was a badge of honour. You were going to

try to do something, you weren't going to just sit at home and collect your dole [money]. Now it's like, 'well there's a job at home that's probably better, so why don't you just go back there? You shouldn't be here and the rest of us have gone through this process to make ourselves legal and we want to be a law-abiding group of the American populous and not classed with the Mexicans.'[35]

IMMIGRATION REFORM

As suggested in the previous chapter, the Irish lobby in the US has grabbed onto the issue of the undocumented in the absence of any other issues which could generate Irish-American activism. The difficulties experienced by the Irish undocumented after 9/11 presented an issue that could potentially unite all shades of green in the US. A mixture of efforts have been tried, ranging from diplomatic discussions between members of the Irish and US governments, information on the scale of the problem provided by specialist NGOs such as the EIIC and Aisling Center, and direct lobbying by advocacy groups such as the AOH and new Irish-American coalitions that have emerged around the issue. The Irish consul general for New York, Niall Burgess, commented in 2008 that these groups performed different roles – NGOs such as the EIIC providing direct assistance and advice to the undocumented while lobby groups played a role in generating momentum for support of new legislation – and that the Irish consulate worked with these in different ways.

> I would distinguish between the way we work with the Emerald Isle [Immigration Center] and the Aisling Center and the way we would work with lobby groups. The mandate of the Emerald Isle Center and the Aisling Center is to work with and help those who find themselves in any kind of distress. They are community centres, they are not a lobby group for immigration reform. But they are on the front line of dealing with people who are undocumented … We work with them very closely on that and we are often the first point of call for people who are in some form of distress here, so we need to have professionals who we can refer people to and we work with them and we support them financially to help build up their structures and their strength here in New York. Lobbying

is a different issue and there we would work pretty closely with
ILIR [Irish Lobby for Immigration Reform] and with other organisations as well. There are other big parts of the infrastructure of
Irish-America that have a very important role to play in this, the
Ancient Order of Hibernians being a good example. They have a
sub-committee dealing with immigration as well. That really
comes into its own when you are involved in public lobbying for
an immigration bill, when you have something to push, and we're
not at that point at the moment.[36]

Lobby groups such as the ILIR emerged in New York at the end of 2005
and campaigned for new federal legislation that would legalise the status of the undocumented, provide them with a means of remaining in
the US and lift the fear of discovery and deportation from their shoulders. ILIR was co-founded by Niall O'Dowd, publisher of the *Irish
Voice*, and his brother-in-law Ciarán Staunton, an Irish-born businessman based in New York who also owns O'Neill's bar in Manhattan.
ILIR lobbied energetically throughout 2006 and 2007 over the undocumented issue, and while they generated publicity and attention for the
plight of such people, achieved little by way of legislative reform. ILIR
claimed that there were around 50,000 undocumented Irish living in
the US, though for obvious reasons a precise figure is difficult to determine, with the Irish government preferring to estimate the number as
being closer to 25,000.

Despite the ILIR campaign and the efforts of the Irish government
and other policy insiders for new legislation to legalise the undocumented, this has so far failed to materialise. Kelly Fincham, executive
director of ILIR, put this failure down to the elongated US presidential
campaign of 2007/8, which had radicalised the debate on immigration
and closed down the option of change until a new administration had
taken office.[37] Fincham, originally from Drogheda in County Louth, has
lived in the US for eight years, having left Ireland in search of better
career opportunities. She suggested that 2006 and 2007 were big years
for ILIR but that both the Democrats and Republicans had backed off
the issue during the election campaign. However, Ray O'Hanlon of the
Irish Echo was blunt in his assessment of the prospects for legislative
reform. 'If I was down to my last dollar and I had to bet on immigration
reform or buy a lottery ticket, I know which one I'd go for ... I'd buy the
lottery ticket!'[38] When Niall Stanage (another Irish-born New York-based

journalist) was asked which of these two alternatives he would spend his last dollar on, he too opted for the lottery ticket.[39] Niall Burgess, Irish consul general in New York, remarked that seeing the issue as broader than an Irish problem may contain the best hope for finding a solution to it.

> I think the chances of addressing that as a distinct Irish problem are pretty slim. I think that it's more likely that when it's addressed it will be addressed as part of an overall package that looks at an amnesty, as opposed to the undocumented. That's political realism and it may prove not to be the case but it's probably a realistic assessment at this stage.[40]

Niall O'Dowd, chairman of ILIR, commented in November 2008 that while life for the undocumented Irish had been difficult, the possibility remained that the situation would improve after President Bush's period in office came to an end. This whiff of optimism was tempered, however, by the realisation that the financial crisis in America would dominate the presidential agenda in the years ahead.

> The past few years have not been kind, with an anti-immigrant sentiment taking hold throughout the Republican Party to the point where any sensible compromise became impossible on the issue. President George W. Bush has proven a grave disappointment in his final days, unleashing immigration agents to corral thousands of frightened workers in meatpacking plants and elsewhere. All the fine rhetoric he used to espouse about seeking a fair and principled solution has utterly evaporated, like much else about his presidency. The worst of those days, I believe, are now over.
> … The abysmal state of the economy probably means that immigration has slipped even further down the food chain … However, while it is unlikely we will see a major bill like Kennedy/Mc Cain, there will very definitely be immigration legislation in the next Congress which will almost certainly be better disposed to it than the outgoing one.[41]

Despite ILIR's valiant attempts to raise awareness of the plight of the Irish undocumented and engage policy makers around the issue, their basic problem – and it was a significant one – was that they were a tiny ethnic lobby seeking legislation that would impact on the whole body politic of the United States. Thus, while mainstream American public opinion might be able to swallow legalising the white Irish, their throats start to collectively gag when this begins to apply to Mexicans, Hispanics and Africans. This is partly explained by the ingrained racism within the United States (one trait shared by Ireland itself) but is more immediately connected to the sheer numbers of illegal immigrants in America.

One of the reasons why ILIR had been unable to achieve its objectives on immigration reform is connected to one of the wider themes of this book, namely the limited political clout of Irish-America within the wider context of American politics. Unlike the Hispanic-American, African-Americans or Jewish-Americans, Irish-America is no longer (if it ever was) electorally significant. Added to this, even if ILIR's figure of 50,000 is accepted, it was relatively insignificant to policy makers given that there are an estimated 12 million illegal immigrants in the US today. It speaks perhaps to an old-time arrogance within Irish-America that they are somehow different from the other hyphenated identities in the US and therefore worthy of special treatment. Niall Stanage encapsulated this point when he reflected on the ILIR campaign in 2008. 'The slogan "legalise the Irish", I have problems with ... I don't see any rationale as to why you should legalise the Irish before the Guatemalans or the Argentinians, the Nigerians or anybody else.'[42]

None of this belittles the difficulties faced by the undocumented Irish community living in the US today, nor the price they have to pay in order to continue doing so. The focus on movement across the US borders and the use of video and computer technology to monitor such traffic has meant that the vast majority of the undocumented Irish in the US are now living under a form of self-imposed imprisonment. If they leave the country, even for a holiday, they may be unable to return, as their illegal status is likely to be detected by immigration officials. Patricia Grogan, former director of the Aisling Center, claimed in 2004 that the undocumented Irish had become a target of federal agencies as a result of the 9/11 attacks and the focus on 'homeland' security. 'Nobody has access to the information about the number of deportations or the number of people being detained at airports. But all we can attest to is the desperate phone calls we get – people saying things like "my girlfriend has been caught trying to cross the Canadian border" or "my boyfriend has been deported from Kennedy airport."[43] Fr Colm Campbell, who founded the Fáilte Center in Long Island, summarised the social impacts of the problems facing the undocumented Irish community in the post-9/11 security environment and the threat this posed to the longer-term future of the Irish community in America: 'I have seen families split over this. One family had a child born in Ireland and when they returned to the States they were told at immigration that they could all enter the country but the baby couldn't ... I have seen people moving home to Ireland because they cannot take the pressure or the insecurity of being illegal.'[44] The fear of detection extended into the cultural realm also, in that Gaelic football and hurling teams in New York found it difficult to travel because several of their players were undocumented. Professor Larry McCarthy, secretary of the New York GAA Board, commented in 2008 that teams were now having to side-step some sensitive issues. 'It's like one of those questions: you don't ask a woman how heavy she is, you don't ask how much money are you making and you don't ask a guy round here [New York GAA] "are you legal?"'[45]

In this sense, the digital age has dealt the undocumented Irish a cruel blow, as the fear of biometric detection of their status has resulted in many undocumented Irish remaining in the US despite family illness or the death of relatives back in Ireland, which in the past would have seen them pay return visits to Ireland on compassionate grounds. The enabling changes in global technology are tempered for some of the Irish abroad, therefore, by the political imperative of the US administration's focus on *homeland* security.

9/11 AND ANTI-AMERICANISM IN IRELAND

For four years I've lived in Dublin. Over that time, especially after September 11, a level of hostility here toward America that once would have been shocking has become expected, normal, even lauded ... Something very new is happening in Irish attitudes towards America. And it goes beyond anger at one man.[46]

While the activities of the Irish-American lobby have changed to take account of the peace process in Northern Ireland and the new security environment within the US, another feature of the post-9/11 relationship between Ireland and the United States relates to feelings of resentment that have surfaced between the two. Whereas some Irish people have been bruised by the tightening of US immigration regulations such as 'expedited removal' or by the implications of legislation such as the Patriot Act, some Irish-Americans have been angered at their treatment when they have visited Ireland and by Irish opposition to the foreign policies of the Bush administration. It was stressed several times by Irish-Americans interviewed for this book that they detected an undercurrent of anti-Americanism when they visited Ireland on holidays and found themselves caught up in having to defend US policies in Afghanistan and Iraq. Jake MacNicholas, an Irish-American detective in the NYPD Terrorism Interdiction Unit and secretary of the NYPD Emerald Pipes and Drums Society, claimed that while he would visit Ireland at least once a year for holidays and to catch up with family members, he had experienced real hostility and anti-American sentiment in recent years. MacNicholas, whose grandfather came from County Mayo and whose parents came from Limerick and Kerry, felt that he had experienced abuse on his last few trips to Ireland from people who equated Americans with the policies of the Bush administration in Iraq.

> I have been travelling to Ireland at least once a year since 1977. Been there on a rugby tour back in 1981 when I went to college. I'm not your typical tourist, not loud or difficult and I'm someone who always manages to treat people with kindness and respect, unless they act otherwise. I have not been happy with the way I have been treated at times on my recent trips. [It has been] rude and uncalled for. People certainly have short memories.[47]

This last reference relates to the long history of migration from Ireland to the US in times of need, which MacNicholas is himself a product of. Another Irish-American with connections to the AOH, who emigrated from Ireland in the 1960s, expressed his irritation at Irish attitudes towards America after 9/11, though he placed a lot of the responsibility for this on the media.

> I've just come back [to the US] from Ireland and it seems like the Irish know more, or think they know more, about American politics than people here ... I met this guy ... he's an in-law and ... one of the first things he said to me was, 'when you go back [to the US] would you shoot President Bush for me?' I mean that's an

awful thing to say. How does he know so much about President Bush and even if I hate the guy's guts, why would he say something like that? ... not all of the Irish are like that now, but I think that the press have brainwashed a lot of them.[48]

Sentiments such as these tended to be expressed more trenchantly from older Irish-Americans sympathetic to the Bush administration rather than being a consistent voice across the community. Niall Stanage commented that one of the underlying reasons that explains the tension is related to the fact that, in political and social terms, Irish-America was further to the right on the political spectrum than the majority of people within Ireland itself.

I think Irish people in Ireland sometimes mis-comprehend, because they do think of Irish-America politically as being pictures of [John F.] Kennedy on the wall. But the centre of gravity within Irish-America is significantly to the right of the centre of political gravity among the Irish-born. Partly because of social issues and the more traditional church-going views that older people would have, but also because they have been very much absorbed into American society to the point of being so-called super-patriots.[49]

This disjuncture was certainly to the fore over the US-led invasion of Iraq, and differences of opinion over the war on terror, allegations of US torture in Abu Ghraib jail and the practice of 'extraordinary renditions' led to a noticeable rise in tension between some Irish-Americans and their kin from the ancestral home.

Cassie Farrelly, former administrative director of the Institute of Irish Studies at Fordham University in New York, differentiated between Irish attitudes towards America and attitudes towards the Bush administration more generally and US policy in Iraq in particular.

My aunts and uncles would go back to Ireland twice a year to play golf and when I came back three weeks ago from Ireland they said to me, 'oh did you find that the people were horribly anti-American?' and I said 'no, they weren't anti-American, they were anti-Bush, which doesn't make them any different from the rest of the world' ... I didn't find anyone to be insulting ... but I think if you go into that thinking that your country is being criticised, then as soon as someone says something [critical] it just confirms in your mind that you are under attack. I didn't find anyone who was anti-American though there were plenty of people who were anti-Bush and that is fair enough.[50]

Bill Flynn, the doyen of corporate Irish-America and one of the pivotal third-party figures in the Northern Ireland peace process who was an aligned Bush supporter during the war in Iraq, agreed with MacNicholas's viewpoint, claiming in 2004 that, regardless of the reasons behind it, the relationship between America and Ireland was at a very low ebb.

> American people of Irish heritage are absolutely taken aback by what they are observing. We are shocked by the response [of the Irish people]. People say 'It's not an anti-American thing, it's an anti-Bush thing.' But they forget that he's our President. He was elected. Some of the things written and said about him have been in very poor taste.[51]

Niall O'Dowd suggested that Flynn's remarks were consistent with many others he had heard from Irish-Americans who have visited Ireland in recent years. O'Dowd's view is that they are explained not by any sustained trend in anti-Americanism so much as opposition to American foreign policies, and in particular the US invasions of Afghanistan and Iraq. 'A good friend was recently on the American Ireland Fund tour to Ireland and called me when he got back to discuss what he found. The unrelenting criticism, the cartoon-like image of the United States and, above all, the deep hatred shown towards President Bush by all sections of Irish society that he met had left him deeply angry.'[52] Stella O'Leary, chair of Irish-American Democrats, suggested that while Irish public opinion was guilty of a lot of generalisations, this had been exacerbated by the actions of the Bush administration which had played into the hands of those who depicted the US as a global bully. 'There has always been a resentment [in Ireland] of America, and sometimes that resentment seems to come from envy. But George Bush has also seemed to confirm some of the worst perceptions people have of America – brashness, ignoring other opinions and so on.'[53] This tension between Ireland and America was even given as a possible motive for an attack on two US basketball players in County Mayo, with one of the assailant's shouting 'Americans think they rule the world' during an attack that left one of the players with a broken jaw and the other with a broken hand.[54]

When President Bush visited Ireland in June 2004, a number of protests took place which focused on US policies in Iraq and, more specifically, the use of Shannon airport by the US air force as a strategic refuelling post, which was seen by some as compromising Ireland's status as a neutral country. These protests were widespread, well organised, and involved a diverse cross-section of activists, including the mayor of Dublin and the dean of St Patrick's Cathedral in Dublin, who attacked the use of Shannon airport by the US military. A group of 170 Irish lawyers signed a petition opposing President Bush's visit to Ireland and argued that US policies in Iraq were in breach of international law.[55]

Aside from the issue of Irish neutrality, none of the US military personnel who landed at Shannon airport were subjected to any inspection by the Irish security services. It was alleged by a number of Irish human rights activists and leading Irish political figures that Ireland had been used as part of the Bush administration's covert 'extraordinary renditions' programme. It has been claimed that under this shadowy scheme, individuals have been kidnapped by US intelligence services and smuggled around the world in unmarked aircraft for questioning/torture by US intelligence operatives and then moved on to Guantanamo Bay. Former Irish Labour Party leader Ruairí Quinn commented that the use of Shannon airport by the US military, without any inspections being made of US aircraft by the Irish police, was extraordinary, 'considering the evidence that exists indicating that people have been illegally kidnapped and transported through Ireland to destinations unknown for torture'.[56]

The *Limerick Leader* newspaper picked up on international media coverage of the US renditions programme in October 2005.

> A recent report in *Newsweek* magazine identified Shannon as one of the airports used as part of the extraordinary renditions programme. The magazine detailed the abduction of a German citizen, Khaled el-Masri, who was snatched from a bus in Macedonia in December 2003 and later taken in shackles aboard a Boeing 737 jet to Afghanistan where he was tortured. Flight records show that the jet flew from Dulles Airport in Washington to Shannon on January 16, 2004. Seven days later, it took off from Skopje, Macedonia, from where it flew to Baghdad and onto Kabul.[57]

On 10 December 2005, the *Limerick Leader* carried an editorial on attempts by US secretary of state Condoleezza Rice to pacify several

European governments over the issue of alleged US mistreatment of prisoners. This editorial linked the issue of extraordinary renditions with Irish neutrality, and suggested that abuse of Shannon airport by the US government in pursuit of its global war on terror could have wider implications for Irish-American relations, if the ambiguity of these 'phantom flights' was not clarified.

> Ms Rice's statement in Europe this week on 'rendition' – the transporting of suspected terrorists outside the normal legal process – raises more questions than it answers. Why are such prisoners being taken to secret interrogation centres if not for torture? And if the CIA are capable of torture, aren't they also capable of covering it up by lying about their business at Shannon [airport]? The US, by word and by deed, must now give this nation a cast-iron guarantee that the CIA are not smuggling prisoners through Shannon. Failure to do so could only add momentum to the campaign stirred up by anti-American elements to outlaw all American military flights in Irish airspace. This would be bad for business at the airport.[58]

Ireland, of course, was not the only European country caught up in the US renditions controversy. The United Kingdom government also became embroiled in arguments concerning what it knew about this policy and the extent to which it had condoned 'torture by proxy' of suspects who were allegedly being denied the right to legal representation, trial, or any form of due process. British human rights group Liberty took up the issue of 'extraordinary renditions' in November 2005 and launched a campaign to stop government involvement in it. The director of Liberty, Shami Chakrabarti, commented that: 'It is troubling that our Government chases Algeria for anti-torture assurances but cowers from confronting the USA on the same issue. It is the abhorrence of torture that distinguishes all democrats from dictators and terrorists. What can we say to those who perpetrate atrocities in London and around the world if we allow ourselves to become complicit in the cheapening of human life?'[59] Condoleezza Rice tried to dampen the row over extraordinary renditions during a tour of European Union countries in December 2005. During a visit to Kiev, Rice commented that: 'As a matter of US policy, the United States obligations under the [convention] which prohibits, of course, cruel and inhumane and degrading treatment, those obligations extend to US personnel wherever they are, whether they are in the United States or outside of the United States.'[60] While this statement reportedly satisfied several EU governments, it did not address the allegation that such inhumane treatment was being administered by non-US citizens in countries with poor human rights records such as Syria, Afghanistan and Turkey and therefore amounted to torture by proxy.

The *New York Times* carried an article by celebrated Irish journalist Nuala O'Faoláin in 2004 under the tag line 'When Irish Ties are Fraying'[61] in which she pointed out that the degree of unease within Ireland towards the forthcoming visit of President Bush was connected to the foreign policies of the Bush administration.

> How can there be so little enthusiasm for welcoming President Bush in as pro-American a country as exists on the face of the earth? Our intelligentsia is pro-American; American popular culture, far from being resisted as it is elsewhere in Europe, has been a precious modernizing influence on the grim patriarchy that dominated Ireland until recent times; our teachers and students work in the United States in the summer, our athletes train there, our doctors and scientists do postgraduate work there, we all have friends and relations there. No wonder Ireland shut down more completely than any other country in the world – schools, pubs, business, transport, everything – on its day of mourning for the Sept. 11 attacks. But nations on the periphery watch the center more keenly than the center realizes. The vacuum where our enthusiasm should be is our response to the perception – the fear – that this administration is indifferent to any world view but its own; that it doesn't care whether a little place like this loves it or not.[62]

The journalist and voice-over artist Seán McCarthy, founder of RadioIrish.com in New York, commented that he too experienced resentment towards the US within Ireland during this period. 'I remember feeling a very great sense of anti-American sentiment at a certain time not too long ago – over the last, let's say, four or five years. America was not popular in Ireland. You had all the stuff going on at Shannon airport and the war [in Iraq] wasn't being supported, and for a while there on the streets in Dublin in the circles that I was moving in, there was a very anti-American sentiment about.'[63]

On a more positive note, much of this criticism was identified with the Bush administration and US foreign policy since 9/11 rather than against America itself. There is the possibility therefore that President Obama will improve the Irish-American relationship indirectly, by altering the focus of US foreign policy and by improving diplomatic relations with transnational organisations such as the UN and the EU. The closure of Guantanamo Bay, military withdrawal from Iraq and the administration's public position on abiding by international human rights standards are all likely to improve attitudes towards the US within Irish public opinion. However, while President Obama may be more palatable to the Irish than his predecessor, he is unlikely to address their concerns directly at the policy level or target the Irish undocumented as a 'special case'. More importantly perhaps, Obama's administration will have little impact on the structural dynamics of Irish emigration to the US or be able to influence the fact that Irish-America is losing its critical mass. The wave of optimism that swept President Obama into the White House in 2008 is liable to reduce some of the tensions caused by US foreign policy, but it is unlikely to lift the more general mood of gloom within the Irish-American community as they watch the slow but steady decline of their social base. President Obama may of course make the pilgrimage to his 'ancestral home', Moneygall in Ireland during his tenure in office (perhaps in the run up to the 2012 election) and an open invitation has already been extended to him by the Irish government. However, this is unlikely to prove significant in policy terms, despite the inevitable febrile bonhomie that would accompany such a visit.

Regardless of how the Obama presidency develops in the years ahead, therefore, it seems clear that traditional notions of the relationship between Ireland and America (as an organic alliance mediated by steady flows of migration, Catholicism and cultural homogeneity) require updating. This faces us with a further question: If the physical connection between Ireland and America is in decline, what effect is this having on the cultural connection between Ireland and its diaspora? Asked another way, how is 'Irishness' perceived and displayed today within Irish-America?

NOTES

1. O'Hanlon, R. 'Illegals Living on a Dream and a Prayer', *Irish News*, 7 December 2004, p.6.
2. President George W. Bush, 'Address to a Joint Session of Congress and the American People', 20 September 2001, http://www.whitehouse.gov/news/releases/2001/09/20010920–8.html.
3. Vincent Doherty, correspondence with author, 17 September 2004.
4. 'Is Ireland Hostile to US?' *Sunday Business Post*, 4 July 2004, p.15.
5. Ibid.
6. Pauline Turley, director, Irish Arts Center New York, interviewed by author, 2 September 2004.
7. 'Kerry For President', *Irish Voice*, 21 October 2004, p.1.
8. Christina McElwaine, interviewed by author, 3 September 2004.
9. Siobhán Dennehy, director, Emerald Isle Immigration Center, interviewed by author, 20 September 2004.
10. Ibid.
11. See CNN Online, 22 September 2004, http://www.cnn.com/2004/US/09/22/plane.diverted. stevens.
12. The only exception to this new regulation were people who claimed asylum on the grounds of fearing persecution or torture if returned to their country of origin. In such cases the US Citizen and Immigration Service (CIS) would conduct a 'credible fear' interview with the individual(s).
13. 'Shackled in Chains for Overstaying', *Irish Voice*, 12 January 2005.
14. Ibid.
15. See Indymedia Ireland website, http://www.indymedia.ie/article/87066.
16. See BBC News online at: http://news.bbc.co.uk/1/hi/northern_ireland/2794277.stm.
17. Éamonn Dornan, interviewed by author, 3 September 2004.
18. Ibid.
19. *Irish Times*, 4 November 2008, p.6.
20. Éamonn Dornan, interviewed by author, 3 September 2004.
21. Ray O'Hanlon, interviewed by author, 17 September 2004.
22. Jack Irwin, special liaison officer on Irish affairs, Office of Governor George Pataki, New York State, interviewed by author, 8 September 20004.
23. See comments by Niall O'Dowd of the *Irish Voice* and Ray O'Hanlon of the *Irish Echo* in Chapter 3.
24. Siobhán Dennehy, interviewed by author, 20 September 2004.
25. 'Irish Government to Debate Undocumented',http://www.irishabroad.com/news/irishin america/news/irish-govt-undocumented-051005.asp.
26. Stanage, N. *Redemption Song: An Irish Reporter Inside the Obama Campaign* (Dublin: Liberties Press, 2008), p.174.
27. 'Outrage Over FBI "Informer" Attempts', *Irish Voice*, 5 October 2005, p.3.
28. Ibid.
29. Ray O'Hanlon, interviewed by author, 17 September 2004.
30. John Francis Mulligan, Irish Queers, interviewed by Professor Rosaleen Duffy, 25 September 2004.
31. Eileen Reilly, Glucksman Ireland House, NYU, interviewed by author, 14 September 2004.
32. Éamonn Dornan, interviewed by author, 3 September 2004.
33. Siobhán Dennehy, interviewed by author, 20 September 2004.
34. A 2005 US immigration bill entitled the 'Secure America and Orderly Immigration Act 2005' failed to pass through Congress.
35. Mary McGlynn, CUNY, interviewed by author, 15 September 2004.
36. Niall Burgess, Irish consul general, New York, interviewed by author, 9 September 2008.
37. Kelly Fincham, executive director, Irish Lobby for Immigration Reform, interviewed by author, 9 September 2008.
38. Ray O'Hanlon, *Irish Echo*, interviewed by author, 11 September 2008.

39. Niall Stanage, journalist, interviewed by author, 13 September 2008.
40. Niall Burgess, interviewed by author, 9 September 2008.
41. O'Dowd, N. 'Reform Still on the Map', *Irish Voice*, 30 October 2008, http://www.irishabroad. com/news/irish-voice/niall-odowd/Articles/reform301008.aspx.
42. Niall Stanage, interviewed by author, 13 September 2008.
43. *Sunday Business Post*, 10 December 2004, p.1.
44. *Daily Ireland*, 7 October 2005, p.8.
45. Professor Larry McCarthy, secretary, New York GAA, interviewed by author, 9 September 2008.
46. 'Irish Eyes No Longer Shine on US', *Irish Voice*, 4 November 2004.
47. Jake MacNicholas, NYPD, interviewed by author, 8 September 2004.
48. Irish-American AOH member, interviewed by author, September 2004.
49. Niall Stanage, interviewed by author, 13 September 2008.
50. Cassie Farrelly, former administrative director, Institute of Irish Studies, Fordham University, New York, interviewed by author, 16 September 2004.
51. 'Is Ireland Hostile to US? *Sunday Business Post*, 4 July 2004, p.15.
52. 'Deep Divisions on Iraq', *Irish Voice*, 25 October 2004.
53. 'Is Ireland Hostile to US?' *Sunday Business Post*, 4 July 2004, p.15.
54. 'Anti-American Attack Claim', *Irish Voice*, 17 February 2005.
55. RTÉ News, http://www.rte.ie/news/2004/0621/bush.
56. 'Troop Numbers at Shannon Soar', *Irish Voice*, 5 October 2005, p.4.
57. *Limerick Leader*, 12 March 2005, p.1. For *Newsweek* story on practice of 'extraordinary rendition', see 'Aboard Air CIA', *Newsweek*, 28 February 2005.
58. *Limerick Leader*, 10 December 2005, p.5.
59. 'Liberty Demands Government Halt CIA "Torture" Flight Stops in Britain', *Liberty* Press Release, 30 November 2005, http://www.liberty-human-rights.org.uk/news-and-events/1-press-releases/2005/torture-flights.shtml.
60. 'Defining Torture in a New World War', BBC News, 8 December 2005, http://news.bbc.co.uk/1/hi/world/americas/4499528.stm.
61. This was an imaginative reworking of the Irish song 'When Irish Eyes Are Smiling'.
62. O'Faoláin, N. 'When Irish Ties Are Fraying', *New York Times*, 23 June 2004, p.12.
63. Seán McCarthy, RadioIrish.com, interviewed by author, 11 September 2008.

5

Paddy Power:
The Evolution of the St Patrick's
Day Parade in New York City

This chapter explores the development of the St Patrick's Day parade in New York, as a metaphor for the changing cultural and political relationship between Ireland and America. It charts the history of the parade from its origins in the eighteenth century to the more recent controversy over the exclusion of gay and lesbian groups by the AOH and the evolution of new pressure groups such as the St Pat's for All Society, Irish Queers and the Lavender and Green Alliance and their alternative cultural celebrations and parades. This micro study of St Patrick's Day relates to the meta-theme which lies at the centre of this book, namely the evolution of the cultural, political and economic relationships between Ireland and America in the twenty-first century.

ST PATRICK'S DAY IN NEW YORK

The New York St Patrick's Day Parade has inspired many imitators all over the world, not least in Ireland itself, where until the 1970s the saint's day was celebrated by closing all the pubs so that a suitably pious and penitent mood might be observed.[1]

St Patrick's Day is one of the most celebrated and widely recognised national festivals in the world. It is a global brand alongside other notable items of Irish cultural iconography such as Guinness and 'Riverdance'.[2] St Patrick's Day is a suitable illustration of modern trends in Irish migration, combining historical and religious legacies with modern cultural celebrations. This national feast day has been exported beyond the island of Ireland as a symbol of the Irish diaspora's global reach.

This chapter examines the evolution of St Patrick's Day in New York

City and what this signifies about the changes that are taking place within the ethnographic profile of Irish-America. The central focus here looks at the way in which more traditional conceptions of Irishness epitomised by the AOH and their control of the 'official' St Patrick's Day parade in Manhattan are increasingly being challenged by those who feel excluded from this event. The AOH-organised parade on Fifth Avenue raises issues about how cultural identity is constructed and about who is (and who is not) defined as being part of the imagined Irish community. Of particular importance here are the tensions centring around the control of the official parade by the AOH and their exclusion of gay and lesbian groups from participation in it. While the major fissure relates to the exclusion of gay and lesbian groups from marching openly in the parade, these tensions are political as well as cultural and have even involved arguments over the commemoration of the victims of the September 11th attacks in New York. To this extent, the chapter parallels several of the main themes of the book and illustrates the intersection of political and cultural pressures within contemporary Irish-America.

The central argument here is that the controversy over the celebration of St Patrick in New York City underscores important changes taking place in the fabric of Irish-American civil society. These changes reflect a move away from traditionally conservative notions of Irishness as represented by organisations such as the AOH, with the emergence of a younger and more diffuse Irish-American community with a more secular focus.

OFFICIAL CONSTRUCTIONS OF IRISHNESS

What you see with the AOH parade is the face of mid-nineteenth century immigrants – they had to live in a hostile world and struggle to survive. They felt unwelcome when they arrived in New York and they then had to assert their identity. A lot of this is mixed up with sentiment. So they sing and have divisions called after counties in Ireland such as the County Louth Division. You might say it is a simple tribal thing. They are now caught in that model.[3]

The St Patrick's Day parade in New York has an impressive history and has been identified as the oldest parade of its type in the United States.[4] According to the website of the organisers of the parade in Manhattan, the festival has an ancient pedigree which, they claim, began on 17

March 1762, 'fourteen years before the signing of the Declaration of Independence … an annual celebration which has continued without interruption ever since'.[5] The organisers go on to claim that the Manhattan parade organised by the AOH is the biggest and best in the world. 'There's no denying the pre-eminence of New York's St Patrick's Day parade. Last year over 400 marching bands … and scores of others made up the 200,000 marchers who followed the course from St Patrick's Cathedral up Fifth Avenue to 86th Street. Over 2,000,000 spectators lined the sidewalks to watch and cheer.'[6]

However, there is an alternative narrative within contemporary sections of Irish-America, which sees the AOH as being out of touch with modern forms of cultural and political identity and views the Fifth Avenue parade as a narrow, exclusionary and aging event, out of sync with the cosmopolitan nature of Ireland and Irish-America. John Francis Mulligan, a representative of the gay activist organisation Irish Queers, claimed that: 'Catholicism has a big part to play in the parade. A lot of the people involved in the AOH emigrated here in the 1940s and 1950s. Ireland was different then and they have held on to this romantic notion. It will only change when they die.'[7] A more traditional perspective is highlighted by John T. Ridge in his history of the St Patrick's Day parade in New York, when he comments that: 'It offers to those of Irish heritage a chance to reaffirm the connection with old traditions while participating in all the enthusiasm of a revival. With the Irish population in America increasingly more scattered and distant from the old ethnic centers, the parade is an all-important reunion.'[8] While the St Patrick's Day parade has today become synonymous with a global party, it began as a combination of religious devotion and nationalistic sentiment towards Ireland. It also functioned to symbolise the right of a rather beleaguered Irish community in the mid-nineteenth century to parade publicly as full US citizens. The commemorative cultural aspects of the parade were therefore fused simultaneously with contemporary political issues relating to the importance of the First Amendment to the US constitution in respect of freedom of assembly and the right to parade peacefully within a democratic society.[9]

In this sense the message it tried to send out was that the Irish were trustworthy law-abiding citizens and not a community to be feared or distrusted. Seen from this perspective, St Patrick's Day was a public relations exercise aimed at improving the image of the Irish community in the US and combating some of the anti-Irish stereotypes that existed until well into the twentieth century. There is evidence, for example, that the custom of 'Paddy-making' took place well into the nineteenth century, which involved parading anti-Irish effigies of St Patrick through the streets on 17 March as a means of irritating and denigrating the Irish immigrant community. This became such a problem that it led to legislation in 1803 to outlaw the practice, with a fine of $10 for anyone found to be inciting the Irish community by doing this on March 17th.[10]

The parade organised by the AOH in Manhattan began to evolve following the large numbers of Irish people who arrived in the US during the 1850s in the wake of the Famine. In 1851 the number of organisations taking part in the parade increased from six to a record seventeen societies, with the increasing numbers of Irish immigrants drawing in people from the New York suburbs as well as labour union organisations. The influx of numbers also increased the role and power of the AOH, which assumed control of the parade from the Convention of Irish Societies in 1853. The parade is unusual in New York in that it is held every year on the actual feast day itself (unless it falls on a Sunday) rather than on the closest weekend available. This is a testament to its status and to the power of the Irish lobby given the disruption this inevitably causes to traffic and commerce in the city. While rapid Irish immigration to the US in the mid-nineteenth century partly explains the growth of the parade in New York, this was amplified by the growing agitation in Ireland for home rule and the activities of Irish nationalist lobby groups abroad. 'All radical groups, such as the Fenians, Clan na Gael and the Land League found support and funds in New York, and the enthusiasm in the city for such causes and for the Irish generally made St Patrick's Day all the more important.'[11]

During the latter half of the twentieth century, the parade had evolved into a full-blown civic festival that owed as much to a celebration of American civic and military culture as it did to its Irish ancestry. In 2006, for example, the parade was dedicated to the 69th Regiment of the National Guard (The Fighting 69th) who had just returned from Iraq where they had lost nineteen soldiers in combat. While there was usually an undercurrent of Irish nationalism, a more overt manifestation in the 1970s related to the drinking culture that became associated with the parade, frowned upon by sections within the AOH due to threats to public order and the reputation of the event as a respectable family day out.

One of the few occasions when the political conflict in Northern Ireland impacted on the parade was with the election of Michael Flannery as grand marshal in 1983. Flannery was a founding member of the Irish Northern Aid Committee (Noraid) and openly sympathetic to the Provisional IRA. His installation by the AOH as grand master led to a boycott of the parade by some participants and an unseemly political row. The doors of St Patrick's Cathedral in New York remained symbolically closed by the Catholic Church to register their disapproval, though as Ray O'Hanlon of the *Irish Echo* points out, 'Flannery took it in his stride, not least because Cardinal Cooke had explained his position and the likely response to Flannery in advance.'[12] One of Flannery's supporters within the AOH commented that Flannery's appointment was an important statement and that the parade was important in the context of the Northern Ireland conflict. 'It's the only day of the year we can get the world to pay attention to the Irish.'[13] Flannery's election was preceded the previous year by the appointment of Bobby Sands (recently martyred in the 1981 republican hunger strikes) as honorary grand marshal of the parade. The elections of Sands and Flannery illustrate the wider point made in Chapter 3, that political attitudes within Irish-America have fluctuated in intensity at particular pressure points in the conflict in Northern Ireland. Their elections were to mark the high point of Irish republican impact on the St Patrick's Day parade in New York.

Unusually for a parade of such magnitude, the AOH has strictly controlled the people who participate in it and the way in which they do so. Floats and non-official political slogans are not allowed in the body of the parade (though what's left of Noraid seem less affected by such regulations). In 2006 the ILIR[14] was prevented from taking part in the parade under its own banner on the grounds that it was an advocacy group. A compromise suggestion that its parade participants take part in the main body of the parade wearing their specially commissioned 'Legalise the Irish' T-shirts was also rejected by the parade's organising committee. This was perhaps due to fears that setting such a precedent would make it impossible for the AOH to exclude the people they *really* wanted to keep out – gay and lesbian groups.

By far the biggest issue for the parade in New York over the last fifteen years relates to the exclusion of gay, lesbian, bisexual and transgender groups from the parade. This raises issues relating to the conservative Catholicism of Irish-America and the control of the modern Manhattan parade by the AOH, which its opponents have argued remains stuck in

a 1950s *Quiet Man* vision of Irishness. This critique was confirmed to
me when I attended a St Patrick's Day Breakfast on 17 March 2006 in
the Waldorf Astoria in New York, hosted by George Pataki, then governor of New York state. The guest speaker, Lieutenant Governor Mary
Donohue, opened her address with the comment, 'Top of the mornin'
to you all', which was the first time I had heard this remark first hand.
In reality this event was connected more to America than to Ireland
and, despite the presence of a representative of the Irish government,
was dominated by symbols of US civic pride and in particular the US
armed forces, FDNY and NYPD.

The next section examines the politics of exclusion associated with
the Manhattan parade, the reaction to this exclusion by gay and lesbian groups, and how this issue fits into the wider context of patterns
of Irish migration to the US.

OUTSIDE THE LOOP: THE POLITICS OF EXCLUSION

It is a uniquely New York kind of row. It involves one of the endless
parades that represent the teeming ethnic groups that make up the
city (with the notable exception of the English) and that gridlock
Fifth Avenue for much of the summer. It involves sexual politics,
sensitive racial issues, the Mayor and even, for good measure, a
couple of cast members of 'The Sopranos'.[15]

I never thought my life would end up being defined by a
parade. It's important though, it is about power and identity. The
men who control the most important cultural expression of Irishness are the AOH. What other parade gets the kind of global coverage that their St Patrick's parade gets?[16]

It is ironic that in recent years the politics of St Patrick's Day have not
revolved around Ireland at all, but have instead been the crucible for
heated debates surrounding the civil rights of the GLBT community
and their right to parade on St Patrick's Day under their own banners,
which has been resisted by the parade organisers. The Irish Lesbian
and Gay Organisation (ILGO), which formed in 1990, has been at the
forefront of public protests against their exclusion, sometimes taking a
confrontational stance as a way of highlighting what they see as their
unjust exclusion from constructions of Irishness in the twenty-first

century. 'Inevitably, Irish gays and lesbians found each other in their new big city homes, and just like their straight fellow Irish, contemporary and long dead, they formed an association.'[17] A number of other groups such as the Lavender and Green Alliance, Irish Queers and St Pat's for All have emerged in reaction to the unwillingness of the AOH to allow the gay and lesbian community to participate openly in the Fifth Avenue parade.

Tensions relating to the exclusion of gay and lesbian groups came to a head during the early 1990s, leading to unedifying confrontations, protests and counter-protests at the AOH parade on St Patrick's Day itself and, eventually, the establishment of alternative St Patrick's Day celebrations designed to be inclusive, gay-friendly events. Anne Maguire, one of the founding members of ILGO, has commented that she became an activist over this issue because she felt excluded from cultural citizenship.

> Our mission was to make it possible for the predominantly immigrant group to be Irish and gay at the same time. Before ILGO we were forced to choose; we could be Irish if we were closeted (which most of our members were) or we could be lesbians and gay men so long as we gave up the benefits offered by the Irish community to immigrants in this city. ILGO changed all that.[18]

In 1991, ILGO picketed the AOH parade to protest at being excluded from marching openly under gay and lesbian banners. 'We're here, we're queer, we're Irish' was a startling departure for many observers used to less colourful declarations of identity. The most pithy headline surrounding the controversy over the 1991 parade was supplied by *New York Newsday*: 'Erin Goes Boo'.[19] The message of one protest banner at the 1991 AOH parade, 'Beware the AIDS of March',[20] indicated that the issues went far beyond St Patrick's Day or even Irishness itself. For many of these protestors, the issues are much broader than the parade and go to the heart of official constructions of identity and who has the right to be the gatekeeper of twenty-first century definitions of Irishness. Anne Maguire's activism in ILGO was based on her objection to the AOH casting Irishness as a white, male, Catholic and heterosexual preserve. 'We see this as a fight for the full participation of all Irish people in the annual celebration of our heritage. The parade committee shouldn't be trying to determine who is Irish enough to celebrate St Patrick's Day.'[21]

Beyond this, some saw the issue as fundamentally one of civil rights, equality and constitutional liberties enshrined in the US Bill of Rights.

This has opened up an examination of the extent to which the AOH representation of Irishness through the St Patrick's Day parade on Fifth Avenue is actually reflective of contemporary Irish-America, with its focus on US military and NYPD participants and its trappings of Catholicism. John Francis Mulligan from Irish Queers claimed that resentment related to the wider issue that the AOH parade was regarded by the wider media as the primary illustration of Irish culture in New York.

> The media give the Fifth Avenue parade all the coverage and it is presented as the pinnacle of Irishness. It is the major event to define Irishness and if you watch the parade you have to ask how Irish is it? All the military institutions of America are there: the army, marines, police and so on; it is a militaristic format and that turns the parade around into a military parade. So the parade has become a flash point over what it means to be Irish. So this issue of exclusion is an important one.[22]

Back in 1991, the struggle between ILGO and the AOH led to aftershocks that destabilised other elements of New York's civic society. The police department entered the fray when the NYPD Emerald Society, a fraternal organisation of Irish-American police officers, approved a resolution seeking the exclusion of ILGO and any other 'homosexual and alternative lifestyle' groups from the parade. This resulted in a letter to the NYPD commissioner Lee Brown from the openly lesbian New York State Assembly member Deborah Glick, which widened the issue beyond St Patrick's Day or even Irishness and turned it into a debate about representative policing and the civil rights of New Yorkers. Commenting on the NYPD Emerald Society's resolution, Glick claimed that: 'This most recent action takes the [police] Department to a new low. It is incredible that a fraternal organization made up of members of the Police Department feels free to openly embrace and encourage extreme homophobia.'[23] The New York mayor at the time, David Dinkins, sided with ILGO and marched alongside them in the 1991 parade under the AOH's Division 7 association, who had invited ILGO to march with them in an effort to defuse the situation. Dinkins was booed and pelted with beer cans by those who felt he had sided with the lesbian and gay groups, while both ILGO and Division 7 of the AOH were banned from the following year's parade by the organising committee.[24]

The AOH's defence to its exclusion of ILGO has generally rested upon two arguments, the first being that the parade is a privately organised event which under the terms of the First Amendment can exclude any group that it believes conflicts with the message of the event and that has a 'confrontational' agenda. The AOH obtained a New York court order to exclude ILGO in 1993. When ILGO challenged its exclusion in a New York court in 1996, the eventual ruling (four years later) found in favour of the AOH, which claimed that ILGO took a position 'contrary to that of the Roman Catholic Church', and were intent on using the parade for 'confrontation'.

Protests linked to exclusion from the Fifth Avenue parade have become quite ritualised, with gay and lesbian activists periodically blocking the route of the parade or walking up and down with placards protesting against their exclusion. These have generated considerable media attention, especially when protestors have been arrested by the police for blocking the route of the parade, and due to the clever use of placard slogans such as '12 July, 17 March – same bigots, different sashes'.[25] In 1999 ILGO campaigned for its supporters to wear orange rather than green on St Patrick's Day as a symbolic protest against their exclusion from the parade. This tactic generated interest from the gay and lesbian media including *Gay Pride* magazine in New York, which saw the St Patrick's Day issue as symbolic of wider elements of discrimination against the gay community.

> If a group of white chauvinists decided to recast the saint's day of a universally revered saint as an occasion on which to stage a parade to celebrate the white race; forbade blacks, Orientals, and people of mixed race from participating; and defended their right to march as a unified white community on 'National No-Nigger Day' on the basis that this is a religious procession the state may not interfere with, how many major politicians would vie to be the most prominent political marcher in that parade each year? How many political and social luminaries would compete for seats at the reviewing stand?[26]

In recent years, alternative parades have become established that seek to provide a more inclusive celebration of St Patrick's Day and these have been gaining in popularity and credibility. Brendan Fay, an Irish-born gay rights activist and founding member of the Lavender and Green Alliance, claimed that the issue of gay and lesbian groups was more complex than simple exclusion. He suggested that it was not simply a case of liberalism versus conservatism, and that there were divisions within gay and lesbian groups and shades of opinion within the AOH.

> At first ILGO was about 60 or 70 people and then within two or three meetings it had descended into a conflict. This is part of the story that isn't acknowledged. It is always cast in terms of us versus them. Us being the gays and lesbians and them being Hibernians, as a sort of liberal versus conservative fight. The AOH present a particular mode of being Irish. But it's not as simple as that, it's too neat. There are differences within the gay and lesbian community and differences within AOH. There are some enlightened ones in AOH, some welcome Irish gays and lesbians and want them to march with AOH on the Fifth Avenue parade. But still the AOH is cast as the enemy. In 1991 gays and lesbians did march in the Fifth Avenue parade and that was thanks to these people within the AOH. There are splits between native-born Irish and Irish-Americans. There are also gender splits, and tension between lesbians and gay men. Often the gay men are dismissed as misogynists.[27]

Kathleen McGreal, an Irish-American teacher whose family come originally from County Mayo, corroborated this opinion, claiming that it was too dismissive to caricature the AOH as being merely homophobes stuck in a time warp of 1950s Ireland. McGreal, whose father had been a member of the AOH for over thirty years, argued that there were liberals within the AOH and that many of them would welcome a more inclusive parade. She suggested that both sides in the argument contained conservative and liberal elements, but that they were represented by their most extreme voices.[28] Niall Stanage took the view that the AOH was liberal in the sense that some of the more forward-thinking within its ranks would welcome new younger members joining so long as they reflected their own traditional attitudes to the parade and other matters, 'and sign up lock stock and barrel to what they [the AOH] believe. But the nature of generational change is that people don't sign up lock stock and barrel to what previous generations believe.'[29]

The profusion of gay and lesbian organisations protesting in different ways about AOH control of the parade in New York is testament to the fact that there is disagreement between them about how to handle their exclusion as well as more philosophical differences related to gender politics. One of the main disagreements relates to those who favour confrontation and others who would rather withdraw and participate in more inclusive St Patrick's Day events. 'It is clear that for some it is easier to sustain the conflict with the leaders of the Fifth Avenue parade – perhaps unconsciously. Instead of resolution that can be agreed by all sides and all groups, the conflict is sustained.'[30] Essentially one of the central tensions within the gay and lesbian community in New York is between reformers and radicals, with some wanting to reduce conflict with the AOH by initiating alternative St Patrick's Day celebrations while others want to continue protesting at their exclusion from the Manhattan parade. This has caused internal splits within the gay and lesbian community, with the Irish Queers maintaining their protest and the emergence of the St Pat's for All group, which has established an increasingly popular alternative parade in the Woodside area of Queens. This was established by gay activists such as Brendan Fay in response to their exclusion from the Fifth Avenue parade, the aim being to provide an inclusive and multi-ethnic celebration of St Patrick's Day. The first St Pat's for All parade was held in 2000 and it has grown in popularity in subsequent years. It is normally held in the week preceding the AOH parade to allow those who wish to, to attend both. The emphasis here is on diversity and the local community and it has none of the military trappings of the AOH-controlled parade: 'The St Patrick's Parade & Irish Fair Committee is committed to celebrating the diversity of the Irish and Irish American communities of New York. First held in 2000, the Parade & Fair has become an annual community endeavour that cherishes and celebrates an inclusive St Patrick's holiday season. Our celebration is the first in the 240 years-plus of Irish parades in New York City to be open and welcoming to all who share the spirit of the day.'[31] In the run-up to the 2009 celebrations, the St Pat's for All website emphasised the event's inclusivity and its cultural diversity.

> The Irish community of Queens hosts the city's only parade to welcome lesbian and gay contingents. The March 1st parade continues a rare spirit of hospitality and welcome that began with the 2000 parade's historical breakthrough. Other participating Irish groups and businesses include the Niall O'Leary School of Irish Dance, Lavender & Green Alliance, a New York-based Irish lesbian and gay group, the Brehon Law Society, the Irish Parades Emergency Committee, The Keltic Dreamers and the All City School march-

ing Band and Irish marriage equality pioneers, Drs Katherine Zap-
pone and Ann Louise Gilligan! Community youth groups will join
as drummers and puppeteers.[32]

In 2009, the St Pat's for All parade included an address by Stella O'Leary,
president of the Irish-American Democrats in celebration of the election
of Barack Obama to the US presidency. O'Leary told the *Irish Times*: 'It's
refreshing to know that there is an Irish group that is so inclusive ... I've
been very impressed by all the ethnic groups involved.'[33]

This new wave of cultural expression loosened the Catholic heterosexual grip on cultural expressions of Irishness during the 1990s and
began to gain popularity and notoriety after the first parade in 2000.
Hillary Clinton attended the St Pat's for All parade in addition to the
AOH parade while campaigning for a New York Senate seat in 2000,
while the mayor of New York, Mike Bloomberg, has also been a regular
supporter of the parade since 2002. The *Irish Echo* pointed out that
Bloomberg was criticised by members of his own party for taking this
step. 'Bloomberg's participation in the Queens parade comes despite a
letter from [Patrick] Hurley and Ed Coyne – district leader and president, respectively, of the Woodside branch of the Republican Party –
urging him to stay away from what Hurley in particular has long argued
is nothing more than a radical left-wing demonstration.'[34] Bloomberg
was also attacked by gay and lesbian activists for accepting an invitation
from the AOH to parade in the Fifth Avenue event because it excluded
them from taking part. Pat Lavery of the Irish Queers group suggested
that 'If Bloomberg marches on Fifth Avenue, he's a bigot, plain and
simple.'[35] Irish Queers have typically taken a more radical approach,
focusing on their exclusion from the AOH parade rather than putting
their energies into the alternative celebrations in Queens. This disagreement has caused a degree of tension between them and the Lavender
and Green Alliance led by Brendan Fay.

> We have got some hostility from the gay community who want to
> continue the fight on Fifth Avenue. They're more committed to
> conflict than conflict resolution. I suppose we all know where we
> stand. Irish Queers want to be in the Fifth Avenue parade, not an
> alternative parade. But what they don't like about us is that it
> means Irish Queers cannot continue with their story that there is
> no gay-inclusive parade in New York. There is. But there is money

in conflict. There are law suits, court cases and websites.[36]

While the gay and lesbian community is itself divided over how to celebrate St Patrick's Day, there were more obvious sources of opposition to the St Pat's for All parade. The *Irish Echo* illustrated the depth of feeling generated by the Woodside parade from more traditional quarters. 'One house on Skillman Avenue displayed posters attacking the parade in its windows, including a statue of the Virgin Mary holding a sign that read, "A blasphemous lesbian and homosexual parade".'[37] Brendan Fay claimed that the St Pat's for All committee had not set out to deliberately provoke more traditional Irish-Americans or the AOH, but was a positive and non-confrontational alternative.

> There are 12 parades in New York for St Patrick's, of which the Fifth Avenue parade is the biggest. But there are others every weekend in March. Some are inclusive, others not. The Woodside Parade is inclusive and that breaks down the idea that there are no gay-friendly Irish parades in New York. Here we have a Chilean group in the St Pat's for All parade ... So people have welcomed the St Pat's parade enthusiastically. It is a different kind of parade. Lesbians and gays bring their own banners. Other religions too: Protestants, Catholics and Jews are included.[38]

While an invitation has been extended to the AOH to take part, they have yet to take up the offer. In recent years some of those involved in the St Pat's for All parade have become frustrated by media portrayals of it being a gay parade and have attempted to get beyond what they see as a ghettoisation of the parade as a gay and lesbian event, depicting it as a community festival which is inclusive of the gay community but not defined by it.

In 2002 the politics of St Patrick's Day became embroiled in the aftermath of the September 11th attacks, with both the AOH and the St Pat's for All parades vying with one another over honouring the heroes and commemorating the memory of the dead victims. The Woodside parade focused on Fr Mychal Judge, a sixty-eight-year-old Catholic priest who was chaplain to the Fire Department of New York (FDNY) and who died while tending to the other victims of 9/11 at the World Trade Center.

Judge was classified by the New York morgue as DM-01-00001, with DM relating to Disaster Manhattan and the number referring to the fact that he was the first victim to be classified. A movement quickly emerged to have Judge canonised, though the Catholic Church backed off this idea when it was subsequently reported that Judge was gay. *USA Today* reported that over 3,000 people attended Judge's funeral on 15 September 2001 and that the then mayor of New York, Rudy Giuliani, called him a saint.[39] Judge marched at the St Pat's for All parade in 2000, and two years later the parade was dedicated to his memory. Brendan Fay, co-founder of the St Pat's for All parade, claimed that Fr Judge was one of the few Catholic Church figures in New York who had openly supported the parade.

> For many priests they won't march in our parade because it's too controversial ... I asked if every church on the route of our parade would open the doors and let people use their toilets or provide drinks for the parade goers. And every church on the route said no. They all said it was because there were gays in the parade. Mychal Judge supported the first parade and we got an anonymous cheque from a donor to give financial support to it. But it was all swept under the carpet [by the Catholic Church].[40]

ILGO used the 9/11 issue to once again attack the AOH policy of discriminating against the gay and lesbian community in their parade on Fifth Avenue. In an interesting twist, they focused on their rights as US citizens rather than any reference to St Patrick or to their Irishness, and explicitly invoked their US patriotism post-9/11 in their attack on the AOH refusal to allow them to take part as members of the gay and lesbian community.

> The St Patrick's Day parade will honor heroes of September 11. We are denied our rightful place in the parade line up. This denies us the opportunity to celebrate the heroes of September 11 and denies the existence of the many LGBT heroes and victims of 9/11 ... help to remind the homophobic organizers and supporters of the parade that ILGO belongs in the parade and that 9/11 is every community's tragedy.[41]

In a predictable counter-punch, the Brooklyn edition of the Catholic newspaper *The Tablet* explicitly invoked the 9/11 attacks in opposing the St Pat's for All parade in Woodside. 'In the spirit of the aftermath of the tragedy at the World Trade Center, we ... ask the public to resist the temptation to view this curiosity.'[42]

While the two sides appear to be entrenched in their opposition to one another, the longer-term demographic changes within Irish-America highlighted elsewhere in this book suggest that the days of AOH control of the Manhattan parade may be numbered. In 2006, the issue of AOH exclusion of open gay and lesbian participation in the parade was once again centre stage. Two prominent Irish-American figures in New York epitomised the entrenched positions that have been in place for well over two decades – Christine Quinn, the speaker of New York City Council on the one hand, and John Dunleavy, chairman of the St Patrick's Day Parade Committee in New York on the other. Quinn, the newly elected speaker, was an Irish-American and a lesbian who was not prepared to take the pragmatic approach of other political figures such as Mayor Bloomberg or Senator Hillary Clinton by marching in both the St Pat's for All event in Queens and the Fifth Avenue parade. Quinn, New York City's first openly lesbian (or Irish) city council leader, attempted to negotiate an agreement with the Fifth Avenue parade organisers that would allow the gay and lesbian community to march under their own banner. 'As a proud Irish-American lesbian, I certainly hope to be able to march in this year's St Patrick's Day Parade with the Irish LGBT community in a way that allows us to openly celebrate our heritage and identity.'[43] However, when Quinn failed to reach an agreement with the organisers she announced that she would not be participating in the Manhattan parade. This decision, announced on 16 March, led the television and newspaper media coverage in conjunction with comments made by John Dunleavy, chairman of the parade committee, in an interview he gave to the *Irish Times*. Dunleavy accused both Quinn and Hillary Clinton of playing politics with the parade and using it to win votes within the Irish-American community. More controversially, he made a parallel between ILGO agitation for their inclusion in the parade and neo-Nazis, the Ku Klux Klan and prostitution.

> The issue was decided unanimously in our favour in the Supreme Court, there is nothing to negotiate. If an Israeli group wants to march in New York, do you allow neo-Nazis into their parade? If African Americans are marching in Harlem, do they have to let the Ku Klux Klan into their parade? … People have rights. If we let the ILGO in, is it the Irish Prostitute Association next?[44]

The comments of Dunleavy, together with Quinn's boycott of the Fifth Avenue parade, framed the New York media coverage of St Patrick's

Day in 2006 and at a wider level epitomised the differences between old and new visions of Irishness that are apparent across the Irish-American diaspora in the twenty-first century. Cronin and Adair have argued that the power struggle between the AOH and groups such as ILGO 'reveal the ever-changing nature of the Irish diaspora in America. They reveal some of the pressures that the traditional custodians of St Patrick's Day are under as the world around them becomes increasingly fluid in terms of notions of identity, difference and morality.'[45]

LOSING CONTROL: DEMOGRAPHIC TRENDS IN IRISH-AMERICA

While the celebration of St Patrick's Day in New York might suggest that Irish-America is vibrant and relatively stable, the reality is that elements of Irish-American civil society such as the AOH, the GAA and cultural groups such as Irish history societies are in a state of flux. The reason for this, as is documented elsewhere in this book, is that the tap of Irish migration has been turned off since the early 1990s, while trends linked to globalisation have changed the behaviour of many who do arrive in the US from Ireland in the twenty-first century.

Ray O'Hanlon of the *Irish Echo* has commented that the slowdown of Irish migration poses a serious dilemma for Irish-America due to the fact that it 'had always needed periodic waves of fresh-faced Irish immigrants in order to reinvigorate its heart and soul'.[46] In cultural terms and within the context of St Patrick's Day conflict in New York between the AOH and gay and lesbian activists, the irony was that Ireland itself had moved on. 'By 1993, the third year of ILGO's storming of the parade ramparts, it was no longer illegal for consenting adults to have homosexual relations in Ireland. Mary Robinson was inviting gays and lesbians to her official residence for tea and gay marching groups were being accepted in St Patrick's Day parades in Irish cities with little or no fuss.'[47]

In addition to the obvious point that fewer Irish people are emigrating to the United States due to the lack of economic or social push factors, the behaviour of the post-1990 wave of Irish migrants is different to that of their predecessors. These changes in the causes of Irish migration to the US are having a significant impact upon Irish-American civil society. It is clear from historical accounts of the St Patrick's Day parade that its early years were characterised by battles against anti-Irish bigotry and that Irish immigrants were often considered to be on the outside of society, struggling economically and culturally to carve out a new life within the US. Groups such as the Hibernian United Benevolent Society, the Young Friends of Ireland and the Independent Sons of Erin formed in the nineteenth century as essentially service-delivery NGOs for the Irish immigrant community in New York. Today, of course, Irish-America is very much within the US political and social mainstream, and the military presence at the St Patrick's Day parade in Manhattan illustrates the extent to which it has been absorbed into the hegemonic centre of US cultural life.

In the twenty-first century, therefore, there is less need for NGOs such as the AOH, as the vast majority of those who arrive in the US today are confident, young and upwardly mobile individuals. They are not driven to join organisations such as the AOH nor are they desperately trying to hang onto home by going to Irish history or Irish dancing classes. The argument here is that the ground is shifting under the feet of the St Patrick's Day parade, due to the decline in Irish migration and the increased transience of the Irish who do enter the US to work. The AOH is entering a period of transition as its numbers decrease and its officers and members get old together. Brendan Fay believes that the AOH is increasingly becoming a beleaguered and defensive organisation, out of step with both modern America and Ireland itself.

> It looks like a group under siege, one which sees their Catholic minority status under attack. At first it was an expression of dignity and pride, and now it's become stuck in a particular model that they cannot change.[48]

AOH numbers are dwindling and they are losing critical mass, particularly in urban areas where Divisions with increasingly elderly demographic profiles and a dearth of younger members are merging or disappearing altogether. John T. Ridge, a noted historian of the AOH, commented that the nature of the membership had changed dramatically in recent years and that this has had an impact on the organisation's profile and role within the Irish-American community.

> The important thing about the Hibernians is that the membership numbers may be the same, which I doubt – but they may be the same – but the membership has changed. In the old days, [AOH] divisions were basically in cities and towns where most people went to the same church and the division was also a part of that

parish, it was part of the neighbourhood. At its centre, each parish almost had a Hibernian division and when you thought of another parish, you thought of another Hibernian division. That has almost gone. There are not enough people left in those areas – in concentration – to form those Hibernian divisions and so in the cities those Hibernian divisions are going very fast. I think [that] in another twenty-five years they will be all gone ... It is going to follow the pattern that it has done across the country.[49]

Eileen Reilly, an academic from Glucksman Ireland House at NYU, suggested that the demographic profile of the AOH was in decline to the point that its control of the St Patrick's Day parade was under threat. 'They will eventually lose their grip on the main St Patrick's Day parade. It will change.'[50] Professor Joe Lee, director of Glucksman Ireland House, suggested that in addition to the Irish-born being less interested in joining groups such as the AOH, those born in the US since the early 1960s who would identify themselves as having an Irish heritage were significantly different to older Irish-Americans. 'It is not only a gap between American-born and Irish-born, but Irish-Americans born after 1960 would almost certainly have a very different image of their place in American society [than their predecessors].'[51] This point was substantiated by Cassie Farrelly, former administrative director of the Institute of Irish Studies at Fordham University in New York. Farrelly suggested that the economic mobility and transience of the Irish community was having an impact on groups such as the AOH among those from her own generation.

> In the 30s you were here to stay. You couldn't go back. It was a one-way ticket. Now that there's more mobility, people are less married to upholding old [Irish] traditions. Like I wouldn't belong to the Ancient Order of Hibernians, but my grandfather would have been ... It [the AOH] captures a particular time in Ireland and a particular way of organising ... Our interest is much more in contemporary Ireland and the feeling of organisations like that [AOH] is that they are stuck in a very 1950s view. They [young Irish-Americans] wouldn't tend to join organisations partly because they tend to be much more economically comfortable [than their predecessors] and they would buy Irish music and watch Irish movies but they wouldn't join Irish organisations

anymore.[52]

St Patrick's Day can be seen to have emerged therefore despite extremely humble beginnings in the middle of the nineteenth century, to the point that today it is a globally recognised cultural celebration of Irishness, but one that owes little to Ireland itself. The most obvious parallel in fact, though perhaps an unwanted one, would be with the Orange Order and those who view the parades on 12 July in Northern Ireland as a celebration of Britishness. Both of these events have evolved through a form of cultural Chinese whispers, to the point that they are virtually unrecognisable to those within the imagined homeland.

The Manhattan parade in New York is the largest of its type and is emblematic of the evolution of the Irish diaspora over several centuries. Current debates concerning the content of the parade and who should be allowed to participate in it are ironically reminiscent of its own origins. This chapter has tried to outline the politics of exclusion highlighted by the AOH parade in Manhattan and the way in which 'official' constructions of Irish identity as being male, Catholic and heterosexual have been challenged by those who do not fit into the hegemonic discourse. The battle over the memory of St Patrick in New York reflects the evolution of Ireland itself. What was a nation of subsistence agriculture, regular emigration and conservative Catholicism has been transformed into an economic powerhouse characterised by inward migration and secularisation in the twenty-first century.

While the AOH have constructed a St Patrick's Day parade in New York that reflects one version of Irishness, it is clear that this does not exist within a cultural vacuum and that other alternative celebrations have emerged after they were excluded from the AOH parade. These emphasise that Irishness is not tied to Catholicism, sexual orientation, gender or nationalism. In an ironic twist, the AOH and the traditional Catholic Irish-America it represents have found that Ireland has liberalised and secularised, while they have been holding the torch for what they believe to be traditional Irish values.

Although the AOH parade on Fifth Avenue remains dominant in New York, the alternative St Pat's for All parade in the Woodside area of Queens is increasingly coming into the political mainstream. While it may always remain a small community event, some believe that it represents the beginnings of the fracture of AOH control over official constructions of St Patrick's Day and of Irish-America more widely. The structural context of Irish migration, within which St Patrick's Day in New York has evolved, would suggest that the life-blood of Irish-America is draining away as Irish emigration slows to a trickle. Others would argue that while the AOH may have to loosen its grip on the Manhattan parade, Irish-America will persist, as it has sufficient new traditions, which stem from the US rather than Ireland, to be a self-sustaining community. John T. Ridge, official historian of the AOH in New York, commented that: 'The interesting thing is that [today] Irish cultural life in America could survive quite well without Ireland, independently [from it].'[53] If patterns of Irish migration are maintained, it may have to, and this 'new variant' Irish culture will move forward as a totally American phenomenon. As Cronin and Adair have remarked: 'The continued success of St Patrick's Day parades in America lies in the psyche of the American rather than Irish nation.'[54]

Whether or not the AOH retains control of St Patrick's Day, those who participate in it like their green beer and will continue to drink it for the foreseeable future. One reason for this is because the theme bars in which they can do so are plentiful, are unthreatening cultural environments and allow them to assume a temporary mantle of Irishness when they want to do so, without disrupting the baseball game on the big-screen television.

NOTES

1. McCarthy, P. *The Road To McCarthy* (London: Hodder and Stoughton, 2002), p.166.
2. 'Riverdance' could also be said to be an import, as the two original leading cast members, Michael Flatley and Jean Butler, are American born.
3. Brendan Fay, Lavender and Green Alliance/St Pat's for All Society, interviewed by Professor Rosaleen Duffy, 22 September 2004.
4. Jarman, N., Bryan, D., Caleyron, N. and de Rosa, C. *The Politics of Difference* (Belfast: Democratic Dialogue, 1998), p.82.
5. See http://www.saintpatricksdayparade.com/NYC/history.htm.
6. Ibid.
7. John Francis Mulligan, Irish Queers, phone interview with Professor Rosaleen Duffy, 25 September 2004.
8. Ridge, J.T. *The St Patrick's Day Parade In New York* (Brooklyn: AOH Publications, 1988), p.iii.
9. Jarman et al., *The Politics of Difference*, p.2.
10. Ridge, *The St Patrick's Day Parade In New York*, p.7.
11. Cronin, M. and Adair, D. *The Wearing of the Green* (London: Routledge, 2006), p.65.
12. O'Hanlon, R. *The New Irish Americans* (New York: Roberts Rinehart, 1998), p.134.
13. Quoted in Trillin, C. 'Democracy in Action', in J.J. Lee and M. Casey (eds), *Making the Irish American* (New York: New York University Press, 2007), p.539.
14. The Irish Lobby for Immigration Reform (ILIR) was founded by Niall O'Dowd in November

2005 to campaign for new legislation to regularise the status of the undocumented Irish. It has been active in supporting the McCain/Kennedy bill on immigration reform, http://www.irishlobbyusa.org.

15. 'Reining in New York's Parade: Organisers of the St Patrick's Day Parade Have Banned People from Marching with Banners Identifying Themselves As Gay', *Guardian*, 14 March 2003.
16. Brendan Fay, interviewed by Professor Rosaleen Duffy, 22 September 2004.
17. O'Hanlon, *The New Irish Americans*, p.136.
18. Maguire, A. *Rock The Sham* (Dublin: Street Level Press, 2005), pp.12–13.
19. O'Hanlon, *The New Irish Americans*, p.138. This was a play on the words *Érin go brágh*, which is Gaelic for 'Ireland forever'.
20. Ibid., p.129.
21. Maguire, *Rock the Sham*, p.79.
22. John Francis Mulligan, *Irish Queers*, (phone interview with Professor Rosaleen Duffy, 25 September 2004).
23. Maguire, *Rock the Sham*, p.80.
24. Reimers, D. 'An End and a Beginning', in R.H. Bayor and T.J. Meagher (eds), *The New York Irish* (Baltimore, MD: Johns Hopkins University Press, 1997), p.433.
25. Cronin and Adair, *The Wearing of the Green*, p.226.
26. 'Wear Orange on St Patrick's Day', Mr Gay Pride New York, autumn 1999, http://www.mrgaypride.org/OrangeOnStPats.html.
27. Brendan Fay, interviewed by Professor Rosaleen Duffy, 22 September 2004.
28. Kathleen McGreal, phone interview with author, 28 September 2004.
29. Niall Stanage, journalist, interviewed by author, 13 September 2008.
30. Brendan Fay, interviewed by Professor Rosaleen Duffy, 22 September 2004.
31. See St Pat's for All website at: http://queens.about.com/gi/dynamic/offsite.htm?zi=1/ XJ&sdn =queens&zu=http%3A%2F%2Fwww.stpatsforall.com.
32. Ibid.
33. 'Taking to the Streets of New York with Pride', *Irish Times*, 28 February 2009, http://www.irishtimes.com/newspaper/weekend/2009/0228/1224241957928.html.
34. O'Hanlon, R. 'Charge of the Right Brigade', *Irish Echo*, 26 February 2002.
35. McKinley, S. 'Protests Yes, But Queen's March Finds its Stride', *Irish Echo*, 16 March 2002.
36. Brendan Fay, interviewed by Professor Rosaleen Duffy, 22 September 2004.
37. McKinley, 'Protests Yes'.
38. Brendan Fay, interviewed by Professor Rosaleen Duffy, 22 September 2004.
39. 'The Making of St Mychal', 19 February 2003, http://www.usatoday.com/news/nation/2003-02-19-mychal-cover_x.htm.
40. Brendan Fay, interviewed by Professor Rosaleen Duffy, 22 September 2004.
41. 'The Impact of 9/11 on the St Patrick's Day Dispute', *Gay City News*, March 2002.
42. Ibid.
43. Deignan, T. 'Parade Conflict is Nothing New', *Irish Voice*, 15–21 March 2006, http://www.irishabroad.com/news/irishinamerica/columnists/sidewalks/ParadeConflict.asp.
44. 'The Politics of Parading in New York', *Irish Times*, 16 March 2006.
45. Cronin and Adair, *The Wearing of the Green*, p.226.
46. O'Hanlon, *The New Irish Americans*, p.231.
47. Ibid., p.140.
48. Brendan Fay, interviewed by Professor Rosaleen Duffy, 22 September 2004.
49. John T. Ridge, interviewed by author, 9 September 2004.
50. Professor Eileen Reilly, associate director, *Glucksman Ireland House*, New York University, interviewed by author, 14 September 2004.
51. Professor J.J. Lee, interviewed by author, 14 September 2004.
52. Cassie Farrelly, former administrative director, Institute of Irish Studies, Fordham University, New York, interviewed by author, 16 September 2004.
53. John T. Ridge, interviewed by author, 9 September 2004.
54. Cronin and Adair, *The Wearing of the Green*, p.211.

6

Exporting the Brand: The Irish Theme Bar and the Diaspora Space

Despite the humble origins of Irish migration, 'Irishness' has become a brand in the twenty-first century, a cultural commodity which has spread on the tide of emigration and been enabled through the processes of globalisation. In his book *Global Ireland*, Tom Inglis remarks that the Irish 'have become one of the most successful ethnic groups in the world, the global "other" with whom it is easy to identify.[1] The waves of Irish migration over several centuries has led to a cultural fusion where American influences have been felt in Ireland and where Irish culture has stretched and mutated in the US to the point that it has almost become a stand alone cultural phenomenon. Nothing illustrates this point more vividly than Chris Byrne's rationale for the music of his band Seanchai and the Unity Squad.

> Seanchai has an Irish element, but it couldn't come out of any city but New York. I wish people would do that in every city where Irish people are. Work with the local flavour and make something new. I think our music is a lot more honest than standing on Fifth Avenue singing 'The Mountains of Fuckin' Mourne' ... A lot of Americans used to feel that the more they read about Ireland, the more they travelled there, at some point in their life they would achieve the rank of being Irish. See, I don't aspire to that. I'm Irish-American and I don't want to be them. I'm real happy being me.[2]

This statement of cultural hybridity provides a perfect illustration of the way in which historical patterns of Irish migration have become indigenous and authentic in themselves, rather than imitations or shadows of the homeland culture. Seanchai represent a new wave of contemporary Irish-America which has morphed into its own artistic milieu and provided a new variant of music which possesses Irish influences but is not possessed by Ireland. Byrne was also the driving force behind the establishment of Rocky Sullivan's bar in New York, which was formed in response to the proliferation of Irish theme bars and their cultural branding of Irishness.

This chapter builds on the previous exploration of the cultural branding of St Patrick's Day in New York, by looking at the commodification of Irishness and its connection with globalisation through the medium of the Irish theme bar. It connects with the previous chapter by illustrating the hyper-reality of cultural representations of Irishness in the modern age, and the way that the cultural construction of the theme bar[3] departs from the contemporary experience in Ireland in a similar manner to the St Patrick's Day parade in Manhattan.

DECONSTRUCTING THE CRAIC

They [Irish theme pubs] represent … the most obvious example of the way in which the packaging of Irishness has been an aspect of recent shifts in the marketing strategies of multinational breweries.[4]

This chapter examines the concept of the Irish theme pub as an illustration of the ways in which globalisation has acted to create a homogenised narrative on Irish culture, a picture of studied authenticity which belies its role within the multi-million dollar drinks industry. What this shares with the St Patrick's Day parade on Fifth Avenue in New York is its hyper-real depiction of Irishness, which has little to do with the reality within contemporary Ireland. While the Irish theme pub represents a form of cultural branding that shares similarities with St Patrick's Day in New York (the emphasis upon community, historical memory and, above all, relaxed ambience), this masks a less romantic economic model where the profit motive is king. The central argument here is that while the theme pub presents itself as a site of community and easygoing friendliness, it is in reality constructed to a carefully studied formula, where a flat-packed cultural authenticity is injected through the financial power of the global drinks industry and its business partners. While the Irish theme pub is to some extent a modern legacy of the Irish diaspora, its homogenised nature reflects the 'diaspora space' referred to elsewhere in this book, namely a parallel universe which – like St Patrick's Day in New York – is clearly infused by Irish iconography but not in a manner recognisable within Ireland itself. At the same time, however, these bars' global reach reduces their meaning and impact beyond being places to get a standardised product and a level of off-the-peg consistency, regardless of location. The Irish theme bar is successful because of this very consistency and uniformity; rather like a major hotel chain, you can have a similar experience regardless of where you are in the world. Ironically, while the Irish theme bar alludes to a rustic small town individuality and charm, it is frequently the opposite, constructed to a flat-pack formula, financed by large business enterprises and patronised by a transient tourist market whose cultural understanding of Ireland may not extend far beyond St Patrick's Day and 'Riverdance'. In this sense the Irish theme pub phenomenon is the antithesis of the authentic, and is to the local bar what Starbucks is to the local coffee shop and McDonald's is to the local greasy spoon café. Irish theme pubs perfectly reflect Atvar Brah's notion of the 'diaspora space' as they transcend the geo-political limits of state boundaries and their cultural uniformity allows people to have the same pint of Guinness in the same surroundings, regardless of what country they happen to be living in. Ironically, the Irish theme bar attracts more than its fair share of English tourists in search of a pint and a chance to watch English premiership football, raising an existential crisis surrounding who is colonising whom?

THE IRISH THEME PUB

The notion of the Irish pub as uniform in its look and orientation is about as credible as the idea that the ploughman's lunch, devised by marketers of English pubs in the 1970s, really represents authentic farmer's fare. Yet this has not stopped entrepreneurs launching Irish pubs in almost all major European cities as well as in a great many American cities.[5]

The starting point for the Irish theme pub is a stereotype of the national character. Firstly, the Irish like to drink. Secondly, they like to have a good time and work to live rather than live to work. This was expressed more poetically by Seán O'Casey when he said that the Irish 'treat a joke as a serious thing and a serious thing as a joke', though this phrase has itself become commodified to the point where it has been etched into 100,000 tea towel welcomes for tourists looking to spend their last few holiday euros.[6] Finally, the Irish have a reputation for plain speaking, which invests their social interactions with an honesty and sense of humour envied by those with more reserved dispositions. At its most extreme, this stereotype is overlaid with a mystic superstitious and sentimental quality, where the Irish have access to tales of banshees, moving statues and, in the words of Patrick Kavanagh, 'at any one time, a standing army of over 10,000 poets'.[7] All of this combines into Irish pubs being identified with the craic, an amorphous concept loosely connected to the pursuit of fun, and if you cannot actually *be* Irish, the theme pub suggests that you can experience what it might be like, for an evening at least.

The Irish theme pub has become as omnipresent in the modern city as Starbuck's, McDonald's and Pizza Hut. Inglis records that Guinness claims to have opened 1,700 Irish pubs between 1992 and 1998 and that it sells over 1.8 billion pints of Guinness globally each year.[8] Kieran Allen points out that Guinness has been so successful in its branding that it has gained a status as a quasi-national emblem and even an asset to public health! 'The visitor who enters an Irish souvenir shop will be encouraged to buy Guinness cups, leprechauns, towels and T shirts. The "Irish pub" has also become a marketing concept for selling the Guinness product abroad. The Irish population has been sold the brand image so successfully that until quite recently Guinness was seen as good for your health. At one time, children used to be encouraged to drink "egg flips" composed of Guinness and beaten egg to help their growth.'[9] Guinness's own advertising slogan in the 1920s was 'Guinness is good for you', though this was discontinued some years ago and parent company Diageo make no claims today about the health benefits of their products. Urban myths remain that Guinness may have restorative benefits, and it was routinely given to pregnant women and blood donors in Britain in the 1940s in the belief that it was high in iron. However, to say that drinking Guinness makes you *feel* good is rather like saying that anti-wrinkle cream makes you *look* younger, as the impact of both is limited to perceptions of cause and effect rather than any objective reality.

Theme pubs are usually constructed to a formula that highlights a perceived stereotypical image of Ireland but owes more to *The Quiet Man* shebeen than it does to the drinking hostelries of contemporary

Ireland. Their names range from the descriptive, The Irish Club – Kabul in Afghanistan, to the more racy such as Pogue Mahone's (Gaelic for 'kiss my arse') in Queenstown, and Auckland, New Zealand, or the traditional Rosie O'Grady's off Times Square in Manhattan. Some of these pubs such as O'Reilly's or O'Neill's[10] are large chains with pubs in several countries. 'All O'Neill's bars are owned by Bass Leisure and they constitute the largest and fastest growing of the Irish theme pub chains.'[11] Other Irish bars, such as Scruffy Duffy's on Eighth Avenue in New York, are owned by individuals and are more authentic in terms of their ownership, though not always in terms of their appearance. Scruffy Duffy's is typical of many New York Irish bars in being privately owned rather than part of a multinational chain. Irish-American co-owner Pat Hughes explained the name and recent development of the bar.

> This bar was originally owned by my uncle ... who now has a place on the Upper East Side called the Kinsale Tavern. He was from Cork and he had this bar originally in 1983 and it was called the Bantry Bar ... He sold it to my father shortly after he opened it because he had a couple of other bars and it was too much to handle three at that time. So he sold it to my father and it was operated as the Bantry for about ten years. The neighbourhood was very, very undesirable at that time, so my sister and I took over in 1991 and we changed the name to Scruffy Duffy's, because the neighbourhood was a scruffy hellhole and we really didn't have the money to fix it up. So we went with this theme of scruffy and we drew in the Irish name, you know you can't lose with an Irish name attached to your bar. So we slowly but surely transformed it into this thing that you see now. It's a sports bar with an Irish background really, trying to maintain a little of the old flavour. So we're attractive to anyone who wants a basic unpretentious place with a good pint and an occasional laugh.[12]

This model of the privately owned Irish bar is typical of New York and differs markedly from the national chains that tend to dominate other regions. McGovern has written about the Irish theme bar phenomenon in Britain (an obvious port of call for the Irish diaspora) and comments on the connection between the cultural brand and the economics behind them.

Complete with 'traditionally painted' exteriors, falsely-aged or reclaimed wooden floors, stools, snugs and bar, and decked out with all manner of nostalgic bric-a-brac, most of these pubs are owned either by the large multinational corporations who dominate the leisure and brewing industries or by local entrepreneurs who often receive backing from the same. As with a number of the products which are sold in these pubs, a major selling point is the imagined 'Irish' character which they are supposed to encapsulate and the 'brand values' with which such a character is associated.[13]

Some so-called 'Irish super pubs' have emerged such as Paddy O's in Boston, which opened in 2005. Part of the Somers Pubs chain in the US, its website mission statement contains a classic exposition of the Irish theme pub persona.

> This latest offering from the Somers Pubs embodies everything that is Ireland and the Irish. From the hand-crafted bar to the authentic furniture, custom made in Ireland, this pub breathes 'one hundred thousand welcomes' from the moment you step through the door. But this is not the home of Saints and Scholars or Mythical Creatures. Paddy O's has just one purpose in mind – FUN![14]

Brown and Patterson suggest that in Britain the prize for themed hyperreality should go to one particular ersatz brand leader who's success has led to the opening of other branches in Glasgow, Manchester and New York.

> The epitome of Oirishness, nonetheless, is Waxy O'Connor's, opened by Glenora Leisure in 1996. An 80,000 sq ft labyrinth in deepest darkest Soho, Waxy's is the superpub to end all superpubs, with its warren of neo-Celtic drinking spaces. Here a fake pharmacy; there a kitsch chapel; over there a replica spirit grocer. A pulpit for storytelling, copious sepia-hued photographs and wall-mounted displays of copper utensils help complete the picture ... Excessive perhaps, extravagant unquestionably and doubtless environmentally unfriendly, but the bottom line is that Waxy's sells over 45,000 drinks per week, making it one of Britain's busiest pubs.[15]

Even Dubai airport has its Irish Village, possibly the saddest version of the Irish theme bar in the world, though it too is bedecked with stage-Irish regalia including Gaelic inscriptions such as 'céad míle fáilte' (a hundred thousand welcomes) on the walls, an upturned fishing boat on the roof and the ever-present Guinness Toucan leering at weary travellers. The history of the Guinness Toucan itself has been influenced by global business priorities.[16] Less obviously, the Irish Village is furnished with a collection of oil lamps on the ceiling and a wall case full of Irish clay pipes, one of which refers (without explanation) to Scottish poet Robbie Burns. The power of the theme pub in the US is illustrated by the fact that several hotel chains have incorporated them into their premises. The Chicago Hilton, for instance, sports Kitty O'Shea's on its ground floor, a perfect complement to its large global business convention clientele.[17] The authors of *Your Guide to the Irish Pubs of Chicago*, a publication which acknowledges sponsorship by Diageo-Guinness USA, overstate the authentic ambience but correctly point out its core business market. 'Kitty O'Shea's is a sharp looking authentic pub decked out with the images of the Irish countryside and other associated nick-nacks, including quite a few shillelaghs, each dedicated to a notable Chicagoan of Irish descent. During the week they mostly cater to the hotel and local business trade, but on weekends, Kitty's is a good destination for anyone looking for some good craic.'[18]

The power of the Irish theme pub within contemporary US cultural iconography has been demonstrated by its appearance in an episode of 'The Simpsons', where Catholic heaven was depicted as an Irish theme bar containing a performance of 'Riverdance', heavy drinking and carousing, while in Protestant heaven, well dressed genteel people spent a boring eternity playing croquet and badminton.[19] This exaggerated stereotype encapsulates the theme bar, which is represented as a hyperreal 'Irishness on speed', and bars which do not reflect many of their counterparts on the island of Ireland. The most extreme version of the hyper-real Irish bar in New York is McSorley's Old Ale House, which designates itself as the oldest bar in New York, dating back to 1854. This is a classic example of a bar that makes a feature of its authenticity and its longevity, serving only two types of beer, 'light' and 'dark'. McSorley's has made a virtue out of its own anti-modernity, refusing to install female toilets until legally obliged to do so in the 1980s, and reflects a snapshot of a historic memory of Ireland taken through an American filter. This reflects the fact that McSorley's presents a hyperreal version of Irishess in New York, which is explicitly directed at the tourist market and is a popular venue where tourists and local New

Yorkers meet and engage with one another. Seán Murphy, owner of the Irish bars internet listings and review site 'Murphguide', commented that most of the Irish bars in New York were privately owned small businesses rather than national chains, and that there was a geographical difference in their character between the midtown and downtown areas of New York. 'Midtown is very different from downtown. 14th Street is the recognised border and the best nightlife is downtown below 14th Street. Midtown and from 14th to 59th street gets a lot of the after work crowd, whereas the downtown bars don't get busy till 9 or 10 o'clock at night and will stay busy till 4 am ... They would be less sports [orientated] because the artistic community [downtown] isn't as interested in sports as the businessman is.'[20]

BRIC-A-BRAC PADDYWHACK: CONSTRUCTING AUTHENTICITY

There are three key components of the Irish theme bar – first, Irish beer (preferably Guinness); second, some form of Irish music; and third, memorabilia or 'bric-a-brac' relating to Ireland. Some Irish bars, especially chains such as O'Neill's, have a specific house style in terms of their décor and music designed to construct a particular type of ambience. This house style is micro-managed to the extent of ensuring that a particular type of music is played at certain volumes during the day and evening, and adjusted to cater for the different markets that the bar is targeting. In the O'Neill's chain of theme bars, for instance, guidelines exist on layout to ensure the existence of snugs and booths, hardwood floors with the word Fáilte (Welcome) etched in the floor at the entrance and Irish Gaelic names on the toilets.[21] While conducting the research for this book I was momentarily inconvenienced when visiting MacGinty's Irish bar at an airport hotel in Johannesburg, as the Gaelic signs designating the toilets (*Mná* for women and *Fir* for men) were positioned the wrong way around!

Guinness have used the theme bar to export their brand at an international level and have utilised them as a vehicle for getting into the drinks market in countries where other brands are dominant, such as Budweiser in the US and Foster's in Australia. Irish music is another standard feature of the Irish theme bar, though unsurprisingly, this tends to be directed at the mass market international audience who form the clientele of the Irish bar, rather than more traditional Irish folk music. Artists most likely to be heard in an Irish theme bar would include U2, Van Morrison, The Pogues, The Corrs and Sinéad O'Connor – in other words, Irish bands that would be recognisable to an international audience that knew little about Ireland or Irish music. A smaller number of Irish bars would include Irish folk music, though this would usually be limited to acts with an international recognition, such as Christy Moore, The Dubliners and The Chieftains.

The other staple ingredient of the Irish theme bar is the Irish memorabilia. This normally falls into three categories: the written word, the pictorial representation and the cultural artefact. The written word often includes quotations or Irish proverbs, the most common of which is 'céad míle fáilte', though there are a number of more toe-curling examples. For the purposes of illustration, 'May the blessed charm and good luck of the horse shoe be with you and yours' is inscribed on the wall of the Irish Village in Dubai airport. Such phrases are seldom uttered in Ireland, of course, other than for the benefit of foreign tourists, nor are they to be found in many pubs, unless these too are explicitly marketed at tourists. In addition to the carefully chosen Irish proverb or Gaelic inscription, the patron of an Irish theme bar will often find a copy of the Irish Declaration of Independence, relating to the 1916 Easter Rising, or references to the work of Ireland's literary glitterati such as James Joyce, Oscar Wilde, Samuel Beckett or, less frequently, Brendan Behan. Many of the theme bars take their names from Irish cultural figures, such as Patrick Kavanagh's and Swift in midtown Manhattan or Ulysses in Hanover Square.

The pictorial architecture of the Irish theme bar covers the political, literary and cultural aspects of Irishness and may include pictures of revolutionary heroes such as Michael Collins, James Connolly, Patrick Pearse, and occasionally Arthur Griffith, founder of Sinn Féin at the start of the twentieth century. The other ever-present pictorial representations are the Guinness signs, represented either by the black and gold Irish harp, or the Guinness Toucan, with slogans such as 'My Goodness, My Guinness'. There may also be photographs of Ireland itself, predominantly images of Dublin and pictures of Irish sporting triumphs in football, rugby and Gaelic games.

In addition to the written word and pictorial representations of Irishness, one of the most interesting facets of the Irish theme bar is presented by the artefact, the physical memorabilia that is included to provide the pheromone of authenticity and originality to these ware-houses of uniformity. Among the most common exhibits are autographed football shirts, hurley sticks, and *bodhrán* drums (sometimes with the word Guinness written across them for added authenticity). More bizarrely, some theme bars have old bicycles strung from the ceiling, rusty typewriters or old sewing machines arranged around the walls, in an effort to recreate the rustic simplicities of de Valera's Ireland and a comfortable ambience within which to eat and drink.

One of the largest suppliers of this memorabilia is the Irish Pub Company (IPC), which outlines its ability to create Irish authenticity for its customers.

> The Company, appointed by Guinness as their sole Irish Pub Con-cept Designer, succeeded by researching pubs in Ireland in great depth and their origins, history, styles, their role in Irish culture, and what made them enduring and successful. Then the Irish Pub Company developed ways of recreating Irish pubs, which would be successful culturally and commercially, anywhere in the world. The Irish Pub Company was established in 1991 and specialises in the design, manufacture and installation of authentic Irish Pubs and creative commercial concepts worldwide.[22]

As the next section of the chapter will illustrate, while an effort has been made to illustrate the originality of a community pub, where the customer will have a relationship with the bar, the reality is that the physical surroundings of the Irish theme bar have been mainstreamed into a global economy where you can artificially construct the authentic from the pages of a catalogue.

THE POLITICAL ECONOMY OF THE IRISH THEME BAR

Don't break your back collecting your pub's bric-a-brac. A pub's unique decorations (or bric-a-brac) can take many years to col-lect. Framed posters, signs, jugs and old bicycles are examples of some items that could help create a comfortable Irish Pub environ-ment. Still, it is the presence of uniquely Irish brands that estab-lish authenticity for your new or refurbished pub. That's why Guinness has offered you some samples of bric-a-brac items to view and the ability to purchase these items directly from the

selected Guinness Approved Supplier. Each item is based on an original piece of classic advertising. Antique-finished boards, individually
created on timber by skilled craftsmen, preserve the original aged
look and feel of an Irish Pub atmosphere.[23]

Ironically, given their attempted rustic small-town ambience, construction
of the Irish theme bar is a big business enterprise which has
become an integral part of a multinational industry. Specialist companies
such as the IPC will design the bar and provide the necessary materials to
create that authentic Irish feeling.[24] The IPC was formed in 1991 and has
close links with Guinness, one of the behemoths of the global drinks
industry. According to McGovern, Guinness sought to combine brand
recognition of its product with appropriate social settings designed to
increase its volume sales in the belief that the consumption of its product
was organically connected to the social context within which this takes
place. In short, if the customer will not come to Ireland, then bring
Ireland (or a stylised version of it) to the customer.

> The atmosphere of the Irish bar, or of what people believed Irish
> bars to be like, was regarded as crucial for this process of appro-
> priate 'setting'. Exporting the 'ambience' of the Irish bar therefore
> became the means to increase the volume consumption of Irish
> alcoholic products. From the early 1990s onward Guinness' world-
> wide operation therefore worked to provide certain services and
> incentives to create a network of Irish bars, run almost invariably by
> Irish staff, that could establish the social setting seen as a necessary
> prerequisite for the consumption of their products.[25]

Rules governing the alcohol industry make it difficult for companies like
Guinness to engage directly in the construction, supply or financing of
bars, but they can do so in association with secondary organisations such
as the IPC. Part of the McNally Design Group, the IPC was founded as
the design and construction partner to Guinness, fitting out the bars and
providing the bric-a-brac and memorabilia. Crucially, the relationship
is not a franchise but rather a loose advisory consultancy where Guinness and the IPC work together voluntarily, with IPC building the pubs
and stocking Guinness products, the pay-off being in the expansion of
the brands' availability worldwide and increased sales. Thus, despite the
whiff of post-modernism that surrounds the Irish theme pub, they are

driven by more normative factors and have a carefully honed and closely monitored political economy in terms of their location, design, products and marketing. For large drinks manufacturers such as Guinness and Bass, therefore, the theme pub is a mechanism through which to connect production with distribution and sales. 'Distribution is a key success factor for Bass' new products. Bass Brewers are able to distribute through the large retail estate owned by Bass Leisure, the retail operation of Bass plc. Distribution is therefore guaranteed at one of their various high profile outlets. The theme nature of their bars is exploited to fit with the positioning of the brand. In the case of Caffrey's, for example, the O'Neil [sic] chain of Irish theme bars provided an ideal fit, benefiting both the bars and the product.'[26]

In design terms, the Irish Pub Company offers a choice of five different styles of Irish theme bar: 'Victorian', 'Shop', 'Country', 'Celtic' or 'Brewery' styles.

> The Celtic Pub captures the character of the Gaelic people, well known for their dedication to merry-making, music and craftsmanship through the centuries. The rough-hewn doors, furniture and bar counters give a natural feel to the interior. Hand-crafted metalwork fixtures complement the texture of the timber, adding a touch of finesse to the overall design. Stories from the rich heritage of Irish folklore and mythology are illustrated in delicately painted wall murals, inspired by distinctively Gaelic art forms. This pub, with its combination of natural materials and artistic traditions, provides the ideal backdrop for modern-day musicians and storytellers to recreate the Gaelic way of enjoying life, or 'craic' as it is known in Ireland.[27]

This brings us back to the Irish diaspora in that the Irish theme bar is often keen to employ Irish people (especially young students on gap years from Ireland) to help create an authentic feeling within the bar. The IPC is responsible for theme bars such as Fitzpatrick's in New York, The Loafing Leprechaun in Atlanta, USA, and Molly Malone's in Hiroshima, Japan. Brown and Patterson suggest that IPC's business model is a sound one: 'In 1998, the company's turnover touched £12 million and it employed 75 people in a variety of roles, including site selection, obtaining liquor licences, pub marketing and promotion, and co-ordinating food and beverage distribution.'[28]

In the US, the IPC has gone to great lengths to ensure that its staff are trained to a level that makes them capable of making the Irish feel comfortable, though this may be at the expense of the staff's own sense of well being. In relation to their construction of the Nine Fine Irishmen pub in Las Vegas, a representative from IPC claimed that:

> The aim was to instil a real sense of Irishness that focuses on the natural personalities of the staff, most of whom are American, and immerses them in traditional and contemporary Irish culture … Tactics to enhance their understanding of modern Ireland included role play to think Irish, learning about Irish sports and culture, plus, uniquely in the heavily branded US market, how to greet and chat with customers in a natural, unformulaic way. At the end of each day and week, all employees were quizzed on what they had learnt, leading to a final competency test with those successful gaining an Irish 'passport'. Standards for all areas of the pub operation are extremely high and are monitored not just by the management team but mystery guest auditors too.[29]

Brendan Gregg, manager of the Bog Irish bar in Christchurch, New Zealand, commented in 2003 that a diverse range of services are available from Guinness, where in return for the supply of a 'vanilla box' you can obtain everything from market research reports on the demographics of your area (age and gender breakdown with drinks preferences and existing drinks sales) to the hardware and memorabilia necessary to turn the venue into an 'authentic' Irish bar.[30] As McGovern notes, Guinness and its partner companies place great emphasis upon the structural elements of the Irish bar business, pre-eminent among which is location. 'Location dictates, in particular, the demographic profile of the potential consumer to be targeted, according to age, socio-economic group, disposable income, etc. At the same time the overall design concept is intended to be adaptable to create different environments to suit different groups of people (as distinct consumer markets) through the day.'[31]

In the United States, through its affiliate **Diageo-Guinness USA,** Guinness provide what they refer to as 'upstream services' designed to prepare the bar prior to opening. These services include market research reports, advice on suitable locations for an Irish bar and of course recommended suppliers of design and building work, together with Irish bric-a-brac suppliers (one of whom is the IPC). Its 'downstream services' targeted at the post-opening period include marketing sales support, bar and kitchen management, and a list of Irish food distributors.

The post-modernist dream was realised when the theme bar began to make incursions into Ireland itself, leading to a situation where the 'fake' replaced the 'authentic'. In the post-modern world, of course, where everything is relative, connected, and ever-evolving and where nothing is truly fixed or quantifiable, labels such as these have little purchase. Whether or not the executives from Bass and Guinness (and their advertisers) have post-modern leanings or not, the fact of the matter was that the sums and the balance sheets added up.

> The sniping of snobs and sceptics notwithstanding, the simple fact of the matter is that theme pubs are staggeringly successful ... So popular have they become that in a classic coals to Newcastle or cappuccino to Copacabana situation, replica 'Irish' pubs are actually displacing 'real' Irish pubs, 'actual' Irish pubs, 'genuine' Irish pubs in Dublin, Cork, Belfast, Enniskillen and elsewhere. Of the forty public houses pictured in the famous 'Dublin Pubs Poster' of 1973, no less than 13 have been given the theme treatment, or some manner of marketing makeover and a further two have been demolished.[32]

Despite reports in the media that the Irish theme pub bubble had burst in 2001, they have proved remarkably resilient for large drinks companies such as Bass and Guinness as well as the other ownership conglomerates that control them. In 2001 the *New Statesman* hinted that the phenomenon had peaked, in an article with the inspired title 'Last orders down at MacFoney's'. The report suggested that while the theme bar had ironically now made it into Ireland itself in order to satisfy a tourist market that had come to expect the rustic idealised charm of the craic, the business model on which they were based had less of a rosy glow to it. 'The trend is towards more women-friendly bars, leaving the future of the Irish theme pub looking shaky.'[33] The *Daily Telegraph* reported in 2003 that market research company Mintel had found the theme bar concept to be in decline in Britain since the high point in 2000 when there were in the region of 500 Irish theme pubs in the UK. 'That trend is now being reversed, and 35 O'Neill's pubs, 23

Scruffy Murphy's and 12 Finnegan's Wakes have been closed by their respective breweries. The Mintel study predicted that another 150 theme bars would shut by 2007.'[34] Despite the slow down in the proliferation of Irish theme pubs, however, they have retained their global presence and, for good or ill, they continue to sell a one-dimensional stereotypical representation of Irishness.

Of course the Irish have not been singled out for special treatment; other ethnic groups have been subjected to the 'theming treatment', with Australia perhaps the closest comparison. Brown and Patterson's entertaining article, 'Knick-Knack Paddy-Whack, Give a Pub a Theme', suggests that the growth of these themed bars was built on the stereotype of the hard-drinking, hard-playing, back-slapping Aussie and were triggered by Australia's heightened profile in the wake of the 2000 Sydney Olympics. 'Greenalls, for instance, has recently opened The Roo Bar in Bristol, which features a surf simulator, a boomerang-shaped serving area, stuffed koalas, Antipodean lagers, a dentist's chair (for downing shots), an imitation Aborigine cave and toilets marked Bruce and Sheila.'[35] The largest of these Australian-themed chains, the Walkabout, owned by Regent Inns, have labelled their toilets 'dunnies', and function primarily as sports bars, while Scottish and Newcastle financed the Bar Oz chain and directed it at the youth market. 'In 1994 the first Walkabout venue was opened in London's Covent Garden. A decade later they have 50 venues, in 42 British cities, up from 20 venues in 2000.'[36] These theme bars are about constructing an Australian version of the craic, with an easy-going, relaxed feel and ethnic signifiers such as menus with names such as the Walkabouts' 'Aussie All-Dayer' breakfast, Aussie bric-a-brac which includes surfboards, didgeridoos, kangaroos, koalas, pseudo-Aboriginal art and Australian tribute acts. This is often topped off with sporting memorabilia, especially relating to rugby, and television coverage of large sporting events.

THE EVOLUTION OF THE IRISH THEME BAR

The flat-pack Irish theme bar has evolved in some places into a new form of Irish bar, where the traditional image of Irishness has given way to a more indigenous and authentic fusion of cultural hybridity. This can be thought of as the fusion Irish bar and is an example of an effort to reflect the realities of modern identities, which are often fractured and fluid. The fusion bar takes aspects of the Irish identity and gives them a local twist, basing them firmly in the present rather than the Ireland of the 1950s. One of the most interesting fusion bars in New York is Rocky Sullivan's, which opened in 1996 and was originally located on Lexington Avenue and 29th Street in Manhattan. It relocated to Red Hook, Brooklyn in July 2007 due to a rise in rental prices in Manhattan and took over the premises of the old Liberty Heights Tap Room. Rocky Sullivan's is named after James Cagney's character in *Angels with Dirty Faces* and it markets itself not as an Irish bar but as an Irish-American bar, with an ambience that is unique to New York and could not be replicated in Ireland itself. Rocky Sullivan's is a less obvious tourist destination than McSorley's Ale House and tends to be frequented primarily by local New Yorkers rather than the tourist market, even when it was located in Manhattan. While Rocky Sullivan's has an obvious Irish heritage and Irish republican ambience, it also contains a tangible New York energy that removes it from the theme bar category.[37] It houses one of the main Glasgow Celtic supporters' clubs in the city, the 'Unrepentant Fenian Bastards', which provides a sense of the gritty flavour of the bar itself. The co-owner of Rocky Sullivan's, Chris Byrne, is a former member of the NYPD and issued the following mission statement when asked by the late Pete McCarthy if Rocky Sullivan's was not just another Irish theme bar. 'No. It ain't themed. It's a New York bar, but with an Irish influence. It's like the music. It couldn't come out of any place but this city.'[38] The bar holds regular public readings by literary luminaries that have included Roddy Doyle, Malachy McCourt and Pete McCarthy, but also has its own resident Irish hip-hop band, Seanchai and the Unity Squad, whose sound typifies the fusion between Irish and New York musical influences.

This brings us back to the remark at the end of the previous chapter by New York AOH historian John T. Ridge, that Irish-America has now become culturally self-sufficient from Ireland itself. Rocky Sullivan's is a bar which does not try to recreate Ireland, but is content with the fact that it is an American bar with an Irish influence. There are also a number of other bars in New York that are/were Irish owned, but now market themselves beyond the traditional theme bar market, such as the Social in Hell's Kitchen and the uber-trendy Tonic in Times Square. These are primarily sports bars that appeal to a broad range of customers and have relatively little connection to the 'theme bar' concept. Seán

Murphy from the 'Murphguide' website commented that there were
Irish-owned bars in New York that have moved away from the standard image and traditional market of the Irish pub. 'There's a place in
the Village called Alibi which is owned by an Irish guy and managed by
an Irish woman, but it plays hip-hop music and you wouldn't know it
was an Irish bar if you walked into it.[39]

Of course, some observers may deduce from all of this that the Irish
theme bar is authentic in its own right, in the manner that copies of
original works of art are themselves original, even if they are copies
of something else. Doubtless legions of post-modern cultural theorists
will be ready to chant that notions of authentic reality are but a false
consciousness of the theoretically ill-informed. Thus, the theme bar is
simply the latest reflection of multiple and overlapping cultural forms
and iterations, which are as authentic in their own right as the 'genuine article', which itself was a particularist and subjective interpretation of local culture in its own way. Brown and Patterson make this
point in the context of the theme pub: 'In post-modernity there is no
such thing as authenticity, only varying degrees of inauthenticity.
O'Neill's, Scruffy Murphy's, Waxy O'Connor's and so on may be several
notches higher on the kitsch-o-meter than 'authentic' Irish pubs, but the
beauty of such fakes is that the conviviality, the communitas, the craic
are certain to appear on cue. This is *not* true of 'genuine' establishments,
where unpredictability reigns and serendipity can't be guaranteed.'[40]

Irish culture, of course, is nothing if not a hybrid mixture of other
cultures and ethnic groups, and has evolved itself during the latter half
of the twentieth century. The Gaelic cultural revival at the end of the
nineteenth century could be said to be something of an invention
itself, where authentic traditions were fast-tracked into existence as part
of Ireland's claim to cultural distinctiveness, nationhood and political
self-determination.

There is nothing sacrosanct about Irish bars in Ireland which gives
them a claim to be the last word in cultural authenticity, and some of
them would not be beyond playing up the stage-Oirishry and Paddy-
whackery themselves to capture tourist dollars and yen. Nevertheless,
most of them exist outside the hyper-real time warp of the international
Irish theme bar and there is a strong chance that the memorabilia within
such bars has not been purchased out of a catalogue. Post-structural
scholars might point out that we live in a world of subjective reality

with fluid boundaries and no points of normative fixity, and thus any search for the authentic is akin to chasing rainbows and just as doomed to failure. However, at its most extreme, the post-structural analysis is just as crude and inflexible as those who would present simple binary choices between the authentic and inauthentic.

Wherever we might stand on the axis of authenticity, it seems reasonable to conclude that the Irish theme pub is an idealisation of Irishness, not a reality. Notwithstanding national stereotypes, Ireland is not a land of saints and scholars baptised by fairy water, and it has not cornered the market in the pursuit of the craic. It is a modern capitalist European state which has evolved dramatically over the last thirty years in political, economic and cultural terms. In order to appreciate the contemporary Irish-American relationship, it is to this other end of the hyphen that we must now turn.

NOTES

1. Inglis, T. *Global Ireland* (London: Routledge, 2008).
2. Chris Byrne, co-owner of Rocky Sullivan's bar in New York and member of house band Seanchai and the Unity Squad, in McCarthy, P. *The Road to McCarthy* (London: Hodder and Stoughton, 2002), p.165.
3. The phrases 'theme pub' and 'theme bar' are used interchangeably in this chapter for linguistic convenience.
4. McGovern, M. 'The "Craic" Market: Irish Theme Bars and the Commodification of Irishness in Contemporary Britain', *Irish Journal of Sociology*, 11, 2 (2002), pp.77–98.
5. Cobley, P. 'Marketing the "Glocal" in Narratives of National Identity', *Semiotica*, no. 150 (2004), p.213.
6. An indication of the global reach of this phrase was its inclusion in an episode of American hit comedy series 'Frasier' in 2004, 'And Frasier Makes Three'.
7. Quoted by Paul Muldoon, 'In the Line of Fire', BBC TV, Belfast 1999.
8. Inglis, *Global Ireland*, p.99.
9. Allen, K. *The Corporate Takeover of Ireland* (Dublin: Irish Academic Press, 2007), p.126.
10. The O'Neill's bar on Second Avenue and East 43rd Street in Manhattan is owned by Ciarán Staunton and is not part of this global chain. Like one or two other bars, this is unusual for Midtown Manhattan Irish bars in not being primarily a sports bar, and having an understated local feel to it.
11. McGovern, 'The "Craic" Market', p.84.
12. Pat Hughes, Scruffy Duffy's, interviewed by author, 6 September 2004. Scruffy Duffy's closed down on 6 February 2008.
13. McGovern, 'The "Craic" Market', pp.77–8.
14. http://www.somerspubs.com/web/   index.php?option=com_content&task=section&id= 1&Itemid=32.
15. Brown, S. and Patterson, A. 'Knick-knack Paddy-whack, Give a Pub a Theme', *Journal of Marketing Management*, no. 16 (2000), pp.651–2.
16. The Toucan first appeared as a Guinness character in 1935, drawn by artist John Gilroy, but was originally intended to be a pelican. Gilroy's original picture showed a pelican with seven pints on its beak and a limerick which read:
    A wonderful bird is the pelican,
    Its bill can hold more than its belly can.

It can hold in its beak
Enough for a week
I simply don't know how the hell he can.
As this was considered too offensive, the lines were reworded for more global acceptability and the Guinness Toucan was born.
If he can say as you can
Guinness is good for you,
How grand to be a Toucan,
Just think what Toucan do.

17. This hotel was also the venue for the 2007 International Studies Association (ISA) World Congress, providing the author with an opportunity to engage in some first-hand participant observational research.
18. Kelley, C. and Molis, J. *Your Guide to the Irish Pubs of Chicago* (New York: Green Line Publishing, 2006), p.20.
19. *Sunday Times*, 22 May 2005, http://www.timesonline.co.uk/article/0,,2091-1622421,00.html. This episode of 'The Simpsons', entitled 'The Father, Son and Holy Guest Star', provoked complaints among some Protestant clergy in Ireland, who were concerned that it depicted them as boring. Homer Simpson converts to Catholicism and declares: 'Catholics rule! We got Boston, South America and the *good* part of Ireland.' The transmission of the episode was delayed in April 2005 due to the death of Pope John Paul II.
20. Seán Murphy, owner of 'Murphguide', www.murphguide.com, interviewed by author, 7 September 2004.
21. McGovern, 'The "Craic" Market', p.85.
22. See http://www.irishpubcompany.com/company_profile.htm.
23. See Guinness website, http://www.irishpubconcept.com/craic/bric.asp.
24. The website of the Irish Pub Company is http://www.irishpubcompany.com/.
25. McGovern, 'The "Craic" Market', p.83.
26. Nwabueze, U. and Clair Law, Z. 'The Journey for Survival: The Case of New Project Development in the Brewery Industry', *The Journal of Product and Brand Management*, 10, 6/7 (2001), p.387.
27. See http://www.irishpubcompany.com/celtic.htm.
28. Brown and Patterson, 'Knick-knack Paddy-whack, Give a Pub a Theme', p.652.
29. From McNally Design Group website, http://www.mcnallydesign.com/newsletter/december 2003newsletter/nfi.htm.
30. Brendan Gregg, manager, Bog Irish bar, interviewed by author in Christchurch, New Zealand, 29 December 2003.
31. McGovern, 'The "Craic" Market', p.83.
32. Brown and Patterson, 'Knick-knack Paddy-whack, Give a Pub a Theme', p.648.
33. West, P. 'Last Orders Down at MacFoney's', *New Statesman*, 27 August 2001, p.6.
34. 'Drinkers Lose Their Taste for "Tacky" Theme Bars', *Daily Telegraph*, 7 June 2003.
35. Brown and Patterson, 'Knick-knack Paddy-whack, Give a Pub a Theme', p.651.
36. West, B. *Engaging with Themed Space: Australian Holidaymakers and Banal Nationalism in Aussie Theme Pubs*, Working Paper, The Georgia Workshop on Culture and Institutions, Flinders University, Adelaide (2003), p.3.
37. Rocky Sullivan's was reportedly opened by owner Chris Byrne because his favourite bar had been turned into an Irish theme pub. McCarthy, *The Road to McCarthy*, p.149.
38. Ibid., p.150.
39. Seán Murphy, interviewed by author, 7 September 2004.
40. Brown and Patterson, 'Knick-knack Paddy-whack, Give a Pub a Theme', p.655.

7

Doing Business Together: Into the Celtic Tiger and Beyond

Once upon a time Ireland was an inward-looking, inefficient, economic basket case, haemorrhaging its population through emigration. Today it attracts the admiration of the developed and the developing world.[1]

We are anxious that the branding of Ireland will be done in as co-ordinated a fashion as possible because those people involved in business, tourism and diplomatic circles can influence the way our country is perceived abroad.[2]

So far this book has focused on the Irish and Irish-American community living in New York. However, there are two sides to every relationship and it is important to look at how Ireland itself has been changing in recent years and how this is affecting its relationship with America. This chapter therefore examines the political, social, economic and cultural changes that have been taking place in Ireland and how this is impacting on Irish attitudes towards, and interactions with, America.

The central argument made here is that in line with the evolution of Irish migration trends discussed in earlier chapters, a paradigm shift has taken place in Irish attitudes towards the United States. In simple terms, this can best be described as a shift from a patron–client relationship, where America took in Ireland's hungry huddled masses, to one based on partnership, if not economic and cultural equity. This has been generated by a number of interconnecting factors which have served to raise Ireland's fortunes, chief among which was the country's entry into the European Economic Community (EEC) in 1973 and its pursuit of external foreign investment for several decades afterwards, which led to the emergence of the Celtic Tiger in the early 1990s.

It is not the intention here to map all of the reasons for the development of the Irish economy over the period as this has been done elsewhere by a number of notable scholarly publications.[3] Instead, the purpose of this chapter is to demonstrate how these changes have impacted on patterns of Irish migration and on the contemporary relationships that are evolving between Ireland and America. Unsurprisingly, attitudes have not remained static as Ireland developed from an insular agricultural economy into an outward-looking business-orientated economy. Ireland's image of itself, and its outward projection through tourist advertising and business connections, suggests a more confident and assertive mentality, which throws interesting light upon the development of its contemporary relationship with America. The chapter is not arguing that this development has damaged the Irish-American relationship, but rather that it is changing it in a number of interesting ways, based on instrumental co-operation rather than through bonds of kinship or traditional diasporic ethnic identification.

As William Butler Yeats lyrically put it in his poem 'Easter 1916', 'All changed, changed utterly; A terrible beauty is born.' This equally pertains to the quieter revolution of recent years which is popularly dubbed the Celtic Tiger. Ireland has been transformed in economic terms from a subsistence, rural, agricultural economy into a hi-tech, industrialised and, in relative terms, affluent urban centre. Paradoxically, at the same time Ireland has remained steadfastly close to the bottom of the EU poverty table, 'with a steady rise in households below the poverty line'.[4] Politically, Ireland finally seems to have settled its troubled relationship with Britain and gained the confidence of a truly independent state, rather than defining itself through constant insecure comparisons with its larger neighbour. There remains, however, a subtle, at times subliminal, political confusion within Ireland relating to the boundaries of its political project. Put more bluntly, the 'partitionist mentality' that often irked Northern nationalists lingers, as the 26-county state morphed easily into the 26-county nation. Thus when people say 'Ireland' they think of the Republic of Ireland. Inglis, for instance, defines Ireland's population as being 4 million (i.e. without the 1.7 million people living in Northern Ireland) and goes on to say that 'what makes Ireland different is that it is an island nation.'[5] At one level this is mere linguistic convenience, but at another it carries implications for our 'imagined communities' and reflects de facto cultural, political and economic realities. Ireland can be Ireland without the North. The winding down of political conflict in Northern Ireland did allow the Irish state to rediscover its history as a cultural asset, rather than as a political incendiary device. This has finally enabled the Irish Republic to celebrate its past without worrying about how this might destabilise the tense political relationships on the northern part of the island. Aoileann Ní Eigeartaigh suggests that this explains the failure to celebrate the 1916 Easter Rising which led (indirectly) to the birth of the Irish state. 'On 16 April 2006, the Irish state officially commemorated the 1916 Rising for the first time since 1966. The intervention of the Troubles in Northern Ireland and the perceived hijacking of Irish nationalism by the Provisional IRA had made its celebration in the intervening years a political impossibility.'[6]

Socially, the country has moved from being a Catholic, some might argue theocratic, state into a secular, relatively liberal, capitalist country. It is worth remembering that over-the-counter contraception for over-18s was only legalised in Ireland in 1985, a referendum to provide a constitutional facility to legalise divorce was lost in 1986 and only passed in 1995, while it took an intervention from the European Court of Human Rights in 1988 to eventually decriminalise homosexuality in Ireland, which finally came into effect in 1993. In many ways the struggle between the forces of conservatism and liberalism over such social policy issues defined the politics of the Irish state in a way that Northern Ireland never managed to do, and led to the emergence of significant political voices such as those of Mary Robinson, Des O'Malley and Garret FitzGerald. O'Malley was expelled from Fianna Fáil because he abstained in the Dáil vote over contraception reform in 1985 while his party opposed it. Robinson, newly elected to the Irish Senate to represent Trinity College Dublin in 1969, introduced a private member's bill the same year to amend the Criminal Law Amendment Act, which had made contraception illegal in 1935. Robinson's argument sought to distinguish between Church and state in social policy issues, and while this failed to become law, it was an important signpost on Ireland's journey towards being a more liberal and open society. While many observers have seen Robinson's election as Irish president to be the coronation of a new 'golden age' where Rome rule was vanquished, paedophile priests were exposed and the Celtic Tiger was born, Brian Girvin reminds us that 'Robinson might have been elected in spite of her views on contraception' rather than because of them.[7] Indeed, her victory as a Labour Party candidate was partly due to the misfire within Brian Lenihan (Snr's) campaign. Lenihan, the Fianna Fáil nominee, entered the race as the favourite and out-polled Robinson significantly in the first ballot, despite being sacked from his own government in the middle of the campaign after discrepancies emerged between public statements he had made about an attempt to pressurise the previous president to dissolve parliament in 1982, and earlier comments he had made in an interview with an academic researcher. Her other opponent was Fine Gael candidate Austin Currie from Northern Ireland. While Robinson had a fight on her hands in 1990 to beat the candidate accused of being 'economical with the truth', she had no problem defeating the northerner, who languished back in a humiliating third place. Had Lenihan won the election as he surely would have done had scandal not overtaken him, Ireland's reform trajectory may have experienced a different pace, and while it would be unwise to overstate the impact of Robinson's non-executive office, her presidency set a new tone within Irish society, which slowly began to unbutton the tight corset that de Valera and Church leaders such as the archbishop of Dublin, John Charles McQuaid, had fastened around it in previous generations.

Much of this quiet revolution has been written and sung about by Ireland's artistic community, including its legion of poets, playwrights and musicians. Back in the 1940s, Louis MacNeice's poem 'Autumn Journal' took a thinly veiled swipe at the conservative morality of the state which he saw as stifling creativity, freedom and progress.

> Let the school-children fumble their sums
> In a half-dead language;
> Let the censor be busy on the books; pull down the Georgian slums;
> Let the games be played in Gaelic.[8]

More recently, Christy Moore has been one of the leading critics of Irish social policy in bands such as Planxty, more overtly with Moving Hearts and through his solo recordings, which castigated Irish government policy over Northern Ireland and the conservative intolerance of the Catholic Church. One of his iconic songs, 'The Middle of the Island', was recorded as a duet with Sinéad O'Connor and charts the death in 1984 of Ann Lovett, a 15-year-old girl who died while giving birth near a graveyard in a small town in County Longford, an event which both shocked and defined the country at the time. In his autobiography *One Voice*, Moore recollects that this was often an uncomfortable but vital part of his live repertoire.

> There was a time when this song angered sections of my audience; nevertheless, the song has become a memorial to a young woman who died that we might confront an appalling ignorance, that we might stand up and face those who would have us crawling like mindless slugs in the dark bog of sin and guilt ... I know this song challenges my audience, but I need to sing it for my own sake. It also does not sit comfortably within the concept of entertainment, but I will strive to present it as palatably as such lyrics about our recent history can be.[9]

In light of this list of socially conservative starting points, it is surprising that such a short time later one of the country's most popular politicians, Bertie Ahern, was openly separated from his first wife while serving several terms as taoiseach. Irish sociologist Tom Inglis explains this shift in attitudes towards public morality as a move away from the subjugation of the self and denial of all temporal pleasures to the celebration of personal consumption and materiality. From this perspective, the Irish 'have moved from being quiet, poor Catholic Church mice embodying a discourse and practice of piety and humility, to becoming busy, productive, self-indulgent rats searching for the next stimulation'.[10] As Kitchin and Bartley have remarked: 'As strange as it may sound to many Irish people who have witnessed the recent changes and are familiar with the ongoing problems in Irish society, other countries proclaim that they want to be "the next Ireland" (for example, Hungary).'[11]

For good or ill, Ireland has been transformed over the last thirty years across every conceivable social and economic indicator from being a largely isolated agricultural economy into a mid-sized European capitalist state. Evidence of the relative decline in the dominance of agriculture in the Irish economy is provided by the fact that the 1926 census reported that over half of the population was employed in the sector, a figure which had fallen to 6 per cent in 2005.[12] A retrospective assessment of a group of political scientists at UCD does not overstate the economic makeover which took place over this period.

In 1960, Ireland had experienced almost 20 years of protectionist policies and an attempt at import-substituting industrial development. It had missed out on the first decade of post-war European trade expansion: some 40 per cent of the workforce was engaged in agriculture; most industrial production was small scale and intended for the domestic market; Britain was virtually the sole trading partner ... By the early 2000s, Ireland was one of the most open economies in the developed world, with a ratio of imports plus exports to GDP of 98 per cent, and 118 per cent in relation to GNP. The Netherlands stood at 97 per cent ... The USA stood at 19 per cent, Britain at 39 per cent; the EU15 average was 54 per cent.[13]

If Louis MacNeice were still alive he might perhaps be reassured to know that the schoolchildren no longer 'fumble their sums in a half-dead language'[14] and that Ireland now sports one of the youngest and best-educated workforces within the EU. This transformation did not happen by accident, but was forged through decades of strategic planning and instrumentalism, where economic, social and foreign policies were fused together in pursuit of material growth. From the Lemass period onwards, the Irish state has had two over-riding goals. Firstly, to get its own economic house in order by having a stable currency; an educated (and relevant) workforce; viable trading partnerships; attractive tax laws and incentives for foreign investment. Secondly, to market Ireland internationally as an economic and cultural opportunity to multinational corporations and the international tourist market. This charge towards modernity produced some notable collateral damage of course, not least massive levels of state corruption encouraged by the 'anything goes' neo-Thatcherite mentality that pervaded Irish society from at least the early 1980s onwards, and growing levels of economic disparity between rich and poor across the same period.

In cultural terms, as explored in the previous chapter, 'Irishness' has global recognition and cache, and is seen by many people as *de rigueur*, or at the very least, non-threatening. Literary figures such as Séamus Heaney and Paul Muldoon have been awarded visiting Chairs at Princeton and Harvard respectively, while 'famous Séamus' won the Nobel Prize for Literature in 1995. Musicians such as Van Morrison, The Chieftains and more recently U2, Enya, Westlife and Snow Patrol can be heard in virtually every city in the world. Other cultural exports such as the Afro-Celt Sound System are an example of the creolisation which frequently accompanies diaspora communities, mixing African and Celtic rhythms and instruments into a modern fusion of contemporary dance trip-hop and techno music. Uber-cool Belfast-born DJ and composer David Holmes is on first-name terms with many Hollywood A-list stars and can cite the soundtracks of the *Ocean's 11* series of films as being among his list of achievements.

The 'Riverdance' phenomenon, meanwhile, represents (depending on one's tastes) the zenith/nadir of Irish-American modernity, where Irish dancing was exported from the homeland, reworked and brought back into it in a new and, many would say, revitalised form. 'Riverdance' suffered from over-exposure to the point that it has become an easy target for accusations that it represents an over-commercialised and hybridised culture, with little authenticity or connection to the historical evolution of Irish culture itself. The constant touring, merchandising and ever-changing cast of performers was regarded in some quarters as symptomatic of commodification and cultural dilution – a plastic-Paddy infestation of Blarneyfication and superficiality.

The 'Riverdance Farewell Tour' formed part of the Manchester Irish Festival in March 2009 and the website contained the following valedictory mission statement on this recent incarnation of Irish cultural fusion.

> The original Irish dance extravaganza. Of all the performances to emerge from Ireland in the past decade, nothing has carried the energy, the sensuality and the spectacle of Riverdance. The show has been revised a couple of times during its greatly extended life. With 9,000 spectacular performances in over 276 venues throughout 32 countries across 4 continents, and a worldwide television audience to date in excess of 1.75 billion people, Riverdance is a truly global phenomenon. An innovative and exciting fusion of Irish and International dance including a spectacular array of talent from Spain, Russia and America propels traditional dance and music into the present day, capturing the imagination of audiences across all ages and cultures.[15]

The fact that its popularity and lack of language barriers opened it up to a global audience, where Irish dancing has become de-territorialised from Ireland itself, has proved uncomfortable for some cultural gatekeepers of tradition. However, for others, 'Riverdance' is indicative of the global reach of Irish culture, which has itself been enabled by waves of Irish migration to America over previous generations. The story of Caroline Duggan, an Irish music teacher working in the Soviet-sounding Primary School 59 in the Bronx, illustrates the way in which the 'Riverdance' phenomenon has decoupled Irish culture from Ireland itself, at least in terms of previous patterns of cultural engagement. According to the *New York Times* who covered the story in 2008, hanging a poster of 'Riverdance' in her classroom to stave off homesickness led to her showing pupils some of the steps, which in turn ended up in her forming the group Keltic Dreams. Duggan then raised money to enable the group to visit Ireland, where they performed for Irish president Mary McAleese and appeared on RTÉ's 'Late Late Show'.[16] While the student body in the school was 71 per cent Hispanic and 27 per cent Afro-American, Irish consul general in New York, Niall Burgess, explained that this was an example where the 'Irish footprint' in the area had helped to facilitate a crossover between cultural forms.

> Caroline Duggan is a teacher from Dublin who teaches in one of the poorest and most under-resourced black and Hispanic communities in the Bronx, and she teaches Irish dance to the kids. This is a community that would have been solidly Irish eighty years ago and the sense of an Irish footprint there today is extraordinary. She has a group of about forty Irish dancers, all of them black and Hispanic ... They've danced up at Stormont for [Ian] Paisley and [Martin] McGuinness, and she's had them back at the *Áras* [official residence of the Irish president] and they've become stars in the Bronx and it shows you how the Irish footprint can stay strong even though Irish immigration has moved on and it also shows you how ... something that was essentially Irish a short while ago has now become a very mainstream form of dance.[17]

The fact that the initial leads of the tap-dancing troupe, Michael Flatley and Jean Butler, were both America born neatly extends the metaphor. Butler was born in Long Island with a mother from County Mayo, while Flatley is from Chicago with parents from Sligo and Carlow. In many ways, 'Riverdance' is a perfect emblem for the changing nature of Ireland, with its economic success, cultural hybridity and shift from a buttoned-down repressed guilt-ridden culture to one that celebrated freedom, the body and sexuality, exuberantly and unashamedly. Inglis captures this lyrically in his book *Global Ireland*: 'Riverdance became a mixture of Ireland and America, folk art and Tin Pan Alley, tangos and reels, the pure and the hybrid. Riverdance made Irish dancing exotic and spectacular.'[18] It also raised a less comfortable thought for many. If 'Irishness' has become de-territorialised and disconnected from Ireland and is now open to all-comers in a permissive fusion of global cultures, then does 'Irishness' have any meaning or authenticity left that it can stake a claim to, or has it become little more than a 'themed nation' sponsored by Aer Lingus and Guinness?

This disentanglement of culture, politics and history was given a more positive spin in *Dance Lexie Dance*, which was nominated for an Oscar for best short film in 1998. Based in Derry, the storyline sees a Protestant widower overcome his resistance to Irish dancing as a Gaelic (and therefore foreign) cultural pursuit, because his young daughter had fallen in love with 'Riverdance' without its associated cultural/political baggage and wanted to learn Irish dancing. The storyline served as an allegory for the peace process, for the decoupling of culture and politics in Ireland and ultimately for personal liberation. Thus, while the father tells his daughter at the beginning that 'we don't dance', by the end he is cheering her on at the Irish dancing Feis because his love for his daughter had overcome his own political and cultural insecurities.

ECONOMIC DEVELOPMENT AND CHANGING PATTERNS OF MIGRATION

Traditionally, Irish migration patterns have paralleled periods of economic decline (most obviously the Famine in the 1840s) together with the possibility of better prospects elsewhere. Between the Famine and the latter half of the twentieth century, Ireland turned emigration into a national characteristic, along with economic isolationism, social conservatism and Catholicism. While migration from Ireland during these periods was cyclical rather than constant, economic upturns more often witnessed a reduction in net emigration rather than a significant reversal of migration patterns over a period of years.[19] The foundations of economic recovery are often identified with Seán Lemass replacing de Valera as Irish taoiseach in the late 1950s and the various programmes for economic expansion that followed in the 1960s. These were built

upon by the opening of the Irish economy to the outside world, prin-
cipally through membership of the EEC in the 1970s and subsequent
entry into the EU's single market at the beginning of the 1990s,
together with the promotion of foreign direct investment into Ireland,
investment in education and a taxation system directed at encouraging
outside investment.[20] Murphy and Puirséil are in little doubt that
Ireland's entry into what was then called the Common Market in 1973
was the foundation upon which today's economic and social policies
have been built: 'Few policy decisions have had such a profound impact
on life in Ireland as its entry to the EEC in 1973. That its importance
in Ireland's economic development would be immense comes as no
surprise, with membership having long been an inextricable element of
Seán Lemass' plans for economic development.'[21]

Assessments of this modernisation strategy vary between those who
see it as a bright new dawn that ended the emotionally stunted and
economically suicidal era of de Valera, and others who highlight the
permissive attitudes of subsequent Irish governments who were eager
to surrender Ireland's economic virtue to any foreign business lothar-
ios who called by. While the latter analysis often seeks to distance itself
from de Valera's small is beautiful/poverty is spiritually enhancing outlook, it points to the divisive, inefficient and corrupting trends which
have often mediated Ireland's relations with multilateral corporations.
Put more bluntly, the charge here is that Irish policymakers have lost the
use of their critical faculties when large external investors have waved
their cheque books in the direction of the Irish economy. Kieran Allen
makes this point in the context of Ireland's relationship with the oil
industry in his book *The Corporate Takeover of Ireland.* 'The Irish state
has long adopted a subservient role to the oil corporations. In the late
1960s, Marathon Oil was granted a licence that effectively gave it control of the south coast of Ireland for a nominal sum of just €635. It
then went on to discover large quantities of natural gas off the Kinsale
Head and signed an agreement with An Bord Gais to supply 125 million cubic feet of gas per day for twenty years.'[22]

While mistakes were certainly made during this period in the head-
long rush for external investment (errors compounded by corporate
and individual greed, corruption and cynical manoeuvrings among
the political class), it did at least provide good news for Irish migrants.
The Lemass economic model produced increased jobs within the Irish

economy which resulted in a marked decline in emigration. Lee has highlighted the impact of the Lemass period on patterns of Irish migration and while the figures illustrate a sharp reduction, the trend during this period remained one of emigration rather than immigration. 'Average net emigration fell from 43,000 per annum between 1956 and 1961 to 16,000 between 1961 and 1966, and to 11,000 between 1966 and 1971, or from an annual rate of 14.8 to 3.7 [%].'[23] The figures for inward migration illustrate the rapid change since the 1970s in comparison with earlier periods. 'During the last half of the twentieth century Ireland's population increased by almost one million, or by about one-third, from 2.9 million in 1946 to 3.9 million in 2002 ... The demographic experience in the first half of this period from 1946 to 1971 was one of stagnation. The population in 1971 was almost identical with the population in 1946, about 2.9 million in both years.'[24]

According to MacLaughlin, this new technocratic era served to de-nationalise the emigration issue and turn it from a negative sense of mass group exile into a more positive notion of pragmatic economic opportunity. 'Indeed, since the 60s, the "blame Britain" ethos of nationalist condemnations of emigration has given way to behavioural and geographical explanations of its causes and consequences. There is an increasing tendency today to treat emigration as a cultural tradition and a voluntary activity which attracts upwardly mobile individuals who are assumed to be leaving Ireland to climb social ladders abroad.'[25]

Data from the annual Labour Force Survey for Irish migration, meanwhile, illustrates the dramatic changes that took place since the early 1990s. 'The figures for emigrants show that the total outflow nearly halved from 35,000 in 1991 to 18,000 in 2004.'[26] This evidence led Ireland's Central Statistics Office to forecast in 2006 that Irish migration patterns would be characterised by immigration rather than emigration over the next thirty-year period. 'In short the country has moved from a long-standing pattern of emigration to a new pattern of relatively strong immigration and it is very unlikely that this will be reversed to any sustained degree over the projection period [2006–2036].'[27] These bold assertions were made before the global economic collapse of 2008 which helped plunge the Irish economy into a deep recession in 2009 and surprised academics as much as it did economists, politicians and bankers. Mac Éinrí's observation in 2007 about the reliance of the Irish economy on foreign investment looks prophetic in retrospect. 'The

Irish economy is extremely exposed to global trends, because of its dependence on FDI and its extremely export-driven growth patterns. However, barring unforeseeable catastrophic events, current projections suggest that continuing strong growth is likely.'[28] The global financial crisis which took hold during 2008 and led to an Irish recession into 2009 has changed the picture somewhat, with more pessimistic predictions being made over economic growth, employment and public spending. By April 2009, Dublin's Central Statistics Office had reversed its earlier enthusiasm on migration trends as a result of the economic recession in Ireland. 'The number of emigrants from the State in the year to April 2009 is estimated to have increased by over 40% from 45,300 to 65,100, while the number of immigrants continued to decline over the same period, from 83,800 to 57,300. These combined changes have resulted in a return to net outward migration for Ireland (-7,800) for the first time since 1995.'[29]

However, while this has increased unemployment in Ireland, especially among traditional sectors such as the construction industry that would in the past have formed a typical migrant group, the situation is not comparable (at least not yet) with previous periods of economic gloom. One reason for this is that Ireland remains one of the more prosperous nations within the EU, it still sports a young well-educated workforce and its birthrate has reduced markedly from that of previous generations.

Today, Ireland is a country transformed by economic success, though not without its fair share of economic and social problems. Despite the damaging side-effects of social and economic rejuvenation in Ireland, many people who left in search of work or a more socially tolerant society have been returning to Ireland in recent years. This tends to be underlined by statistics from 2005 which suggest a growth in the Southern Irish population to over 4 million and a marked reduction in migration flows.

> The total immigration flow into Ireland in the twelve months to April 2005 is estimated at 70,000 – the highest figure on record since the present series of annual migration estimates began in 1987. The estimated number of emigrants in the same period was 16,600, resulting in a net migration figure of 53,400, compared with 31,600 in the twelve months to April 2004. The natural increase in the population (i.e. births less deaths) for the year ending April 2005 was

33,500. The combined effect of the natural increase and migration was a population increase of 87,000 (+2.2 per cent), bringing the population to 4.13 million in April 2005.[30]

The 2005 Human Development Report, compiled by the UNDP, suggested that Ireland had become the second wealthiest country in the world as a measure of per capita GDP, but had also become one of the most unequal economies over the same period.[31] Tom Inglis points out the rather substantial caveat to these statistics which obscures the fact that if we take gross national product (GNP) rather than gross domestic product (GDP) as the criteria for examination, Ireland falls to seventeenth position. 'The reason for the difference [between GDP and GNP] is that transnational companies have been the source of the Celtic Tiger. The profits which they make are often exported out of the country. Thus while exported profits are included in GDP, they are not included in GNP figures.'[32]

Despite applying the necessary health warnings to such league tables, in social, cultural and economic terms Ireland is undoubtedly a very different country to the one that many emigrants left during the 1950s. De Valera's Ireland has largely vanished, his 1937 constitution has been reformed to reflect contemporary Irish social views, and the influence of the Catholic Church on public policy has diminished markedly during this period, while the roar of the Celtic Tiger has been well documented. As Paus highlights, this did not take place by serendipity alone, as Ireland established the Industrial Development Authority in the 1950s 'charged with aggressively pursuing potential foreign investors'.[33] Today, many people would accept that Ireland has moved from being a peripheral state on the edge of Europe to being an EU success story and is held out as being an example to follow for those countries that have recently joined the EU. 'We are there because Ireland is very pro-business, they have a very strong educational infrastructure, it is incredibly easy to move things in and out of the country, and it is incredibly easy to work with the government. I would invest in Ireland before Germany or France.'[34] This remark made by the president of Intel would have been inconceivable before the 1990s and is indicative of the economic progress made by Ireland, which bears a direct relationship to the changing patterns of migration.

The US has also played a major part in the Irish economic success story. FDI from US businesses (especially in the IT sector) in conjunction with Irish tax policies (particularly low corporation tax) was one of the central drivers of Irish economic success throughout this period. 'The role of FDI in the growth of the Irish economy is illustrated by the fact that foreign-owned firms now account for about 47% of Ireland's industrial employment, 77% of net industrial output, and 83% of merchandise exports.'[35] FDI took advantage of a growing US economy during the 1990s and Ireland's position as a stable, low-tax, low-wage, high-skilled economy within the EU. As Bradley notes: 'Directly as well as indirectly, FDI has affected every corner of the Irish economy.'[36]

In response to the economic progress of the 1990s, Ireland began to witness an influx rather than an exodus of people, including relatively large numbers of eastern Europeans, Chinese and Africans, into its social and cultural mix. There had been virtually no immigrants coming to Ireland before this, beyond a small trickle of British workers, as it was not thought by many to be an attractive option. This changed dramatically during the 1990s and accelerated after EU enlargement in May 2004 when migrant workers from the ten new EU states were allowed free access to the Irish labour market. The government of the day were eager to attract foreign workers as foot-soldiers for the Celtic Tiger economy, though it did introduce 'habitual residence' conditions which restricted the full range of welfare benefits to these workers for a period of two years. Mac Éinrí demonstrates the impact that this combination of a vibrant economy with an open labour market had on the ethnic profile of the country. He reports that by May 2006, over 206,000 workers from the EU accession countries had been given approval to work in Ireland, which was, pro rata, six times higher than the number of immigrants accepted into the United States.[37]

This has increased Ireland's claim to be in the process of developing a multicultural society – at least in comparison with the past. Figures from the 2006 census suggest that the number of migrant workers in Ireland doubled from 2002 to 2006 to around 420,000 or 10 per cent of the population.[38] While the economic recession in Ireland since 2008 has seen a reduction of inward foreign migration, this has not yet changed the diverse social profile of the Irish workforce. The Irish Labour Market Review for 2008 suggested that the medium term outlook indicated that foreign nationals would remain in Ireland, despite the economic downturn of recent years.

With regards to migration, while there has been a marked slowdown in inward flows from Central Europe, it has not been as pronounced as the slowdown in jobs growth. Significantly, the improvement in the labour market performance of the EU10 countries that took place over the first four years of EU enlargement seems to have come to an end, making return migration a less attractive option. Indeed, the sharp increase in the number of EU12 nationals and construction workers signing on the Live Register over the last year would suggest that many made redundant from the housing slowdown are, for the time being at least, choosing to remain in Ireland, despite the dramatic reduction in job opportunities.[39]

A recent European Migration Network report indicates the rising trend in the number of non-EU nationals since the early 1990s. 'In 1991 the number of non-EU nationals who came to Ireland amounted to 3,200 or a little less than 10 per cent of all immigrants. By 1996 the number of non-EU immigrants had more than doubled in absolute and percentage terms to 8,200 and 21 per cent respectively. Since then these rising trends have continued. In 2004 the inflow of non-EU nationals amounted to 21,300 or 42 per cent of all immigrants.'[40] The more cosmopolitan make-up of Ireland's population has also led to claims that some immigrants have been using Ireland as a means of gaining an EU passport. The Irish citizenship referendum in June 2004 resulted in 80 per cent of people supporting the constitutional amendment to restrict the citizenship rights of non-nationals.[41] The debate surrounding the 2004 referendum brought immigration to the top of the Irish political agenda and raised questions about the depth of Irish claims to multiculturalism, despite the wave of non-Irish-born migrants who arrived since the early 1990s. 'The country of 100,000 welcomes, which still remembers the "no dogs, no blacks, no Irish" signs that greeted its emigrants in 60s Britain, has woken up to face a new accusation from its liberals: that it has morphed into a nation of racists and xenophobes.'[42] John Larkin's insightful and often whimsical 2002 travelogue of his Irish-Australian pilgrimage to the homeland, entitled *Larkin About in Ireland*, recounts an experience of casual racism in Dublin from a refuse collector.

One of them was singing, well, *yelling* a curious Indian or Pakistani song about a woman who was sweeping her front step when what she really ought to have been doing was catching the next boat home to India or Pakistan. It may not have actually been India or Pakistan that the garbo was singing about – perhaps it was Bangladesh, I wasn't sure because his diction was so unclear – but it was clearly sub-continental. He was wailing and warbling as if his testicles had been caught in his sitar strings. I was immediately heartened by the garbo's willingness to embrace multiculturalism – a relatively recent phenomenon in Ireland – until I saw the focus of his song: an elderly Indian woman sweeping her front step. This wasn't the last overtly racist incident I was to encounter either … It seems that the Irish, more accustomed to sending people out, were still coming to terms with welcoming them in.[43]

This throws up one of the supreme ironies of Ireland's recent history and one of the least flattering side-effects of its economic success since the early 1990s. For a country which has been built on the shoulders of its migrant population (de Valera after all was born in America) and which sent its own citizens out because it was unable to provide them with employment, it seems reluctant to accept the 'huddled masses' from other countries. To this extent Ireland appears to have forgotten its own history or, worse still, is wilfully ignoring it, as having climbed up the ladder of economic prosperity, Ireland has pulled that same ladder up behind it, institutionalising its own form of the 'no dogs, no blacks, no Irish' policy within its own borders. Lentin argues that the 2004 citizenship referendum represented the racialisation of the diaspora nation, where membership was defined along blood lines rather than through the geographical limits of the state. Paradoxically, while outwardly and rhetorically embracing its diaspora, Ireland has simultaneously reconfigured membership of the imagined community along racial lines as a means of exclusion. For Lentin, the needs of the Celtic Tiger produced an instrumental racism within the state that separated out the migrant workers from the asylum-seekers. This was done within an official discourse that legitimised the former as useful and legal and de-legitimised the latter as criminal outsiders sponging off the benefits system. All of this was wrapped up in a legal framework where immigration policy was defined through racial background rather than residency.

My argument is that Ireland's exponential economic growth since the 1990s has meant its restructuring as an exclusive racist state, where labour migrants needed to ensure continuing economic growth are welcome ... while asylum seekers, seen as superfluous to Ireland's economic growth, are increasingly prevented from landing to present their applications and where citizenship parameters are being redefined away from birth right (*jus soli*) to blood right (*jus sanguinis*).[44]

The juxtaposition of Ireland's treatment of its own migrant population, with its simultaneous requests for immigration reform legislation in America, is one of the less flattering facets of contemporary social policy.

Regardless of the actual numbers of migrants working in Ireland today and the debate surrounding their treatment by the state and by the indigenous community, it is clear that the experience of relatively high migration levels in recent years has left an indelible mark on the social fabric of the country. Reluctant cosmopolitans though some might be, Ireland is no longer as socially and culturally homogenous as it once was. To this degree it is conforming to the pattern of many other European states with populations composed of people from mixed ethnic backgrounds.

REDISCOVERING THE DIASPORA

Notwithstanding the criticisms that economic migrants have felt unwelcome due to both state legislation and casual racism from the indigenous population, Ireland is (statistically at least) a less homogenous country today than it used to be. Economic expansion has shifted the balance from emigration to immigration and membership of the EU has led to an influx of Eastern European and other nationalities coming to Ireland in search of employment opportunities. Coinciding with these changes and in order to feed the avaricious appetite of the Celtic Tiger economy, Ireland has sought to reconnect with its diaspora communities through tourism and trade in recent years and has built this into a central component of its economic and its foreign policies. To this extent, cyclical migration has been transformed from Ireland's dirty little secret into a post-modern national attribute, where the emigrant has been heralded as a de-territorialised member of the spiritual nation and an ambassador for the ancestral homeland. In recent years, the estimated 70 million members of the Irish diaspora worldwide have been identified as a lucrative market to be exploited in terms of tourism and trade through the enabling features of the global economy.

This recognition led to an increased focus on the economic and social condition of the diaspora by the state, leading to its Task Force report of 2002.[45] Before this point, the diaspora were viewed as an unfortunate and inevitable fact of life, a human safety valve which eased the pressure on land, jobs and food in the homeland. Regular migration also allowed both Church and state to continue its advocacy of large families and its opposition to effective birth control. Until relatively recently, therefore, out of sight was out of mind and once they left, the Irish state paid little attention to where its migrants went, what they thought or how they fared in their new lives abroad. There was even less enthusiasm to provide financial assistance to Irish migrants abroad, as Taoiseach Seán Lemass made clear in 1965 when he rejected a plea from the Catholic Church for the government to provide a state subsidy for Irish welfare groups in Britain. 'The government remains of the opinion that the diversion of Irish state revenue to the support of Irish centres in England would be unsound from the point of view of State finance and would, in practice, be incapable of being kept within fixed limits.'[46] Such indifference to the condition of the Irish abroad was a far cry from the contemporary official discourse where, rhetorically at least, the diaspora are being 'cherished' and seen as an invaluable part of the nation. This was perfectly illustrated in a keynote address given by Taoiseach Brian Cowen in 2008 when visiting New York. His speech, given at an awards dinner for the Irish-American business community, placed the Irish diaspora at the front and centre of his government's economic policy and indicated that Irishness was no longer to be territorially defined.

> The great challenge in Ireland today therefore in this new place which now exists for us is how to harness that tremendous font of goodwill, wisdom and expertise that is represented by the Irish diaspora in the world today. How do we establish the new networks that are required, the new relationship that is required to make sure that your sense of participation, your sense of being Irish, is fully encapsulated as it now must be since we amended Article 2 of our constitution, which recognises the Irishness of all of those people who not only reside at home or vote at home but all those who are dispersed throughout the world who have a great sense of Irishness and who remind many of us at home of the importance of what it is to be Irish, values that we sometimes take for granted at home.[47]

This represents the modern manifesto for engagement with the twenty-first century Irish diaspora and presents an interesting contemporary definition of the nation as being a de-territorialised entity with the imagined community extending well beyond the geographical borders of the Irish Republic. The concern to re-engage with the diaspora is not purely altruistic of course, as the reported figure of 70 million people of Irish descent around the world represents a potentially lucrative market for Irish tourism and trade. The possibilities for such synergy have been crystallised in part by the faltering Irish economy over recent years and by the enabling powers of globalisation and digital communication. Ireland possesses a number of competitive advantages from the point of view of global capital, not least its young, well educated workforce eager to connect into multinational corporations, who can in turn take advantage of attractive tax laws, low levels of state bureaucracy, a lightly unionised workforce and the obvious time zone advantages. Having an outlet in Ireland allows US companies to extend the working day by over five hours, sending work between the two countries by e-mail and through the internet in ways that take advantage of the time difference, thereby helping to maximise efficiency and productivity.

Following Cowen's speech in New York, the Irish government initiated a 'strategic review' of Ireland–US relations in an effort to put flesh on the bones of the aspirational rhetoric. The document produced by the Irish embassy in Washington in March 2009 was entitled *Ireland and America: Challenges and Opportunities in a New Context* and it identified economic co-operation as the government's first priority.

> The Ireland–US economic relationship is one of mutual benefit and is stronger now than at any time in our history. US foreign direct investment accounts for 95,000 jobs in Ireland. Ireland is among the top ten investors in the US. Combined investment in our two countries is some 65 billion euro, directly generating as many as 170,000 jobs. The US is Ireland's second largest trading partner and our largest export market, with annual trade in goods and services between the two countries at over 50 billion euro. The US is one of our most consistent and valuable sources of tourism. Around one and a half million people travel annually between our two countries. Open skies and new pre-clearance arrangements at Shannon and Dublin agreed in November 2008 offer real potential to bring new visitors to Ireland.[48]

The marketing of Ireland through its culture, sporting achievements and business connections has become a central component of Irish economic and foreign policy. The establishment of a thriving film industry during the 1990s was an extension of Irish economic policies which sought to entice external investment into Ireland through attractive tax rates. The growth of 'Paddywood' provided obvious direct benefits to the Irish economy but perhaps more importantly added to the wider cultural capital, where Ireland was displayed on the global stage. Films such as *My Left Foot* in 1989 and *In the Name of the Father*, *The Commitments*, *The Crying Game* and *Michael Collins* achieved international acclaim and elevated directors such as Jim Sheridan and Neil Jordan to global attention. *My Left Foot* resulted in Oscars for both Brenda Fricker and Daniel Day Lewis, who was also nominated for an Oscar following his portrayal of Gerry Conlon in the 1993 film *In the Name of the Father*. In addition to films with Irish subject matter, Ireland became a popular location for the making of big budget box office films such as *Braveheart* and *Saving Private Ryan*, due to favourable tax rates. On St Patrick's Day 2009, 'The Simpsons' premiered an episode entitled 'In the Name of the Grandfather'[49] which encapsulated the changing nature of the relationship between Ireland and America. The storyline focuses on the Simpsons visiting Ireland in search of the quaint simplicities of yesteryear, only to find an Americanised culture and a cosmopolitan, urbanite, hard-working and abstemious community. They are conned into buying a failing Irish pub and open a 'smoke-easy' to get new customers. Following their arrest for breaking the smoking ban, Homer defends himself in court by saying to the judge: 'I hope you'll forgive two well-meaning Americans for trying to take Ireland back to the good old days of *Angela's Ashes*.'[50] This was the first occasion that an episode of the show was given a world premiere outside the US, which perhaps tells us something about the global cultural reach of the Irish diaspora.

In the sporting arena, the hosting of golf's Ryder Cup at the K Club near Dublin in 2006 provided a similar function, boosting the Irish economy through increased tourism and providing the sort of positive global exposure that advertising would have been unable to buy. The significance of the event to Ireland was illustrated by the fact that the winning European team were presented with the trophy by then taoiseach Bertie Ahern. In terms of direct revenue, the Irish tourist body, Fáilte Ireland, commissioned a report from Deloitte and Touche which estimated that the Ryder Cup boosted the Irish economy by around €143 million in direct income, with other indirect impacts pushing the figure up to around €240 million. 'The bulk of the impact came from event organisers and from spectators, who each spent an average of €350 per day while at the event. American spectators spent the most, at €526 per day. In the corporate sector the average guest spent €500 each day, with those from the United States again being the "big spenders" at an average of €600 per day.'[51] Of course this event was perhaps more important in reputational dollars than it was worth in actual ones, as explained by Fáilte Ireland chair, Gillian Bowler: 'While this report demonstrates the value of the Ryder Cup to Ireland, the real value of the event is in its legacy to the country. The Ryder Cup was a fantastic platform to promote Ireland and Irish golf to a worldwide audience and images of the country were broadcast throughout the world during a memorable few days.'[52] This intersection of economic policy and national identity has been mediated and engineered through Irish tourism and connects with the country's foreign policy in the sense that it has helped to develop the country's brand image at an international level.

IRELAND THE BRAND: THE DEVELOPMENT OF IRISH TOURISM

First came the Vikings, then the Normans, the Saxons. All of them found Ireland irresistible. So think what a grand time we'll show you. Especially since you'd be the only ones of the lot we actually invited.[53]

This quote comes from an advertising campaign commissioned by Bord Fáilte (the Irish Tourist Board) in 1993, which tried to use humour to convey a serious message to its American audience. Ireland was a historic land with a tradition of fighting foreign invaders, but like America itself had prevailed and prospered. At the risk of psycho-analysing the advertisers, the subliminal message here was that the Irish and the Americans had something in common with each other and this could be rekindled through Irish hospitality and their infectious sense of fun. On a broader level, this example raises an important set of issues and questions linked to a country's collective narrative and its projected sense of national identity to the outside world. Mary McGlynn, an Irish-American academic from City University of New York, commented in 2004 that Mastercard were running an advertising campaign with a particular and stylised image of Ireland. 'Over and over again, Ireland is being marketed as a kind of soothing retreat where you can relax. It's being marketed like a spa, as a way to ease your pain.'[54]

While tourism is obviously a major element of economic policy, it also connects into issues surrounding national identity. Clancy emphasises the role that 'branding' plays in the construction of the national identity as a product for external marketing through tourism and trade. The suggestion here is that countries have a brand in the same way that commercial companies do, and are more frequently paying attention to how this is marketed internationally. Thus McDonald's, Starbucks, BMW, Bang & Olufsen, Apple and ASDA all conjure up different sets of reputational images and perceptions among their consumers. 'If companies possess such qualities, so too do places. We think of San Francisco differently than we do Newark, Amsterdam differently than Zurich, Baghdad differently from Casablanca. Location or place branding is becoming ever more important as places become centres of entertainment and tourism.'[55] This connects back into the previous chapter in the way in which theme bars have attempted to market positive aspects of national stereotypes. Thus Australia's location branding emphasises the great climate, relaxed people and healthy outdoor lifestyle; Norway is known for its commitment to quiet diplomacy and international conflict prevention activities; Germany is known for its sober efficiency, reliable machinery and an ability to win penalty shoot-outs in football World Cups. Ireland (leaving generations of violent conflict aside) is known for its craic and its *'céad míle fáilte'*, a hundred thousand welcomes. A fascinating example of this location branding was illustrated when the Czech Republic took over the EU presidency in 2009 and commissioned an artist to provide a visual representation of the member states. The piece that resulted, entitled 'Entropa', depicted the EU's twenty-seven member states in terms of unflattering national stereotypes. Thus Holland was represented as being underwater apart from a few minarets, Bulgaria featured a Turkish toilet, Denmark sported a picture of the prophet Mohammed made out of Lego, Romania's entry was dominated by Dracula, and Germany was shown as a series of autobahns which together formed a thinly disguised swastika. The UK was missing altogether from this artistic map of Europe. Following complaints from several of the member states, David Cerny's creation was withdrawn by the Czech government from its place in the European Council offices in Brussels.

How contemporary Ireland markets its 'brand' internationally tells us something about its preferred self-image, how it wants to be seen by others rather than how it actually is. The changing nature of this international marketing connects back to other themes within this book relating to the changing nature of contemporary Ireland, how it sees its place in the world and how it interacts with those beyond its borders. In this regard the development of Irish tourism maps onto the changing economic and cultural character of Ireland itself, which, as has been explained earlier in this book, has affected relations with other countries, including America. Tourism can be seen to be the pivot on which the old and new images of Ireland have turned, moving us from John Ford's *Quiet Man* to Alan Parker's *Commitments* and beyond.

The branding of Ireland as a tourist destination has changed subtly from the traditional agrarian and spiritual land idealised in de Valera's infamous St Patrick's Day address to America in 1943 to incorporate a more modern image and national identity. Clancy outlines the evolution of this marketing and the Tourism Brand Ireland (TBI) campaign which began in 1996. 'The TBI campaign, first titled "Ireland: An Emotional Experience" reinforced Ireland as a differentiated, untouched, even magical place. "Is there magic in the air?" asked one ad.'[56]

In 2005 Tourism Ireland launched a global advertising campaign under the title 'Discover Your Very Own Ireland' suggesting a chameleonic country with diverse possibilities and identities encompassing history, scenery, outdoor sporting opportunities and welcoming people. The message of this campaign was that Ireland was whatever you wanted it to be, and that it held sufficient diversity to satisfy the global tourist market. This evolved in January 2009 into a new campaign entitled 'Go Where Ireland Takes You'. This continued but refined the message, that there was more to Ireland than the shamrocks, thatched cottages, leprechauns and old historic buildings emphasised by previous advertising campaigns. The television wing of the latest incarnation of Ireland's tourism marketing suggested that the experience of visiting would itself provide some added value to the individual by personalising the authentic rather than providing an off-the-shelf series of experiences. As explained by the Tourism Ireland website: 'The new global TV advertisements are designed to convey a sense of fun and spontaneity and instil the message that there is more to Ireland than just what can be found in a guidebook and some of the most wonderful things can only be stumbled on by chance!'[57] This modern branding of Ireland is a long way from marketing during the 1960s and 1970s, which tended to promote it as an anti-modernist destination, an unchanging (even ancient) environment, a spiritual, magical retreat from the pressures of contemporary life. Negra illustrates this within the context of an advert run by the Pan Am airline during the 1960s where, to the background of traditional flute music, a voiceover intoned a message of romantic and unchanging rural simplicity. 'The hills are as green as they've always been. Life is as quiet as it ever was. And time has a way of standing still. Let Pan Am take you there.'[58]

In pure monetary terms, tourism has become the backbone of the Irish economy in recent years, along with the financial services and technology sector, with American tourism being one of the key markets. By 2000, agriculture, which had in the past been a dominant factor in Ireland's economic viability, had been reduced to a mere 4 per cent of the country's GDP. In addition to a series of deliberate policies which were put in place by successive Irish governments to maximise Irish tourism, wider events also helped, such as the 1998 Good Friday Agreement in Northern Ireland, which reduced the fear factor for potential visitors and created good headlines for the whole island. The figures for international tourism in Ireland in recent years are astonishing given the relative size of the country. Clancy reports that: 'Arrivals to the Republic of Ireland grew from less than 2 million visitors in 1986 to 7.7 million in 2006. Earnings grew from €927 million to just below €4.6 billion during the same period.'[59] As Kelly points out, however, the impressive figures on foreign tourism into Ireland have to be set against the increasing number of Irish people who travelled out of the country during the same period and spent their money abroad: 'For the first time, foreign expenditure by Irish travellers exceeded expenditure in Ireland by foreign visitors in 2003.'[60] Figures from Dublin's Central Statistics Office for the third quarter of 2008 would suggest that this trend is continuing. 'Earnings from visitors to Ireland accounted for €1,734m while expenditure by Irish visitors abroad amounted to €2,366m in Q3 2008, resulting in a net outflow of €632m.'[61]

Tourism marketing connected into the cultural and sporting calendar with examples such as the Ryder Cup in 2006, as mentioned above, and the annual St Patrick's Day festivities, to take advantage of wider publicity opportunities that existed. In a press release on 13 March

2009, Tourism Ireland made the link between the Irish diaspora and the homeland through that year's St Patrick's Day celebrations.

> Tourism Ireland will be tapping into the tremendous interest and goodwill generated by the St Patrick's celebrations next week, as the spotlight focuses on the island of Ireland around the world. Over seventy million people claim links with Ireland and Tourism Ireland will be hosting a range of media, travel trade and consumer events to capitalise on the global interest in all things Irish ... Tourism Ireland's 2009 spring campaign is the most intensive and targeted ever mounted by the organisation. As the global recession continues to bite on consumer confidence, affordability and great value for money dominates all advertising, consumer and trade promotional activities in overseas markets this year.[62]

As part of this effort, Tourism Ireland's New York office combined with the St Patrick's Festival in Dublin and leading US morning television show the 'Today' programme, watched by 8 million viewers, for a live broadcast of the St Patrick's Day celebrations in Dublin. Paul O'Toole, chief executive of Tourism Ireland, commented that such exposure was critical to raising the profile of Ireland as a tourist destination, especially in the difficult market caused by the global recession.

> This live broadcast on the 'Today' show is a fantastic opportunity to convey our message about the wonderful tourism product around the island of Ireland to a huge audience across the US ... The US is a key market for tourism to the island of Ireland and we have a very strong and comprehensive promotional programme under way there for 2009. It is absolutely essential that we convey the message that there has never been a better time for Americans to visit the island of Ireland.[63]

DOING BUSINESS TOGETHER

A debate is currently taking place between Ireland and Irish-America about how the relationship should move forward. Much of this centres around corporate funding and the desire of business interests to build entrepreneurial links between the two countries. This is taking place at a time when (as examined elsewhere in this book) Irish migration has slowed to a trickle and where Irish-American political interest in Northern Ireland has declined as the peace process has progressed. Aside from the thorny issue of immigration reform there is little that binds the Irish-American community together and even less that binds the Irish-born to those of Irish descent. Some of the memories are fading, others are being mis-remembered while a few more are mutating and finding new creolised forms.

The question this poses is what is Irish-America for today? In terms of recent trends, the answer to this question is that it is about tourism, trade and economic investment between the two countries and a relationship which is based on business models and equality. The current relationship between America and Ireland has certainly gone a long way beyond the traditional diaspora remittances model and revolves around developing economic and cultural connections between the two countries. The Irish-America Forum held in New York on 7–8 November 2007 was the embodiment of this new relationship, where business elites from the two countries tried to tease out possible areas for mutual cooperation. This initiative was sponsored by the American Ireland Fund (which has spent over $USD300 million on projects in Ireland since 1976), University College Dublin, *Irish America* magazine, the Irish government and Aer Lingus, and brought together influential people from both countries to discuss the future of the relationship between them. Much of the discussion at this forum centred on opening up new markets and utilising the potential of the Irish diaspora to sustain a very sickly Celtic Tiger, but tied this into the idea of cultural fusion and understanding between Ireland and Irish-America.

The event was a who's who of the Irish and Irish-American business and social elites, with speakers that included Loretta Brennan Glucksman, chair of the American Ireland Fund; former 'Riverdance' and 'Lord of the Dance' star Michael Flatley; author and celebrated journalist Pete Hamill; Atlantic Philanthropies chief executive Gara LaMarche; Dr Hugh Brady, president of UCD, publisher of *Irish America* magazine and the *Irish Voice*, Niall O'Dowd and the Irish consul general in New York, Niall Burgess. The general conclusion of this two-day meeting was that the relationship between Ireland and the US had changed unalterably, both politically and economically, with Irish companies now employing as many people in the US as American businesses do in Ireland, but that it was imperative to proactively develop structures that would maintain these networks and connections into the future.

Niall Burgess, when interviewed in September 2008, summed up the current relationship between Ireland and America by suggesting that it had become more of a two-way connection than it had been in the past, a change mediated by the global economy.

> The economic relationship is now one which is flowing with very strong benefits in two directions. If you look at the city of New York you can see that Ireland is the fifth largest provider of overseas tourism into New York after Canada, Britain and Japan and for a country of Ireland's size that's just a stunning statistic ... But I think there is also a sense that we have benefited from the strong connections that the diaspora have with Ireland and that's not going to change. If anything, the fact that we are a diaspora has a greater value now in a globalised environment, an even greater value than it did ten or fifteen years ago.[64]

This note of optimism needs to be tempered of course by the fact that in line with the world financial crisis that hit Western economies during 2008, Ireland was one of the first countries to enter a recession, which it did in September 2008 for the first time since 1983. This may see a new wave of Irish people trying to enter the US in search of employment opportunities, but as explained in Chapter 4, this trend is unlikely to revitalise Irish-American civil society. Unlike in previous recessions when many Irish people entered the US, found work and deliberately overstayed their visas, a less tolerant climate now prevails in the US towards the undocumented.

All of these trends point to the fact that the relationship between Ireland and Irish-America is evolving in political, economic and cultural terms. As this chapter has outlined, Ireland has changed hugely over the last forty years and this has, perhaps inevitably, led to the beginning of a new phase in its relationship with America. Joe Lee concludes his introduction to the valuable edited collection *Making the Irish American* by suggesting that while Irish-America was at a crossroads, the final destination remains uncertain: 'Who knows what the future may hold? Irish America is changing rapidly. But then so is America. So is Ireland. But change is the law of life. It may mean death. But it need not.'[65]

The final shape of this new relationship has yet to be determined and will depend to a large degree on the actions of those who try to develop it and the economic needs of both countries. What seems certain, however, is that it will continue to evolve in ways that are based on equality and common interests rather than on charity and deference. For better or worse, Ireland has grown up and become a modern mid-sized European state. Its future relationship with America is likely to develop in ways that reflect that.

NOTES

1. Bradley, J. 'The Irish Economy in International Perspective', in W. Crotty and D. Schmitt, (eds), *Ireland on the World Stage* (London: Longman, 2002), p.46.
2. Former tourism minister Enda Kenny speaking in 2007, quoted in Clancy, M. 'Re-Presenting Ireland: Tourism, Branding and Changing Conceptions of the Nation in Contemporary Ireland', unpublished paper prepared for the 49th Annual International Studies Association Convention, 26–9 March 2008, p.16.
3. See, for instance, the following books on the emergence of the Irish Celtic Tiger phenomenon: Coulter, C. and Coleman, S. (eds), *The End of Irish History? Critical Reflections on the Celtic Tiger* (Manchester: Manchester University Press, 2003); Kirby, P. *The Celtic Tiger in Distress: Growth with Inequality in Ireland* (Basingstoke: Palgrave, 1999); MacSharry, R. and White, P. *The Making of the Celtic Tiger: The Inside Story of Ireland's Boon Economy* (Cork: Mercier Press, 2000).
4. Hayward, K. and MacCarthaigh, M. (eds), *Recycling the State: The Politics of Adaptation in Ireland* (Dublin: Irish Academic Press, 2007), p.2.
5. Inglis, T. *Global Ireland* (London: Routledge, 2008), p.154.
6. Ni Eigeartaigh, A. 'Mise Éire: Recycling Nationalist Mythologies', in K. Hayward and M. MacCarthaigh (eds), *Recycling the State* (Dublin: Irish Academic Press, 2007), pp.18–42.
7. Girvin, B. 'Contraception, Moral Panic and Social Change in Ireland 1969–79', *Irish Political Studies*, 23, 4 (December 2008), p.573.
8. MacNeice, L. 'Autumn Journal', in *Collected Poems* (London: Faber and Faber, 1998).
9. Moore, C. *One Voice: My Life in Song* (London: Hodder and Stoughton, 2000), p.42.
10. Inglis, *Global Ireland*, pp.189–90.
11. Bartley, B. and Kitchin R. (eds), *Understanding Contemporary Ireland* (London: Pluto Press, 2007), p.2.
12. Walsh, J. 'Agriculture in Transition', in Bartley and Kitchin *Understanding Contemporary Ireland*, p.158.
13. Hardiman, N., Murphy, P. and Burke, O. 'The Politics of Economic Adjustment in a Liberal Market Economy: The Social Compensation Hypothesis Revisited', *Irish Political Studies*, 23, 4 (December 2008), p.603.
14. MacNeice, L. 'Autumn Journal', in *Collected Poems* (London: Faber and Faber, 1998).
15. Manchester Irish Festival, March 2009, http://www.manchesteririshfestival.com/content/riverdance-the-farewell-tour.
16. Gootman, E. 'For Bronx School Dancers the Moves are Irish', *New York Times*, 14 March 2008, http://www.nytimes.com/2008/03/14/nyregion/14educ.html?pagewanted=1&_r=1.
17. Niall Burgess, Irish consul general, New York, interviewed by author, 9 September 2008.
18. Inglis, *Global Ireland*, p.102.
19. See Fahey, T. 'Progress or Decline? Demographic Change in Political Context', in W. Crotty and D. Schmitt (eds), *Ireland and the Politics of Change* (London: Longman, 1998), p.53.
20. Paus, E. *Foreign Investment, Development and Globalization: Can Costa Rica Become Ireland?* (Basingstoke: Palgrave, 2005), pp.45–9.
21. Murphy, G. and Puirséil, N. '"Is It a New Allowance?" Irish Entry to the EEC and Popular Opinion', *Irish Political Studies*, 23, 4, p.533.

22. Allen, K. *The Corporate Takeover of Ireland* (Dublin: Irish Academic Press, 2007), p.xvii.
23. Lee, J.J. *Ireland 1912–1985: Politics and Society* (Cambridge: Cambridge University Press, 1989), pp.359–60.
24. Mac Éinrí, P. 'Some Recent Demographic Developments in Ireland', *Études Irlandaises*, 22, 1 (Spring 1997), http://migration.ucc.ie/etudesirlandaises.htm.
25. MacLaughlin, J. *Ireland: The Emigrant Nursery and the World Economy* (Cork: Cork University Press, 1994), p.31.
26. Hughes, G. and Quinn, E. *The Impact of Immigration on Europe's Societies: Ireland* (Dublin: European Migration Network, 2004), p.6.
27. Central Statistics Office (CSO), *Population and Labour Force Projections: 2006–2036* (Dublin: CSO, 2006), pp.18–19.
28. Mac Éinrí, P. 'Immigration: Labour Migrants, Asylum Seekers and Refugees', in Bartley and Kitchin, *Understanding Contemporary Ireland*, p.242.
29. Central Statistics Office, Dublin, 'Population and Migration Estimates – April 2009', p.1. http://www.cso.ie/releasespublications/documents/population/current/popmig.pdf.
30. Central Statistics Office, *Population and Migration Estimates* (Dublin: CSO, 2005), http://www.cso.ie/releasespublications/pr pop.htm.
31. 'Ireland Ranked as Second Wealthiest Country', *Irish Times*, 8 September 2005, p.1.
32. Inglis, *Global Ireland*, p.19.
33. Paus, *Foreign Investment*, p.199.
34. President of Intel, Craig Barrett, quoted in Bradley 'The Irish Economy in International Perspective', p.46.
35. Walsh, B. 'Taxation and Foreign Direct Investment in Ireland,' in H. Grubel (ed.), *Tax Reform in Canada: Our Path to Greater Prosperity* (Vancouver: The Fraser Institute, 2002), p.214.
36. Bradley, 'The Irish Economy in International Perspective', p.54.
37. Mac Éinrí, 'Immigration: Labour Migrants, Asylum Seekers and Refugees', p.241.
38. Lentin, R. 'Illegal in Ireland, Irish Illegals: Diaspora Nation as a Racial State', *Irish Political Studies*, 22, 4 (December 2007), p.436.
39. FÁS, *Irish Labour Market Review 2008* (Dublin: FÁS, 2009), p.20, http://www. fas. ie/NR/rdonlyres/9ABC5EE1-CF20-4AA5-ACA4-C5B81DD9FE5E/474/LabourMarket 2008_REVISE098.pdf.
40. Hughes and Quinn, *The Impact of Immigration on Europe's Societies*, p.6.
41. This referendum voted for a constitutional amendment which would allow the Irish parliament to introduce legislation that did not give automatic rights to citizenship to children of non-nationals. The legislation in the form of the Irish Nationality and Citizenship Act 2004, came into effect in June 2004.
42. 'Country's Emigrant Past Lies Forgotten as Irish Accused of Racism', *Guardian*, 21 June 2004, http://www.guardian.co.uk/uk/2004/jun/21/ireland.
43. Larkin, J. *Larkin About in Ireland* (Sydney: Hodder, 2002), pp.223–5.
44. Lentin, 'Illegal in Ireland, Irish Illegals', p.441.
45. *Ireland and the Irish Abroad*, Task Force Report on Emigration, Dublin, 2002.
46. Seán Lemass, cited in Delaney, E. *Demography State and Society* (Liverpool: Liverpool University Press, 2000), p.259.
47. Brian Cowen speech, New York, 17 July 2008.
48. *Ireland and America: Challenges and Opportunities in a New Context*, Irish Embassy, Washington, March 2009, p.4.
49. This was a reference to the 1993 film *In the Name of the Father* about the miscarriage of justice case involving the Guilford Four in the 1970s. The film was directed by Jim Sheridan, starred Daniel Day Lewis and Emma Thompson and was nominated for seven Oscars.
50. 'The Simpsons', 'In the Name of the Grandfather', broadcast on Sky television, 17 March 2009.
51. 'Economic Impact of Ryder Cup Exceeds Pre-Event Predictions', Fáilte Ireland, 26 April 2007, http://www.failteireland.ie/About-Us/News-and-Events/Economic-Impact-of-Ryder-Cup-Exceeds-Pre-Event-Pre.
52. Ibid.

53. Quoted in Negra, D. 'Consuming Ireland: Lucky Charms Cereal, Irish Spring Soap and 1-800-Shamrock', *Cultural Studies*, 15, 1 (2001), p.92.
54. Mary McGlynn, interviewed by author, 15 September 2004.
55. Clancy, M. 'Re-Presenting Ireland', p.5.
56. Ibid., p.16.
57. 'Go Where Ireland Takes You', Tourism Ireland Press Release, http://www. tourismireland.com/Home/Our_Marketing_Overseas.aspx.
58. Negra, 'Consuming Ireland', p.89.
59. Clancy, M. 'Re-Presenting Ireland', p.10.
60. Kelly, C. 'Tourism and Heritage', in Bartley and Kitchin, *Understanding Contemporary Ireland*, p.171.
61. Central Statistics Office, *Tourism and Travel* (Dublin: CSO, 23 December 2008).
62. 'Massive Tourism Promotional Drive Under Way as World Spotlight on Ireland for St Patrick's Week', Tourism Ireland Press Release, 13 March 2009, http://www.tourismireland.com/Home/about-us/press-releases/Massive-Tourism-Promotional-Drive-Under-Way-as-Wor.aspx.
63. '8 Million Americans See Dublin Live on St Patrick's Day', Tourism Ireland Press Release, 10 March 2009, http://193.120.252.10/Home/about-us/press-releases/8-Million-Americans-See-Dublin-Live-on-St-Patrick%E2%80%99.aspx.
64. Niall Burgess, Irish consul general, New York, interviewed by author, 9 September 2008.
65. Lee, J.J. 'Introduction', in J.J. Lee and M. Casey, *Making the Irish American* (New York: New York University Press, 2007), p.49.

8

Redefining Irish-America in the Global Age

This book began by making the case that we are in a transitional phase in the historic relationship between Ireland and America, where the ties between the two were loosening due to a combination of structural and more behavioural factors in migratory trends. Perhaps most fundamentally, the periodic waves of Irish migration that provided Irish-America with its life-blood have ceased and are unlikely to recur. There has been some speculation in recent times (mainly byactivists in the immigration reform lobby) that the economic recession in Ireland will lead to a new wave of migrants in the manner of those who left for America during the recession of the 1980s. There remains the possibility that the failing Irish economy will produce a new wave of emigrants who leave in search of better opportunities elsewhere. At the time of writing (August 2009) Ireland has been in a formal recession for over a year and its informal effects have been felt for a lot longer than that. During the halcyon days of the Celtic Tiger, the unemployment rate was around 5 per cent, while it hit 17 per cent in the summer of 2009. Forecasts on the Irish labour market produced by the Economic and Social Research Institute (ESRI) in the spring of 2009 indicate the severity of Ireland's economic downturn. Unemployment stood at 100,000 in 2007, rose to 137,000 in 2008 and was estimated to reach 292,000 in 2009 and an eye-watering 366,000 in 2010.[1] This represents a rise of 114 per cent in 2009 from the numbers unemployed in the preceding year.

In light of such frightening forecasts it is not hard to imagine that a new wave of emigration is going to accompany Ireland's economic decline. However, it is unlikely that this will reinvigorate the fabric of Irish-America or its ethnic associations, nor is it likely to change the underlying patterns explored in the preceding chapters of this book. One of the main reasons for this is because immigration into America is more strictly controlled today in the wake of the 9/11 attacks than it was during the 1980s. It is more difficult today to overstay or evade US visa restrictions than it was in previous generations. The current mood of the US, within both public opinion and among the political elite in Washington, is not a positive one when it comes to 'illegal aliens'. The post-9/11 atmosphere witnessed a securitisation of migration (and not just within America) and the fostering of a climate where migrants were treated with suspicion or even hostility and the undocumented were regarded as being a threat to national security. This was given institutional form when the traditional gatekeepers of entry into the US, the INS, were subsumed by the Department of Homeland Security in the wake of the 9/11 attacks. Despite the fact that the 9/11 bombers were actually in the US legally, the psychological impact of the attacks made a subliminal connection between immigrants, national security and terror. Thus, to be undocumented today in the US is literally to be un-American – at best an irritation, at worst a threat to public safety.

Given the economic crisis that has shaped the beginning of President Obama's tenure in office, it is unlikely that the immigration issue will be resolved in a way that opens the door for significant numbers of new migrants to arrive into the US when the country is struggling to find jobs for those who are already there. It is also unlikely that the Irish will be singled out for special treatment as this would open the Obama administration up to accusations of partiality and inconsistency, and more cynically, this is likely to lose Obama more votes than he would gain in his re-election campaign in 2012. While Australia managed to winkle out a special deal for its citizens, this was primarily a product of the 'special relationship' between former Australian prime minister John Howard and former US president George W. Bush and the former's eager participation in the latter's 'coalition of the willing', put together in an effort to help legitimise the war on terror. Obama has little to gain from treating 'neutral' Ireland as an exceptional case on the immigration reform issue. Consequently, he will have to either enact comprehensive legislation that, given its complexity, would take time away from his administration's economic and foreign policy activities, or he will have to push the issue further down the policy 'to do' list, perhaps identifying it as a second term priority.

While there may well be another wave of Irish migration in the years ahead, these people are unlikely to go to the US in the same numbers as they did in the past, and even if they do manage to get in and evade detection by the Department of Homeland Security they are not going to display their presence there by joining cultural or political civil society groups such as the GAA or for that matter the AOH. So the tap that gushed in previous generations providing Irish-America with its pool of cultural and political activists has now all but dried up and, apart from a few powerful squirts in the 1980s, looks set to provide little more than a trickle to slake the thirst of parched Irish-American throats as the twenty-first century proceeds. This does not mean necessarily that Irish-America is dying, but it is certainly changing, as of course is Ireland itself.

The other central theme of the book has been the role of globalisation as a catalyst in this evolving relationship between Ireland and America. While at times 'globalisation' might seem to be an overused or rather nebulous concept, more valued by academics anxious to increase their citation scores than by 'real' people, its impact on the relationship between Ireland and America is certainly visible. In the cultural realm, global communications have brought the two countries (and their people) closer together. At its most basic, it is much easier and, relatively speaking, much cheaper to travel between the two places today than it was during previous generations. The growth of digital technology has helped to muddy the geographical waters, disconnecting our sense of place from our sense of self and providing increased layers of separation between where we live and who we are. To this extent, while globalisation has certainly not replaced the dominance of the state in our lives, it has removed its omnipotence and provided us with cultural alternatives beyond its borders. Once again it is important not to get carried away by the shiny lustre of the latest intellectual fad, but it is certainly not an exaggeration to say that globalisation has changed the rules for diaspora communities. Ulf Hannerz has referred to the phenomenon of globalisation as 'increasing long-distance interconnectedness'[2] and this can certainly be observed in the case of the Irish diaspora.

Global communications now make it possible to keep in touch with home and even experience it much more easily than was the case for previous generations. In fact, it has allowed migrants to reconfigure the whole meaning of 'home', and change it from a physical linear journey (where we move from home to elsewhere and perhaps back again) into an experiential state of mind which transcends the realities of geographical space. In this sense the products and tools of globalisation (the emergence of e-mail and the internet as well as Skype, webcams, digital satellite television, mobile phones, electronic banking, online shopping etc.) have helped to de-territorialise the state. A few examples of this illustrate the point. Today it is possible to keep in touch with family and friends instantly though text messaging, read the local news online, watch the football game in real time without waiting for letters from home or going to the community hall for the delayed showing of the match. Today we can live beyond the shores of Ireland and go online to order our soda farls directly from international suppliers, paying for it via our electronic bank accounts. We can of course have multiple bank accounts within Ireland and beyond it, and even multiple passports. All of this has allowed us to engage in what David Fitz Gerald has termed 'citizenship à la carte', where we can tap into aspects of citizenship that appeal to us and reject those that do not.

> Scholars of migrant 'transnationalism' share the globalists' goal of understanding broken linkages between territory and polity. Transnationalists call for a reconceptualization of terms like community, citizenship, and the nation-state. For them, 'deterritorialization' signifies the uncoupling of residence in a territory with membership in a community and the displacement of culture from geography. Numerous observers argue that international migrants and the governments of their countries of origin are primary agents of deterritorialization. According to this perspective, countries of emigration are becoming 'deterritorialized nation-states' as citizens abroad are incorporated by their homelands.[3]

We should not overstate this case, of course, as not everyone is partaking of this political and cultural smorgasbord. Nevertheless, it is reasonable to argue that diasporic individuals have more freedom of movement today than they had in the past. To continue the culinary metaphor, globalisation has allowed members of diaspora communities to have their cake and eat it, to travel back and forth as they please (if their documentation and wallets permit) and opt in and out of economic arrangements, citizenship requirements, political engagement and cultural offerings between their country of birth and place of residence as they so choose.

The downside to all of this globally inspired hedonistic freedom in the context of Irish-America is substantial. While technology and communication has liberated us from the apron strings of 'Mother Ireland', it has also made us ungrateful to her for the nurturing that we received in the past. In other words, today's migrant community living in America do not feel the same need to build and maintain ethnic networks as their predecessors did in previous generations. As explained in earlier chapters, this is partly because these people do not think of themselves as having *actually emigrated* from Ireland in any real sense and prefer to view their situation as a temporary secondment within America rather than anything more permanent. Allied to this, today's Irish community in the US (notwithstanding the problems of the undocumented) do not feel the same need to congregate within ethnic civil society organisations for protection from the hostile WASP environment experienced by their predecessors in the nineteenth and early twentieth centuries. Finally, there is not the same political cohesion within Irish-America today as the alignment with the Democratic Party has declined and as the uniting pole of the Northern Ireland conflict has effectively disappeared off the map altogether. Many Irish people do still link up together of course and (the time difference being what it is) can be found squeezed into Irish bars in New York at 9 am on a Saturday morning watching Ireland playing in the Six Nations rugby tournament, or in the basement of Jack Dempsey's bar under the shadow of the Empire State Building to watch Glasgow Celtic play Glasgow Rangers in the Old Firm derby of the Scottish Premier League (SPL). Those social and cultural connections still remain but they lack the dynamic force of their predecessors where the Hibernians would show the match and where people would meet to build strong social and political networks and where social clubs and bars would inter-connect with the GAA and the Catholic Church in mutually reinforcing bonds of ethnic civil society. In the context of New York, a critical mass of Irish people remains in areas such as Woodside and Woodlawn in Queens, and streets such as McClean Avenue in Yonkers still retain their Irish character. Nevertheless, forms of civic associationalism have changed from previous generations as the numbers of Irish have declined and as they have evolved as a diaspora community into the political, economic and social mainstream of American life.

As a result of these trends, fewer Irish people are entering America for anything more than a pragmatic short-term stay or an even more pragmatic over-stay. For the majority of those who do remain, either documented or undocumented, the psychological act of hanging onto home does not seem to be at the forefront of their minds and many are coming from an Americanised Ireland in the first place and are eager to sample American culture before they return 'home' rather than immediately registering with the local church or checking in with the nearest GAA club. Equally importantly, the Ireland they are coming from has turned them into individualistic cosmopolitan capitalist consumers, educated in the ways of the international market. In this sense post-de Valera Ireland, perhaps going back to the economic revolution initiated by Seán Lemass in the 1960s, turned Ireland and its people into a nursery, preparing us for and giving us the tools to deal with our American cousins. From this perspective, globalisation was the economic and cultural vehicle for a new hegemony where, without actually leaving Ireland or even having a passport, we owed our livelihoods to high-tech American companies and our sympathies/allegiances to JFK, Maureen O'Hara, James Cagney and subsequent icons of the silver screen. To this extent, America crept up on and seduced Ireland, achieving what the English could not despite centuries of trying to Anglicise and pacify the place.

Stereotypes inevitably simplify and risk over-statement; however, there is an argument to be made that the Americanisation of Ireland has been ongoing for generations and was accelerated by the forces of globalisation. Taken to its logical conclusion, this thesis argues that the process goes way beyond us watching the David Letterman show or being amused by Wolf Blitzer's bombastic hyperbole in CNN's 'Situation Room'. It suggests that the Irish have been changed in terms of how they think and act, in terms of their core values, beliefs and wants. The opening up of Ireland and the sinews that grew between it and other nations and economic actors forced us to adapt and conform to the structures and expectations of others. Thus the spiritual, unpredictable streak, which has at times been seen as unreliability or even aggression ('the Fighting Irish' or cast as a racial insult, 'having a Paddy') has given way to the whimsical nostalgia of nation-branding by Tourism Ireland for external consumption. Irish sociologist Tom Inglis makes this argument forcefully in his book *Global Ireland*, alluding to the fact that this global interconnectedness and interdependency forced the Irish to become predictable rational actors who talked the talk and walked the walk required for the smooth operation of capitalist ventures. 'Now we willingly embrace rational predictable behaviour as part of the global habitus. It is central to the trust that makes the world go round ... Increased interdependency can only succeed if people become more rational and civilized. Irish people have become self-restrained. They do not spit, belch, fart, puke, pee and shit as openly as they used to or with the same sense of freedom ... They have learnt to control their instincts, passions and emotions.'[4] In fairness, the Irish are hardly alone in this and it could be argued that Inglis's focus on contemporary Irish ablution trends differs little from those of other cultures. Nevertheless, globalisation has certainly had a big impact on Ireland and on issues relating to identity and migration. As mentioned in Chapter 2, it has allowed us to forestall questions of emigration and has reduced the psychological impact on individuals, families and communities caused by the act of leaving. Irish journalist Ray O'Hanlon has gone as far as saying that modernity has produced a new form of Irish migrant, set apart from their predecessors by their de-territorialised environment and characterised by 'the mid-Atlantic duel citizen, maintaining business interests in both the US and Ireland. In some cases, movement depends less on a consideration of country of residence than it does on prospects within multi-national corporations, industries or technologies. Arguably a form of third country is emerging, populated by an Irish diaspora pulled together by airline schedules, fiber-optic lines and web pages.'[5]

THE NEW IRISH DIASPORA

It seems clear therefore that the political, cultural and economic relationship between Ireland and America is in a state of flux. The question is not so much is change taking place – as the connections have been constantly evolving over time – so much as where will this change lead to in the context of relations between the two countries and their peoples? The answer to this is necessarily speculative as this is a process that is ongoing and will remain so for the next twenty years at least. However, it is reasonable to conclude that while there will always be an historic connection between the two countries, the political link is receding while the cultural link is morphing into a new phenomenon, which is more American-Irish than it is Irish-American. That is to say, due to the weakening imprint of Irishness on the American psyche, as second generation becomes third and third becomes fourth, the ever-dimming and refracted remembrance of the ancestral motherland, combined with the reality for generations of being an American-American, has had an indelible impact on cultural identities and expressions within Irish-America. Within the context of the GAA in New York, this social and cultural evolution is evident in the minor league, which is dominated by Irish-Americans rather than Irish-born players. Professor Larry McCarthy, secretary of the New York GAA, explained that while the minor league had a healthy new wave of Irish-Americans involved in the sport, they did not graduate in large numbers into the major league due in part to the structure of American society and the link between sporting activity and the education system.

> The minor board, the underage section, is an Irish-American phenomenon which is distinct from the senior board which is an Irish phenomenon. That doesn't mean that there isn't people in both; there is, but there is a lot of fathers and mothers of the kids who are involved in the minor board who are Irish and most of the kids are American ... I'd say about 70 per cent of the kids who are playing are probably American born ... but they do not graduate to the senior level very well. There's a drop off everywhere round the world at that age group, but I would argue even more so in America, because kids go away to college, they don't stay at home ... So you get a significant disconnect there [between minor and senior levels]. The other thing is that there is not a tradition of sports clubs in America. The sports system is very much tied to the education system here, so most of the competition for kids comes from the schools ... Arguably as well, we're at fault. Maybe we haven't been as encouraging of those [American] kids and bringing them on because of the divide that exists in some cases between the Irish guys and the Irish-Americans.[6]

This suggests that while the motivation still exists from Irish parents to instil an understanding of Irish culture to their children through participation in the GAA, the structure of American society makes it difficult to maintain this activity over time. Despite the best of intentions, there are competing demands on the time of young Irish-Americans, and for all but the most energetic it is difficult to squeeze a sporting and cultural heritage into the structure of a twenty-first century American lifestyle. David Reimers has pointed out that the historical, social and economic evolution of Irish-America has had an impact on its patterns of associationalism and spheres of activity.

Irish American ethnicity was no doubt most alive among the first and second generations. It was they who participated in and supported the city's Irish American cultural institutions, including such public displays as the St Patrick's Day parade. It was mostly the first generation that rallied to the cause of Northern Ireland. But most Irish New Yorkers are members of the third or greater generations. Many have married non-Irish, no longer live in predominantly Irish American communities and no longer partake of Irish American culture. With the decline of anti-Catholicism and anti-Irish bigotry after World War II, Irish Americans found new opportunities that their grandfathers never dreamed of. They could identify with their Irishness, however vague, or could choose to ignore it, and many did.[7]

It seems clear that Irish-America is likely to evolve over forthcoming years as an indigenous ethnic category that is as different from Ireland as the Francophones in Quebec are from the French. More provocatively perhaps, the same parallels could also be drawn within Ireland itself, between North and South, as despite the constitutional small print, the Irish Republic and its people have developed over time to the point that the 26-county state has become synonymous with the nation – i.e. Ireland has reconciled itself to the de facto reality of partition and realised that Ireland can be Ireland without the North.[8]

This trend in relations between Ireland and America has already been happening of course, as the previous chapters in this book have illustrated. However, as time progresses this is likely to become more apparent because the differences between Ireland and America will be more clearly evident. Chapter 5 highlighted the way in which the celebration of St Patrick's Day in New York presents a cultural disconnect between the US and Ireland today. This has been recognised by Irish-Americans themselves, such as the late Daniel Moynihan, former senator for New York and one quarter of the 'Four Horsemen' within Irish-American politics who played an important role in US policy towards Northern Ireland during the 1970s and 1980s. In a rambunctious essay, Moynihan pointed out the disjuncture at the Fifth Avenue St Patrick's Day parade between the AOH officials and the Irish dignitaries

who come over for the occasion. 'The sleek porcine judges and con-
tractors, all uneasy bravado, simply don't know what to make of the
smallish, dour Irish officials and emissaries gathered for the occasion.
Neither do the guests from Éire seem to know quite what to make of
the "O'Donnell Abu," Fighting 69th, "Top o' the Marnin" goings on.'[9]

The suggestion here is that instead of a cultural crossover taking
place represented by the hyphen in Irish-America, the Irish-born and
those of Irish ancestry in America are likely to continue along separate
tracks that become increasingly distinct from one another. This may
happen imperceptibly, but function like a receding echo, refracting,
distorting and perhaps ultimately disappearing. While this sounds quite
negative, it is not meant to be, as this suggests that Irish-America can
finally stand alone, confident and independent in its own identity, as of
course can post-conflict Ireland. Writing in 1999, the celebrated Irish-
American journalist Pete Hamill cast this evolution in a positive light
and suggested that this community had overcome the obstacles that had
faced it in previous generations to a point that it had come of age within
mainstream American society.

> At the end of a century that began with much poverty and even
> more hope, the immigrants who are still alive and the children who
> are charged with remembering have much reason to rejoice. There
> are now few doors closed to Irish Americans. Irish Americans run
> vast corporations, control great wealth and have triumphed in
> every field in American life – from the great universities to the
> halls of Congress, from movies and television to journalism and
> literature. We have our scientists, our doctors, our athletes, our
> scholars. Irish America can say with confidence: we have won all
> the late rounds.[10]

This evolution of Irish-America to the point that it can stand alone from
contemporary Ireland represents not so much a divorce as a mutually
agreed separation. It is amicable, even contented, in the recognition
that the future will be based on a looser, less intimate relationship
between the two countries and their peoples.

This is perhaps not the most romantic ending to a book on Irish-
America that has ever been written, but it is a realistic one. Irish-America
will no doubt continue, in cultural if not in political terms, but it will do
so within an overtly American context which, over time, will resonate

less and less with the contemporary Irish experience. Irish poet Louis MacNeice (himself a member of the diaspora before the word was invented) explained this refracted impact of Ireland in his epic poem 'Autumn Journal' in 1939.

> Though yet her name keeps ringing like a bell
> In an under-water belfry.[11]

This verse may help explain the next phase in the relationship between Ireland and Irish-America. It can certainly be heard, but it is muffled, distorted and dimmed.

Perhaps the final irony is one with an historical hue. It is generally accepted in recent scholarship that the pre-Famine waves of Scotch-Irish and Irish Protestants came to America and integrated relatively quickly within that society, disappearing beneath the radar screen rather than building a critical mass based on ethnic group consciousness. Today's Irish migrants (to the extent that this term even applies) are similarly individualistic in behaviour, and are equally disinterested in 'hanging onto home' as were this group of their predecessors who succeeded in 'rising without trace', as Professor Joe Lee puts it.[12] While it is important not to extrapolate too freely for the purposes of neat conclusions, an argument could be made that this trend resonates with contemporary patterns of Irish migration.

This brings us back to the impact of globalisation on Ireland and the outlook of its people. While de Valera may be spinning in his grave, a consumer culture has gripped Ireland as it has done elsewhere, producing a national consciousness which emphasises material individualism. The emergence of the Celtic Tiger during the 1990s, perhaps in conjunction with the self-inflicted decline of the Catholic Church in Ireland during the same period, promoted an acquisitional culture where the personal was elevated alongside (if not above) the social. Once again, it is important not to overstate this case as Ireland remains a traditional, conservative society with a high proportion of Church attendance relative to other European countries. Despite this, the individualism promoted as a by-product of economic and cultural global connections is having an impact on Ireland's twenty-first century diaspora. The Irish who enter America today mostly do so as individuals rather than as families or communities, and they want to consume America as an individual experience. There is a certain irony in the fact that today's diaspora are behaving like their Scotch-Irish ancestors, feeling comfortable with the idea of integrating within American culture rather than forming group associations to deal with the antagonistic environment that surrounds them. On one level, this is a positive reflection of the fact that Irish migrants have made their peace with WASP society and feel that they have just as much access to the 'land of opportunity' as anyone else. The more sobering thought, however, comes from the realisation that the Scotch-Irish and others who came and integrated into American society have all but disappeared from the ethnographic map. If the future of Irish migration into America repeats this pattern of individualistic integrationism (leaving aside their endemic pragmatism) then it is unlikely to strengthen the fabric of Irish-America as a recognisable ethnic group in subsequent generations.

Irish-America looks set to move forward in a number of interesting ways. In political terms it has become diffused for two central reasons. Firstly, as Irish-Americans have climbed up the socio-economic ladder they have moved into different areas and taken on a range of political and social views which have led many to move away from support for the Democratic Party. To this extent the political power of Irish-America as an ethnic bloc vote no longer exists (if it ever did) as the overwhelming majority of the supposed 35 million Irish-Americans vote with an American-American agenda. The economic success story of the Irish-American community has led to a loss of political cohesion, aided and abetted by the relative decline of ethnic civil society organisations such as the AOH. The second reason behind the political dealignment of Irish-America relates to the fact that its project has become uncertain in the wake of the denouement in the Northern Ireland conflict. While difficulties in the peace process remain and will do so for at least another generation, a political settlement has been reached and is being implemented by the people of Ireland. Crucially, the British military and administrative role in Northern Ireland has diminished and there remains very little for potential Irish-American activists to get their teeth into, apart from lobbying the Northern Ireland government itself. This fact was thrown into sharp relief by US secretary of state Hillary Clinton's statement in August 2009 that she would not be taking up the role of special envoy to Northern Ireland. This had been rumoured for several months by Irish-American activists and by the Irish media itself, and indicates the disconnect between the past and the future of the

Irish-American relationship. The idea that a US secretary of state could be spared from key international relations issues facing the Obama administration to encourage or cajole the people of Northern Ireland to pursue their peace process is indicative of how unrealistic some people are about the importance of Irish issues in American politics. Niall Stanage, a journalist who has written extensively about Irish-American affairs, made this point clear in an *Irish Times* article in the wake of Clinton's statement.

> The Clinton saga also illuminates larger truths, however: about the sheer wrong-headedness of so many prevalent perceptions of Irish-America, and about our national delusions of grandeur regarding where Ireland ranks on the American political agenda ... The widespread and largely uncritical dissemination of the original tale [by the Irish media] was made possible by the survival of two intertwined fictions: that the Irish-American community has serious political muscle, and that Ireland is at the forefront of American political debate ... The reality is that Irish-America does not matter very much.[13]

While some regard this as being a harsh truth of the contemporary Irish-American condition, others see it as being an exaggeration, arguing that the power and influence of Irish-America remains potent. In August 2009 this difference of opinion was aired in the Irish media between Niall Stanage and Niall O'Dowd, when the latter took issue with the former's piece in the *Irish Times*, from which the above quote is taken.

O'Dowd responded to this article with his own contributions in the *Irish Times* and elsewhere and while the direct focus remained on the role that Hillary Clinton might play in Northern Ireland, the wider themes related to the health of the Irish-American lobby and, more personally, whose was the legitimate voice of the Irish-American community.

> With regard to Irish America: Stanage is not long enough in America to understand what occurred during the peace process here. It was Irish America which won the visa for Gerry Adams which helped create the IRA ceasefire. It was Irish America which first put forward the envoy proposal which became the George Mitchell initiative and most importantly it was Irish America which first reached out to then Arkansas governor Bill Clinton to

become involved in Ireland. How this signals a lack of clout is a mystery.

He tosses off the usual cockamamie quotes about no Irish Americans ever voting en masse on Irish issues. Whoever said they did? What we in Irish America have done is harnessed support around positions of interest to us such as immigration reform and Northern Ireland. To that end we have cultivated important relationships through fundraising, extensive canvassing at elections and creating personal contacts with many key figures. We are no different in that respect to any other ethnic group.[14]

While some of this analysis is well observed, it would be fair to say that the majority of the achievements outlined by O'Dowd relate to the past efforts of Irish-America rather than to current or even future possibilities. It is difficult to avoid the conclusion that the halcyon days of Irish influence experienced in the 1990s are unlikely to be revisited, at least with the vigour they assumed under the Clinton presidency.

The one remaining uniting pole for Irish-America is immigration reform legislation and this involves lobbying the American government rather than London or Dublin. This issue is complicated of course by the fact that it goes beyond the undocumented Irish, and requires many conservative Irish-Americans to countenance legalising the status of large numbers of Mexicans, Hispanics and other nationalities. The following comment made by an Irish-American businessman in New York in 2004 illustrates the point that this represents a bridge too far for some. 'If you are here illegally now you can't go home [to Ireland] and expect to get back ... If they would just simply kick out the Arabs and the Muslims – that's what we should be doing, but you can't do that in today's world.'[15]

The lack of political cohesion within Irish-America has been accompanied by a wider decline in ethnic civil society as groups such as the AOH are increasingly seen as being out of touch with younger generations and with the Irish-born living in the US. As mentioned above, Irish-American social capital is unlikely to be replenished by new waves of Irish migration, despite the chronic decline of the Irish economy in recent years.

What all of this suggests is that Irish-America is becoming an indigenous ethnic category. While the notion of there being 'an Irish-America' will remain, and may do so vibrantly at the cultural level, it will do so as an element of America's rich heritage, not its contemporary political reality. In other words, Irish-America will assume a role which is critical to understanding the country's past, but marginal to interpreting its political future. It is likely that the next US census will record a figure lower than the 35 million in the 2000 poll and that the vast majority of that number will have an extremely weak affiliation with the first part of their Irish-American identity, in political terms at least.

For their part, the Irish will no doubt seek to maintain ethnic networks for mutual benefit, but this will be based on equality rather than charity and cold calculations of advantage rather than feelings of duty, obligation or guilt. The umbilical cord between Ireland and America is being severed in the twenty-first century and both countries are going their own way. This does not mean that they are turning their faces away from each other, as the historic relationship will always be there. It does, however, suggest that we are on the threshold of a looser, less intense and more pragmatic relationship between the Irish and the Irish-American communities. In the final analysis, that is probably a mature, sensible and sustainable way for Ireland and America to move forward.

NOTES

1. Callan, T. (ed.), *Quarterly Economic Commentary: Research Bulletin 09/1, Summary Table* (Dublin: Economic and Social Research Institute, Spring 2009).
2. Hannerz, U. *Transnational Connections: Culture, People, Places* (London: Routledge, 1996), p.17.
3. FitzGerald, D. *'Citizenship à la Carte': Global Migration and Transnational Politics*, Working Paper No. 3 (March 2008), Center for Global Studies, George Mason University, Fairfax, Virginia, p.2.
4. Inglis, T. *Global Ireland* (London: Routledge, 2007), p.183.
5. O'Hanlon, R. *The New Irish Americans* (New York: Roberts Rinehart, 1998), p.219.
6. Larry McCarthy, secretary, New York GAA, interviewed by author, 9 September 2008.
7. Reimers, D. 'An End and a Beginning', in R.H. Bayor, and T.J. Meagher (eds), *The New York Irish* (Baltimore, MD: Johns Hopkins University Press, 1997), p.438.
8. For more on this argument see Cochrane, F. 'Any Takers? The Isolation of Northern Ireland', *Political Studies*, 42, 3 (September 1994), pp.378–95.
9. Moynihan, D.P. 'The Irish (1963, 1970)', in J.J. Lee and M. Casey (eds), *Making the Irish American* (New York: New York University Press, 2007), p.497.
10. Hamill, P. 'Once We Were Kings', in Lee and Casey (eds), *Making the Irish American*, p.528.
11. MacNeice, L. 'Autumn Journal', quoted in *Collected Poems* (London: Faber & Faber, 1998).
12. Lee, J.J. 'Introduction', in Lee and Casey (eds), *Making the Irish American*, p.4.

13. Stanage, N. 'Clinton Saga Highlights Ludicrous Notions about Importance of Ireland to America', *Irish Times*, 8 August 2009, p.5.
14. O'Dowd, N. 'Irish Clout Real and Hard Won', *Irish Times*, 15 August 2009, http://www. irish times.com/newspaper/opinion/2009/0815/1224252584171.html.
15. Irish-American businessman interviewed by the author in New York, September 2004.

Bibliography

Akenson, D.H. *The Irish Diaspora: A Primer* (Chester Springs, CA: Dufour Editions, 1997)

Allen, K. *The Celtic Tiger? The Myth of Social Partnership in Ireland* (Manchester: Manchester University Press, 2000)

Allen, K. *The Corporate Takeover of Ireland* (Dublin: Irish Academic Press, 2007)

Appadurai, A. *Modernity at Large: Cultural Dimensions of Globalization* (Minneapolis, MN: University of Minnesota Press, 1996)

Arthur, P. *Special Relationships: Britain, Ireland and the Northern Ireland Problem* (Belfast: Blackstaff Press, 2000)

Augé, I. *Non-Places: Introduction to an Anthropology of Supermodernity* (London: Verso, 1995)

Bartley, B. and Kitchin, R. (eds), *Understanding Contemporary Ireland* (London: Pluto Press. 2007)

Basu, P. 'Hunting Down Home: Reflections on Homeland and the Search for Identity in the Scottish Diaspora', in Bender and Winer (eds), *Contested Landscapes: Movement, Exile and Place*

Bayor, R.H. and Meagher, T.J. (eds), *The New York Irish* (Baltimore, MD: Johns Hopkins University Press, 1997)

Beck, U. *What Is Globalization?* (Cambridge: Polity Press, 2000)

Bender, B. and Winer, M. (eds), *Contested Landscapes: Movement, Exile and Place* (Oxford: Berg. 2001)

Bielenberg, A. (ed.), *The Irish Diaspora* (London: Longman, 2000)

Bradley, J. 'The Irish Economy in International Perspective', in Crotty and Schmitt (eds), *Ireland on the World Stage*

Brah, A. *Cartographies of Diaspora: Contesting Identities* (London: Routledge, 1996)

Brown, S. and Patterson, A. 'Knick-knack Paddy-whack, Give a Pub a

Theme', *Journal of Marketing Management*, vol. 16 (2000), pp.648–62

Brubaker, R. 'The "Diaspora" Diaspora', *Ethnic and Racial Studies*, 28, 1 (2005), pp.1–20

Callan, T. (ed.), *Research Bulletin 09/1 Quarterly Economic Commentary*, 'Summary Table' (Dublin: Economic and Social Research Institute (ESRI), Spring 2009)

Castells, M. *The Rise of Network Society* (Oxford: Blackwell, 1996)

Central Statistics Office, *Population and Labour Force Projections, 2006–2036* (Dublin: Central Statistics Office, 2006)

Chambers, I. *Migrancy, Culture, Identity* (London: Routledge, 1994)

Clancy, M.A. 'The United States and Post-Agreement Northern Ireland 2001–2006', *Irish Studies in International Affairs*, vol. 18 (2007)

Clancy, M. 'Re-Presenting Ireland: Tourism, Branding and Changing Conceptions of the Nation in Contemporary Ireland', unpublished paper prepared for the 49th Annual International Studies Association Convention (26–9 March 2008)

Cobley, P. 'Marketing the "Glocal" in Narratives of National Identity', *Semiotica*, no. 150 (2004), pp.197–225

Cochrane, F. 'The End of the Affair: Irish Migration, 9/11 and the Evolution of Irish-America', *Nationalism and Ethnic Politics*, 13, 3 (2007), pp.335–66

Cochrane, F. 'Irish-America, the End of the IRA's Armed Struggle and the Utility of "Soft Power"', *Journal of Peace Research*, 44, 2 (2007), pp.215–31

Cohen, R. *Global Diasporas: An Introduction* (London: UCL Press, 1997)

Coogan, T.P. *Wherever Green is Worn: The Story of the Irish Diaspora* (London: Hutchinson, 2002)

Corrigan, C. 'Real IRA, Other Dissidents Use Social Nets to Catch Teenagers', www.IrishCentral.com (23 April 2009)

Coulter, C. and Coleman, S. (eds), *The End of Irish History? Critical Reflections on the Celtic Tiger* (Manchester: Manchester University Press, 2003)

Cox, M. 'Bringing in the "International": The IRA Ceasefire and the End of the Cold War', *International Affairs*, 73, 4 (October 1997) pp.671–93

Cox, M., Guelke, A. and Stephen, F. (eds), *A Farewell To Arms?* (Manchester: Manchester University Press, 2000)

Cronin, M and Adair, D. *The Wearing of the Green* (London: Routledge, 2006)

Crotty W. and Schmitt, D. (eds), *Ireland on the World Stage* (London: Longman, 2002)

Crotty, W. and Schmitt, D. (eds), *Ireland and the Politics of Change* (London: Longman, 1998)

Cullen, K. 'America and the Conflict', *Frontline* (June 1998), http://www.pbs.org/wgbh/pages/frontline/shows/ira/reports/america.html

Dawson, A. and Johnson, M. 'Migration, Exile and Landscapes of the Imagination', in Bender and Winer (eds), *Contested Landscapes: Movement, Exile and Place*

De Breadún, D. *The Far Side of Revenge* (Belfast: Blackstaff Press, 2001)

Dee, J. 'Irish America Stunned by RIRA Attack', *Belfast Telegraph*, 10 March 2009

Delaney, E. *Demography State and Society* (Liverpool: Liverpool University Press, 2000)

Dempsey, G.T. 'The American Role in the Northern Ireland Peace Process', *Irish Political Studies*, vol. 41 (1999), pp.104–17

Diner, H.R. '"The Most Irish City in the Union": The Era of the Great Migration 1844–1877', in Bayor and Meagher (eds), *The New York Irish* (Baltimore, MD: Johns Hopkins University Press, 1997), pp.87–106

Dowling Almeida, L. 'Irish America, 1940–2000', in Lee and Casey, *Making the Irish American*, pp.548–73

Fahey, T. 'Progress or Decline? Demographic Change in Political Context', in Crotty, and Schmitt (eds), *Ireland and the Politics of Change*

Fanning, C. (ed.), *New Perspectives on the Irish Diaspora* (Carbondale, IL: Southern Illinois University Press, 2000)

Featherstone, M., Lash, S. and Robertson, R. (eds), *Global Modernities* (London: Sage, 1995)

Finnegan, R. 'Irish-American Relations', in Crotty and Schmitt (eds), *Ireland on the World Stage*, pp.95–110

FitzGerald, D. *'Citizenship à la Carte'*: *Global Migration and Transnational Politics*, Working Paper No. 3 (March 2008), Center for Global Studies, George Mason University, Fairfax, Virginia

Garvin, T. *Preventing the Future: Why was Ireland So Poor for So Long?* (Dublin: Gill and Macmillan, 2005)

Giddens, A. *Beyond Left and Right: The Future of Radical Politics* (Cambridge: Polity Press, 1994)

Gilroy, P. 'It Ain't Where You're From, It's Where You're At: The Dialectics of Diasporic Identification', *Third Text*, no. 13 (Winter 1991), pp.3–16

Girvin, B. 'Contraception, Moral Panic and Social Change in Ireland 1969–79', *Irish Political Studies*, 23, 4 (2008) pp.555–76

Global Commission on International Migration (GCIM), *Migration in an Interconnected World: New Directions for Action* (London: GCIM, 2005)

Gootman, E. 'For Bronx School Dancers the Moves are Irish', *New York Times*, 14 March 2008, p.8

Grey, B. *Women and the Irish Diaspora* (London: Routledge, 2003)

Guelke, A. 'Northern Ireland: International and North/South Issues', in Crotty and Schmitt (eds), *Ireland and the Politics of Change*

Guelke, A. 'International Dimensions of the Belfast Agreement', in R. Wilford (ed.), *Aspects of the Belfast Agreement* (Oxford: Oxford University Press, 2001), pp.245–63

Hall, S. 'Cultural Identity and Diaspora', in Rutherford (ed.), *Identity, Community, Culture, Difference*, pp.222–37

Hanley, B. 'The Politics of Noraid', *Irish Political Studies*, 19, 1 (2004), pp.1–17

Hannerz, U. *Transnational Connections: Culture, People, Places* (London: Routledge, 1996)

Hardiman, N., Murphy, P. and Burke, O. 'The Politics of Economic Adjustment in a Liberal Market Economy: The Social Compensation Hypothesis Revisited', *Irish Political Studies*, 23, 4 (2008), pp.599–626

Hayward, K. and MacCarthaigh, M. (eds), *Recycling the State: The Politics of Adaptation in Ireland* (Dublin: Irish Academic Press, 2007)

Hughes, G. and Quinn, E. *The Impact of Immigration on Europe's Societies: Ireland* (Dublin: European Migration Network, 2004)

Inglis, T. *Global Ireland* (London: Routledge, 2008)

Irish Voice, 'Outrage Over FBI "Informer" Attempts', 5 October 2005, p.3

Irish Voice, 'Shackled in Chains for Overstaying', 12 January 2005, p.1

Irish Voice, 'Kerry For President', 21 October 2004, p.1

Jarman, N., Bryan, D., Caleyron, N and de Rosa, C. *The Politics of Difference* (Belfast: Democratic Dialogue, 1998)

Kearney, R. (ed.), *Migrations: The Irish At Home and Abroad* (Dublin: Wolfhound Press, 1990)

Kelley, C. and Molis, J. *Your Guide to the Irish Pubs of Chicago* (Chicago: Green Line Publishing, 2006)

Kelly, C. 'Tourism and Heritage', in Bartley and Kitchin (eds), *Understanding Contemporary Ireland*

Kenny, K. 'American-Irish Nationalism', in Lee and Casey, *Making the Irish American*, pp.289–301

King, R., Connell, J. and White, P. (eds), *Writing Across Worlds: Literature and Migration* (London: Routledge, 1995)

Kinnealy, C. *This Great Calamity: The Irish Famine 1845–52* (Dublin: Gill and Macmillan, 2006)

Kirby, P. *Celtic Tiger in Distress: Growth With Inequality in Ireland* (Basingstoke: Palgrave, 2002)

Laffan, B. and O'Donnell, R. 'Ireland and the Growth of International Governance', in Crotty and Schmitt (eds), *Ireland and the Politics of Change*

Larkin, J. *Larkin About in Ireland* (Sydney: Hodder and Stoughton, 2002)

Lee, J.J. *Ireland 1912–1985: Politics and Society* (Cambridge: Cambridge University Press, 1989)

Lee, J.J. and Casey, M. (eds), *Making the Irish American* (New York: New York University Press, 2006)

Lentin, R. 'Illegal in Ireland, Irish Illegals: Diaspora Nation as a Racial State', *Irish Political Studies*, 22, 4 (December 2007)

Lynch, T. *Turf War* (London: Ashgate, 2004)

MacÉinrí, P. 'Some Recent Demographic Developments in Ireland', *Études Irlandaises*, 22, 1 (Spring 1997), http://migration.ucc.ie/etudesirlandaises.htm

MacLaughlin, J. *Ireland: The Emigrant Nursery and the World Economy* (Cork: Cork University Press, 1994)

MacSharry, R. and White, P. *The Making of the Celtic Tiger: The Inside Story of Ireland's Boom Economy* (Cork: Mercier Press, 2000)

Maguire, A. *Rock the Sham* (Dublin: Street Level Press, 2005)

Makki, L. 'Refugees and Exile: From Refugee Studies to the National Order of Things', *Annual Review of Anthropology*, vol. 24 (1995) pp.495–523

Mallie, E. and McKittrick, D. *Endgame in Ireland* (London: Hodder and Stoughton, 2001)

McCarthy, P. *The Road to McCarthy* (London: Hodder and Stoughton, 2002)

McDowell, C. *A Tamil Asylum Diaspora: Sri Lankan Migration, Settlement and Politics in Switzerland* (Oxford: Berghahn, 1996)

McGovern, M. 'The "Craic" Market: Irish Theme Bars and the Commodification of Irishness in Contemporary Britain', *Irish Journal of Sociology*, 11, 2 (2002), pp.77–98.

McKittrick, D. 'The Afterlife of the IRA: The Dissident Groups Bent on Shattering the Peace in Northern Ireland', *Independent*, 8 November 2008, p.3

Mitchell, G. *Making Peace* (London: Hodder and Stoughton, 1999)

Mol, A. and Law, J. 'Regions, Networks and Fluids: Anaemia and Social Topology', *Social Studies of Science*, vol. 24 (1994), pp.641–71

Moloney, M. 'Far From the Shamrock Shore: The Irish-American Experience in Song' (Shanachie Entertainment Corp., 2002 – sleeve notes)

Moore, C. *One Voice: My Life in Song* (London: Hodder and Stoughton, 2000)

Moynihan, D.P. 'The Irish (1963, 1970)', in Lee and Casey (eds), *Making The Irish American*

Murphy, G. and Puirséil, N. '"Is it a New Allowance?" Irish Entry to the EEC and Popular Opinion', *Irish Political Studies*, 23, 4 (2008), pp.533–54

Negra, D. 'Consuming Ireland: Lucky Charms Cereal, Irish Spring Soap and 1-800-Shamrock', *Cultural Studies*, 15, 1 (2001)

Ní Eigeartaigh, A. 'Mise Éire: Recycling Nationalist Mythologies', in Hayward and MacCarthaigh (eds), *Recycling the State: The Politics of Adaptation in Ireland*, pp.18–42

Nwabueze, U. and Clair Law, Z. 'The Journey for Survival: The Case of New Project Development in the Brewery Industry', *The Journal of Product and Brand Management*, 10, 6/7 (2001), pp.380–92

Nye, J. *Power in the Global Information Age: From Realism to Globalization* (London: Routledge, 2004)

Nye, J. *Soft Power: The Means to Success in World Politics* (New York: Public Affairs, 2004)

Nye, J. *Understanding International Conflicts: An Introduction to The Story and History* (New York: Longman, 2000)

Nye, J. *Bound to Lead: The Changing Nature of American Power* (New York: Basic, 1990)

O'Clery, C. *The Greening of the White House* (Dublin: Gill and Macmillan, 1997)

O'Dowd, N. 'Irish America Played Pivotal Northern Role', *Sunday Business Post*, 7 August 2005, p.4

O'Faoláin, N. 'When Irish Ties Are Fraying', *New York Times*, 23 June 2004

O'Hanlon, R. 'Illegals Living on a Dream and a Prayer', *Irish News*, 7 December 2004

O'Hanlon, R. *The New Irish Americans* (New York: Roberts Reinhart, 1998)

Ormsby, F. *A Rage For Order* (Belfast: Blackstaff Press, 1992)

Paus, E. *Foreign Investment, Development and Globalization: Can Costa Rica Become Ireland?* (Basingstoke: Palgrave, 2005)

Quinn, P. 'The Future of Irish America', in Lee and Casey (eds), *Making the Irish American*

Rapport, N. and Dawson, A. (eds), *Migrants of Identity: Perceptions of Home in a World of Movement* (Oxford: Berg, 1998)

Reimers, D. 'An End and a Beginning', in Bayor and Meagher (eds), *The New York Irish*, pp.419–38

Ridge, J.T. *The St Patrick's Day Parade in New York* (Brooklyn: AOH Publications, 1988)

Robinson, M. 'Cherishing the Irish Diaspora', address by President Mary Robinson to the Houses of the Oireachtas, 2 February 1995, http://www.oireachtas.ie/viewdoc.asp?fn=/documents/addresses/2Feb1995.htm

Rutherford, J. (ed.), *Identity, Community, Culture, Difference* (London: Lawrence and Wishart, 1990)

Safran, W. 'Diasporas in Modern Societies: Myths of Homeland and Return', *Diaspora: A Journal of Transnational Studies*, 1, 1 (1991), pp.83–99

Schmitt, D.E. 'The US War on Terrorism and its Impact on the Politics of Accommodation in Northern Ireland', in C. Farrington (ed.), *Global Change, Civil Society and the Northern Ireland Peace Process* (Basingstoke: Palgrave, 2008)

Scholte, J.A. *Globalization: A Critical Introduction* (Basingstoke: Palgrave, 2000)

Stanage, N. *Redemption Song: An Irish Reporter Inside the Obama Campaign* (Dublin: Liberties Press, 2008)

Stanage, N. 'Is Ireland Hostile to US?', *Sunday Business Post*, 4 July 2004

Stark, O. *The Migration of Labour* (Oxford: Basil Blackwell, 1991)

Sweeney, P. *The Celtic Tiger: Ireland's Continuing Economic Miracle* (Dublin: Oak Tree Press (2nd edition), 1999)

Trillin, C. 'Democracy in Action' in Lee and Casey (eds), *Making the Irish American*

Urry, J. *Sociology Beyond Societies: Mobilities for the Twenty-First Century* (London: Routledge, 2000)

Van Hear, N. *New Diasporas: The Mass Exodus, Dispersal and Regrouping of Migrant Communities* (London: UCL Press, 1998)

Vertovec, S. and Cohen, R. (eds), *Migration, Diasporas and Transnationalism* (Cheltenham: Edward Elgar, 1999)

Walsh, B. 'Taxation and Foreign Direct Investment in Ireland,' in H. Grubel (ed.), *Tax Reform in Canada: Our Path to Greater Prosperity* (Vancouver: The Fraser Institute, 2002)

Walsh, J. 'Agriculture in Transition', in Bartley and Kitchin (eds), *Understanding Contemporary Ireland*

West, B. *Engaging with Themed Space: Australian Holidaymakers and Banal Nationalism in Aussie Theme Pubs*, Working Paper, The Georgia Workshop on Culture and Institutions, Flinders University, Adelaide (2003)

West, P. 'Last Orders Down at MacFoney's' *New Statesman*, 27 August 2001, pp.6–7

Wilson, A.J. '"Doing the Business": Aspects of the Clinton Administration's Economic Support for the Northern Ireland Peace Process, 1994–2000.' *The Journal of Conflict Studies*, XXIII, 1 (2003)

INTERVIEWS CITED

Niall Burgess, Irish Consul General, New York (interviewed by author, 9 September 2008)

William Cobert, director, American Irish Historical Society (interviewed by author, 1 September 2004)

Siobhán Dennehy, executive director, *Emerald Isle Immigration Center*, New York (interviewed by author, 20 September 2004)

Vincent Doherty (e-mail correspondence with author, 17 September 2004)

Éamonn Dornan, formerly of Smith, Dornan and O'Shea Attorneys (interviewed by author, 3 September 2004)

Barry Doyle, organiser of the Wellington St Patrick's Day Festival,

Wellington, New Zealand (interviewed by author, 15 December 2003)

Cassie Farrelly, former administrative director, Institute of Irish Studies, Fordham University, New York (interviewed by author, 16 September 2004)

Brendan Fay, St Pat's for All Society (interviewed by Professor Rosaleen Duffy, 22 September 2004)

Kelly Fincham, Irish Lobby for Immigration Reform (interviewed by author, 9 September 2008)

Pat Hughes, owner/manager, Scruffy Duffy's, New York (interviewed by author, 6 September 2004)

Jack Irwin, special liaison officer on Irish affairs, Office of Governor George Pataki, New York State (interviewed by author, 8 September 2004)

Martin Kelly, former AOH state president (interviewed by author, 9 September 2004)

Liz Kenny, director, Fáilte Irish Center, Long Island city, New York (interviewed by author, 10 September 2008)

Jake MacNicholas, New York Police Department (interviewed by author, 8 September 2004)

Professor Larry McCarthy, secretary, New York GAA (interviewed by author, 9 September 2008)

Seán McCarthy, co-founder, RadioIrish.com (interviewed by author, 11 September 2008)

Christina McElwaine (interviewed by author, 3 September 2004)

Mary McGlynn, associate professor of English literature, Baruch College, City University of New York (interviewed by author, 15 September 2004)

Kathleen McGreal (phone interview with author, 28 September 2004)

John Francis Mulligan, Irish Queers (phone interview with Professor Rosaleen Duffy, 25 September 2004)

Seán Murphy, 'Murphguide' (interviewed by author, 7 September 2004)

Ray O'Hanlon, senior editor, *Irish Echo* (interviewed by author, 17 September 2004 and phone interview, 12 September 2008)

Niall O'Leary (interviewed by author, 15 September 2004)

Professor Eileen Reilly, associate director, Glucksman Ireland House, NYU (interviewed by author, 14 September 2004)

John T. Ridge, AOH historian (interviewed by author, 9 September 2004)

Niall Stanage, journalist (interviewed by author, 13 September 2008)

Pauline Turley, executive director, Irish Arts Center, New York (interviewed by author, 2 September 2004)

Index